MATHEMATICS
FOR BUSINESS

MATHEMATICS FOR BUSINESS

By Bert Miller

Media Materials, Inc.　　•　　Baltimore, Maryland

THE AUTHOR:

Bert Miller, Ph.D.
Mathematics Teacher
Baltimore County, Maryland, Public Schools

Assistant Professor of Mathematics
Essex Community College
Catonsville Community College
Community College of Baltimore

CONSULTANT:

Winda L. Rich
Business Mathematics Instructor
Strayer Business College
Baltimore, Maryland

Editor: Barbara Pokrinchak, Ed.D.
Editorial Consultant: M. E. Criste

Printed in the U.S.A.   06 88 VG/ATB 5.0   ISBN: 0-86601-544-2

CONTENTS

Preface

Mathematics for Business provides students with the necessary information and skill development to be successful in a business environment.

Features of the Lessons

Lessons are short, self-contained, and are designed to minimize the reading difficulties usually encountered in business mathematics textbooks.

Business vocabulary terms are defined at the beginning of lessons. The discussion of background information in each lesson is brief. Illustrative problems have detailed, step-by-step solutions.

Each lesson contains numerous practice problems. The answer to the first problem is provided in the text so that students can verify that they are proceeding correctly.

In most sets of practice exercises, every tenth problem is marked with an asterisk. This indicates that the problem is slightly more difficult than the others, and will be more challenging to solve.

The wealth of practice exercises ensures that instructors will have enough problems to assign, not only for initial practice, but also for subsequent review.

Features of the Chapters

Each chapter contains a calculator activity. There is also a computer program in each chapter. These short programs afford students insight into how programs work and how they are used.

The special Basic Skill Review page in each chapter integrates problem solving and computation with whole numbers, decimals, and fractions.

At the end of each chapter is a Chapter Review that contains representative exercises for the topics in that chapter.

Teacher's Guide

The *Teacher's Guide and Answer Key* that accompanies this text contains objectives, identification of target skills, teaching suggestions, and complete answers. A section of reproducible pages includes chapter tests and supplementary exercises.

Chapter 1

Earning Money By the Hour

It is important for all workers to know and understand the methods of computing wages. Workers who understand how their wages are computed can check to see that their employers are paying them the correct amount of money. Do you know why taxes and other amounts subtracted from wages are called "deductions"? This chapter presents the concepts of *gross pay, net pay,* and *overtime pay.*

GROSS PAY

Business Vocabulary:

Gross pay — Total earnings.

Deductions — Amounts subtracted from gross pay.

The total pay a person earns, before taxes and other deductions, is called *gross pay*. To compute gross pay, you multiply the hours times the rate.

Example A:

Joe worked 38 hours at $4.10 per hour. Compute Joe's gross pay.

```
    $4.10   Rate
  ×   38    Hours
    3280
    1230
  $155.80
```

Joe's gross pay was $155.80.

Example B:

Sara worked 23 hours at $5.85 per hour. Compute Sara's gross pay.

```
    $5.85   Rate
  ×   23    Hours
    1755
    1170
  $134.55
```

Sara's gross pay was $134.55.

▶ Compute the gross pay. The answer to Number 1 is $170.00. Special challenging problems are marked with an asterisk (*).

Hours Worked	Hourly Rate	Hours Worked	Hourly Rate
1) 40	$4.25	26) 36	$3.97
2) 13	$3.79	27) 33	$5.41
3) 12	$3.42	28) 18	$6.33
4) 30	$6.20	29) 39	$6.56
5) 20	$6.65	30* 10	$57.00
6) 32	$4.48	31) 20	$5.44
7) 38	$5.76	32) 29	$7.04
8) 22	$4.10	33) 34	$4.96
9) 16	$4.83	34) 22	$5.64
10* 10	$57.80	35) 10	$4.96
11) 38	$5.93	36) 16	$5.68
12) 18	$3.52	37) 18	$4.01
13) 9	$3.67	38) 38	$4.99
14) 14	$3.92	39) 11	$6.90
15) 27	$3.38	40* 27	$50.10
16) 31	$6.85	41) 32	$3.62
17) 15	$7.19	42) 40	$5.90
18) 27	$5.99	43) 28	$7.33
19) 33	$4.24	44) 15	$3.96
20* 27	$65.70	45) 28	$4.63
21) 40	$7.28	46) 23	$5.61
22) 7	$6.14	47) 18	$6.91
23) 20	$3.85	48) 26	$7.28
24) 15	$5.76	49) 36	$7.04
25) 17	$4.81	50* 18	$72.20

ROUNDING AMOUNTS OF MONEY

In business, there are three main rules for rounding. The best-known rule is to round to the nearer cent or nearer dollar. This rule asks you to look at the digit one place to the right of where you are rounding. The rule requires rounding *up* if that digit is 5 or greater. The rule requires rounding *down* if that digit is less than 5.

The second rule is to round to the next higher cent or next higher dollar. This rule requires rounding *up* in all cases where there is not a whole number of cents or dollars.

The third rule is to round to the next lower cent or next lower dollar. This rule requires rounding *down* in all cases where there is not a whole number of cents or dollars.

Examples:
  A. Round $31.347 to the nearer cent.
      The 7 tells you to round up. The answer is $31.35.
  B. Round $357.09 to the nearer dollar.
      The 0 tells you to round down. The answer is $357.
  C. Round $23.002 to the next higher cent.
      $.002 is not a whole number of cents. Round up. The answer is $23.01.
  D. Round $54 to the next higher dollar.
      $54 is a whole number of dollars. Do not round. The answer is $54.
  E. Round $654.11 to the next lower cent.
      $.11 is a whole number of cents. Do not round. The answer is $654.11.
  F. Round $87.99 to the next lower dollar. $87.99 is not a whole number of dollars. Round down. The answer is $87.

▶ There are two amounts of money given in each item below. Round them according to the directions. The answers to Number 1 are $14.62 and $6.83.

1)	Nearer cent:	$14.615	$6.8338
2)	Nearer cent:	$32.074	$6.0375
3)	Next higher cent:	$77.298	$4.4576
4)	Next lower cent:	$19.377	$5.9961
5)	Nearer dollar:	$610.86	$61.898
6)	Next higher dollar:	$989.85	$96.651
7)	Next lower dollar:	$707.80	$2.071
8)	Nearer cent:	$39.563	$7.5949
9)	Next higher cent:	$40.887	$2.509
10)	Next lower cent:	$33.953	$2.6244
11)	Nearer dollar:	$208.16	$80.442
12)	Next higher dollar:	$319.59	$73.33
13)	Next lower dollar:	$284.85	$86.931
14)	Nearer cent:	$31.475	$3.0164
15)	Next higher cent:	$76.84	$.3237
16)	Next lower cent:	$61.629	$3.4151
17)	Nearer dollar:	$490.71	$71.836
18)	Next higher dollar:	$950.06	$60.631
19)	Next lower dollar:	$651.59	$9.073
20)	Nearer cent:	$17.803	$6.8783
21)	Next higher cent:	$41.157	$.4769
22)	Next lower cent:	$69.661	$6.5838
23)	Nearer dollar:	$846.44	$73.997
24)	Next higher dollar:	$797.39	$80.68
25)	Next lower dollar:	$563.46	$44.248

TIME CARDS

Business Vocabulary:

Time in — The time when a person arrives at work.

Time out — The time when a person leaves work to go to lunch, to go home, etc.

Time card — The card on which employees have their times recorded.

Time clock — The device that stamps the current time on each employee's time card.

Many employees who are paid by the hour record their time in and time out with a time clock. At the end of the week, the manager computes the total time worked by each employee.

Example A: This is part of Ellen's time card. How long did she work yesterday?

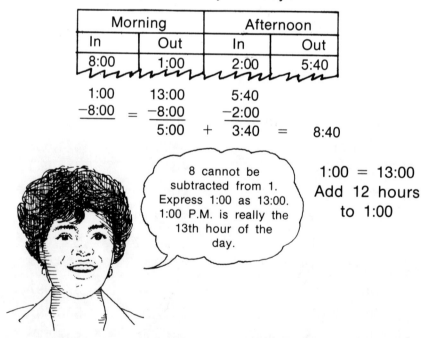

Morning		Afternoon	
In	Out	In	Out
8:00	1:00	2:00	5:40

$$\begin{array}{ccccc} 1{:}00 & & 13{:}00 & & 5{:}40 \\ -8{:}00 & = & -8{:}00 & & -2{:}00 \\ \hline & & 5{:}00 & + & 3{:}40 & = & 8{:}40 \end{array}$$

8 cannot be subtracted from 1. Express 1:00 as 13:00. 1:00 P.M. is really the 13th hour of the day.

1:00 = 13:00
Add 12 hours to 1:00

Ellen worked 8 hours and 40 minutes.

Example B: This is part of John's time card. How long did he work yesterday?

Morning		Afternoon	
In	Out	In	Out
8:30	12:15	1:00	4:30

$$
\begin{array}{l}
12{:}15 \\
-8{:}30
\end{array} =
\begin{array}{l}
11{:}75 \\
-8{:}30 \\
\hline
3{:}45
\end{array} +
\begin{array}{l}
4{:}30 \\
-1{:}00 \\
\hline
3{:}30
\end{array} = 6{:}75 = 7{:}15
$$

30 minutes cannot be subtracted from 15 minutes. 1 hour = 60 minutes. Rename 12 hours as 11 hours. Add the 60 minutes to the 15 minutes.

12:15 = 11 hours + 60 minutes + 15 minutes
12:15 = 11 hours + 75 minutes
12:15 = 11:75

John worked 7 hours and 15 minutes.

▶ Compute the total time worked each day. The answer to Number 1 is 7 hours and 37 minutes.

Morning		Afternoon	
Time In	Time Out	Time In	Time Out
1) 7:53	12:57	1:59	4:32
2) 8:40	12:18	1:37	5:04
3) 7:07	12:20	2:42	6:57
4) 8:52	1:43	2:56	6:58
5) 6:50	10:37	11:32	4:49
6) 6:00	11:06	12:56	4:31
7) 7:45	11:43	12:21	4:55
8) 6:50	11:11	1:55	6:08
9) 8:20	12:55	1:29	4:52
10) 8:35	12:12	2:04	6:32

NET PAY

Net pay is also called "take-home pay." It is the amount of money your employer pays you after subtracting the deductions. Common deductions are taxes, social security, union dues, and health insurance.

Example A: Find Harry's net pay.

Harry earned a gross pay of $210.91. His employer deducted these amounts:

$43.07   Federal tax
 6.93   State tax
 5.87   Social Security
 2.14   Health Insurance
+ 3.85   Union dues
—————
$61.86

$210.91   Gross pay
− 61.86   Total deductions
—————
$149.05   Harry's net pay

Example B: Find Frances's net pay.

Frances earned a gross pay of $483.05. Her employer deducted these amounts:

$138.27   Federal tax
  28.91   State tax
  38.04   Social Security
   5.07   Health insurance
+   0   Union dues
—————
$210.29

$483.05   Gross pay
−210.29   Total deductions
—————
$272.76   Frances's net pay

To compute net pay, add the deductions first. Then subtract that total from the gross pay.

▶ The deductions and gross pay are listed below for twenty-five workers. Compute the net pay for each worker. The answer to Number 1 is $727.92.

	Federal Tax	State Tax	Soc. Sec. Tax	Union Dues	Health Ins.	Gross Pay
1)	$50.38	$17.26	$54.06	$4.19	$8.78	$862.59
2)	19.69	15.04	26.28	1.15	8.15	384.52
3)	34.71	16.69	35.49	1.23	9.81	589.40
4)	8.64	6.33	10.10	7.94	2.89	144.60
5)	42.01	73.73	50.08	7.58	.68	730.52
6)	15.33	7.07	17.78	2.56	5.04	263.13
7)	23.25	31.45	27.16	5.95	7.53	449.96
8)	35.31	57.65	39.75	1.61	2.03	639.84
9)	38.24	14.25	46.82	4.29	1.97	693.19
10)	40.31	19.61	47.87	2.53	1.28	750.96
11)	38.87	16.22	42.30	7.32	6.75	652.66
12)	11.49	14.32	13.18	3.74	8.12	198.77
13)	5.88	5.62	6.91	8.95	6.89	106.89
14)	51.18	13.06	57.24	5.50	8.92	905.94
15)	13.99	14.19	15.55	2.82	3.69	241.74
16)	56.21	21.54	62.42	9.43	8.12	999.90
17)	14.99	8.86	16.32	6.80	7.96	263.36
18)	21.72	8.35	25.08	8.91	2.21	411.88
19)	49.73	16.22	57.83	.13	4.55	900.83
20)	17.57	8.81	21.76	5.50	1.97	349.04
21)	24.98	9.84	29.49	.51	8.72	479.09
22)	36.95	10.22	45.59	7.57	8.96	684.42
23)	44.28	22.73	50.88	1.62	4.70	814.66
24)	38.26	10.48	43.40	5.53	3.18	659.51
25)	31.71	16.59	42.06	5.12	5.96	625.11

FRACTIONAL RATES

Usually the wage rate is fixed at whole number amounts. Occasionally, however, some workers may be paid at a rate that includes a fraction of a cent.

Example A:

Joan is a construction worker who earns $8.127 per hour. Joan worked 33 hours last week. Find Joan's gross pay. Round fractional answers to the nearer cent.

$$
\begin{array}{r}
\$8.127 \text{ Rate} \\
\times \quad 33 \text{ Hours} \\
\hline
24381 \\
24381 \\
\hline
\$268.191
\end{array}
$$

Joan's gross pay was $268.19.

Example B:

Joan worked 37 hours this week. Find Joan's gross pay.

$$
\begin{array}{r}
\$8.127 \text{ Rate} \\
\times \quad 37 \text{ Hours} \\
\hline
56889 \\
24381 \\
\hline
\$300.699
\end{array}
$$

Joan's gross pay was $300.70.

▶ Compute the gross pay and round to the nearer cent. The answer to Number 1 is $126.09.

Hours	Rate	Hours	Rate
1) 29	$ 4.348	26) 14	$ 4.934
2) 40	$ 3.557	27) 16	$ 6.085
3) 25	$ 6.585	28) 23	$ 5.836
4) 34	$ 4.976	29) 15	$ 4.732
5) 35	$ 5.032	30* 30	$49.435
6) 21	$ 5.100	31) 35	$ 5.531
7) 16	$ 5.026	32) 37	$ 6.393
8) 26	$ 5.120	33) 7	$ 4.260
9) 11	$ 5.317	34) 27	$ 3.821
10* 31	$73.133	35) 22	$ 5.771
11) 31	$ 4.856	36) 8	$ 7.094
12) 32	$ 3.486	37) 39	$ 6.677
13) 37	$ 4.875	38) 34	$ 4.221
14) 21	$ 3.680	39) 12	$ 6.296
15) 27	$ 6.855	40* 39	$45.136
16) 10	$ 3.771	41) 27	$ 3.495
17) 30	$ 4.386	42) 19	$ 4.743
18) 21	$ 5.743	43) 24	$ 6.542
19) 20	$ 4.101	44) 34	$ 4.031
20* 28	$52.643	45) 23	$ 4.336
21) 31	$ 4.706	46) 35	$ 5.620
22) 12	$ 4.616	47) 39	$ 6.893
23) 10	$ 6.373	48) 26	$ 3.821
24) 37	$ 6.725	49) 11	$ 4.903
25) 37	$ 3.987	50* 37	$37.246

DOUBLE OVERTIME

Business Vocabulary:

Double overtime — Twice the rate per hour for extra hours that are worked.

Under law most workers must be paid at a higher rate after they have worked 40 hours in one week. When some people work on Sundays and holidays, they earn double their regular hourly wages.

Example:

Cosimo earns $5.95 per hour and double overtime after 40 hours. This means that he earns $5.95 times 2, or $11.90, for each hour he works after 40 hours.

This week Cosimo worked 40 hours at his regular rate, and 11 hours overtime. This is how Cosimo computed his gross pay.

Step 1:

$5.95   Regular rate
× 40   Regular hours
$238.00   Regular wages

Step 2:

$5.95   Regular rate
×   2
$11.90   Overtime rate

Step 3:

$11.90   Overtime rate
×   11   Overtime hours
1190
1190
$130.90   Overtime wages

Step 4:

$238.00   Regular wages
+130.90   Overtime wages
$368.90   Gross pay

Cosimo's gross pay was $368.90.

▶ Compute the gross pay. Use double overtime for any time over 40 hours. The answer to Number 1 is $417.12. Round answers down to next lower cent.

Hours Worked	Regular Rate	Hours Worked	Regular Rate
1) 53	$6.32	26) 56	$6.41
2) 38	$4.33	27) 88	$5.62
3) 49	$6.17	28) 47	$6.39
4) 46	$3.58	29) 76	$6.49
5) 60	$6.86	30* 51	$8.236
6) 63	$7.95	31) 35	$5.37
7) 61	$6.65	32) 87	$5.43
8) 87	$7.13	33) 51	$5.08
9) 73	$6.33	34) 52	$4.43
10* 63	$4.436	35) 90	$4.99
11) 66	$5.26	36) 85	$4.82
12) 53	$4.86	37) 59	$4.97
13) 85	$5.81	38) 55	$7.24
14) 41	$4.48	39) 36	$6.48
15) 90	$8.03	40* 57	$5.846
16) 54	$6.78	41) 49	$6.42
17) 57	$3.83	42) 90	$4.96
18) 69	$3.75	43) 79	$3.85
19) 45	$5.12	44) 46	$6.83
20* 49	$4.831	45) 62	$3.63
21) 76	$3.49	46) 82	$6.68
22) 41	$6.99	47) 47	$7.08
23) 86	$8.32	48) 80	$7.42
24) 52	$8.01	49) 73	$5.61
25) 80	$6.38	50* 44	$6.811

TIME AND A HALF

Business Vocabulary:

Time and a half — You earn 1.5 times as much per hour for extra hours that you work.

Some workers earn time and a half when they work late or on weekends. In many companies, overtime refers to hours worked beyond 40 per week.

Example:

Tyrone earns $5.22 per hour and time and a half after 36 hours. This means that he earns $7.83 ($5.22 × 1.5) each hour he works after 36 hours.

Last week Tyrone worked 36 hours at $5.22 per hour and 5 hours at time and a half. This is how Tyrone computed his gross pay:

Step 1:

```
  $5.22   Hourly rate
 ×  36    Hours
  31 32
 156 6
$187.92   Regular wages
```

Step 2:

```
  $ 5.22   Hourly rate
 ×    1.5
  2 6 10
  5 2 2
 $ 7.8 30  Overtime rate
```

Step 3:

```
  $7.83   Overtime rate
 ×   5
 $39.15   Overtime wages
```

Step 4:

```
 $ 187.92   Regular wages
 +  39.15   Overtime wages
 $227.07    Gross pay
```

Tyrone earned $227.07.

▶ Compute the gross pay. Use time and a half for any time over 40 hours. The answer to Number 1 is $376.04. Round answers down to the next lower cent, if necessary.

Hours Worked	Regular Rate	Hours Worked	Regular Rate
1) 53	$6.32	26) 70	$5.50
2) 66	$4.12	27) 87	$5.08
3) 88	$6.58	28) 85	$4.16
4) 75	$7.56	29) 59	$7.09
5) 40	$7.11	30* 49	$4.417
6) 43	$4.41	31) 88	$4.36
7) 77	$8.35	32) 49	$8.03
8) 81	$4.64	33) 51	$4.08
9) 55	$5.45	34) 50	$5.18
10* 77	$6.611	35) 55	$8.03
11) 67	$4.05	36) 56	$5.83
12) 50	$5.08	37) 68	$7.79
13) 88	$6.91	38) 89	$6.34
14) 74	$8.21	39) 47	$4.43
15) 86	$7.76	40* 83	$3.815
16) 47	$7.03	41) 72	$5.28
17) 58	$8.08	42) 37	$4.83
18) 78	$8.26	43) 34	$5.34
19) 53	$7.64	44) 46	$3.57
20* 67	$6.501	45) 80	$6.58
21) 72	$8.07	46) 82	$6.40
22) 46	$3.73	47) 56	$4.22
23) 34	$7.66	48) 47	$6.06
24) 41	$3.82	49) 89	$7.04
25) 50	$7.07	50* 48	$7.076

COMPUTING PAYROLL DEDUCTIONS
With a Calculator

Many companies have a payroll deduction plan to benefit employees. Workers may pay their insurance premiums, pay union dues, pay off a loan, or even donate to charity with this plan. It is very convenient and efficient because the money is deducted directly from the workers' paychecks. The system works automatically.

Example A:

Ethel worked 36 hours at $8.55 per hour. Her deduction for life insurance was 2.77% of her gross pay. Find the amount of the deduction.

2.77% = .0277

.0277 × 36 × $8.55 = $8.52606

Round to the next higher cent.

Ethel's deduction was $8.53.

Example B:

Eugene worked 38 hours at $6.97 per hour. His deduction for union dues was 2.093% of his gross pay. Find the amount of the deduction.

2.093% = .02093

.02093 × 38 × $6.97 = $5.5435198

Round to the next higher cent.

Eugene's deduction was $5.55.

▶ Use a calculator to compute these payroll deductions. Round to the next higher cent. The answer to Number 1 is $1.84.

	Deduction Rate	Hours Worked	Hourly Rate
1)	2.87%	14	$4.59
2)	1.84%	22	$7.79
3)	1.9%	31	$4.77
4)	1.51%	32	$8.61
5)	1.48%	35	$7.86
6)	3.46%	37	$8.63
7)	1.84%	14	$8.83
8)	1.8%	19	$8.64
9)	3.19%	24	$6.44
10*	.149%	33	$6.95
11)	1.2%	16	$7.56
12)	1.94%	26	$6.73
13)	3.09%	10	$5.95
14)	2.59%	11	$7.33
15)	1.79%	30	$7.00
16)	2.33%	14	$4.96
17)	3.24%	33	$7.64
18)	1.11%	32	$7.12
19)	1.18%	18	$4.94
20*	.153%	35	$4.32
21)	1.14%	24	$5.16
22)	3.26%	16	$5.78
23)	2.03%	34	$5.65
24)	2.79%	37	$7.97
25)	3.12%	29	$5.79

BASIC SKILL REVIEW

1) During the last 4 weeks, Fran worked 54, 39, 68, and 47 hours. How many hours did she work?

2) Joe works 9 hours per day. He worked 27 days last month. How many hours did Joe work last month?

3) Sally is often late for work. Last year she was scheduled to work for 1907 hours. She lost pay for 39 hours because of lateness. For how many hours was Sally paid?

4) Two-thirds of 429 employees reported early for work. How many reported early?

5) Juan answered the phone for $2\frac{1}{2}$ hours in the morning and $3\frac{1}{4}$ hours in the afternoon. For how much time did Juan answer the phone?

6) Sue-Ellen can tune $2\frac{1}{2}$ truck engines in a day. How long will she need to tune the engines of 75 trucks?

7) Henry's car repair bill listed the repair times in hours: muffler, 1.2; tune-up, 3.5; alignment, .7; and brakes, 1. Find the total labor time.

8) Gerry's new pay rate is $8.126 per hour. His old pay rate was $7.689 per hour. What was his hourly raise?

9) Pens cost $.45 apiece. How many pens can be bought for $9.90?

10) 17% of 1200 workers earned overtime pay. How many earned overtime pay?

Computer Program: **OVERTIME RATES**

This program computes gross pay and overtime rates from an hourly rate.

Type the program into a computer and run it. Use an hourly rate of $4.88. If you type it in correctly, the computer will compute:

- the gross pay as $195.20,

- the time and one-half rate as $7.32,

- and the double time rate as $9.76.


```
10  REM PAY RATE PROGRAM
20  PRINT "TYPE IN THE REGULAR HOURLY PAY RATE
        AND PRESS RETURN."
30  INPUT W
40  PRINT "THE GROSS PAY FOR A FULL 40-HOUR WEEK
        = $"; 40 * W
50  PRINT "THE TIME AND ONE-HALF RATE IS $"; 1.5 *
        W ; " PER HOUR."
60  PRINT "THE DOUBLE TIME RATE IS $"; 2 * W; " PER
        HOUR."
70  END
```

Note: On some computers the return key is labeled ENTER.

Run the program several times with different hourly rates. How do you think this program would simplify the work of a payroll clerk?

CHAPTER REVIEW

▶ Number each calculation on your paper. Work neatly. Round answers 3 and 4 to the nearer cent.

	Hours Worked	Rate	Gross Pay
1)	38	$ 5.28	?
2)	29	7.92	?
3)	34	9.162	?
4)	39	15.439	?
5)	47	8.65 } (Double time	?
6)	54	12.45 } after 40 hours)	?
7)	53	7.84 } (Time and a half	?
8)	67	9.52 } after 40 hours)	?

	Morning In	Morning Out	Afternoon In	Afternoon Out	Total Time Worked
9)	6:22	11:10	12:43	5:51	?
10)	7:54	12:20	1:25	5:00	?

	Fed. Tax	State Tax	FICA	Union Dues	Health Ins.	Gross	Net
11)	$92.16	$14.22	$32.16	$2.66	$ 7.20	$405.10	?
12)	79.24	12.25	29.98	4.03	8.90	360.11	?

	Fed. Tax	State Tax	FICA	Union Dues	Health Ins.	Hours	Rate	Net
13)	33.00	9.34	20.76	—	15.98	35	$8.94	?
14)	54.92	7.49	37.64	5.91	13.87	40	5.50	?

▶ Round these amounts of money:

15)	To the nearer cent:	$ 84.644	$ 8.4153
16)	To the next higher cent:	$ 59.196	$ 2.68
17)	To the next lower cent:	$ 41.921	$ 8.7883
18)	To the nearer dollar:	$368.37	$12.323

Chapter 2

Earning Money in Sales And Manufacturing

Most people who work in the sales field earn a commission on their sales. Employers use commissions to reward employees for how much they sell. Salespersons who are paid on the percentage of what they sell are motivated to make as many sales as possible.

Many people who work in manufacturing earn a certain amount for each unit they produce. This is called piecework.

Why are commission sales and piecework both called "incentive" pay?

This chapter will give you practice in computing earnings for commission sales and piecework.

COMMISSION

Business Vocabulary:

Commission — Pay based on a percentage of sales.

Many salespersons earn commission. Stores and companies pay commissions to reward their employees for hard work in selling goods and services.

Example A: David earns 6% of his sales of men's clothing. This week his sales totaled $3,150.00. Compute David's commission.

Step 1: 6% = .06

To change a percent to a decimal, move the decimal point two places to the left.

Step 2:

$3150 Sales
×.06 Rate
——————
$189.00 Commission

David earned a commission of $189.00.

Example B: Susan earned 11% commission on sales of $2,175.00. Compute Susan's commission.

Step 1: 11% = .11

Step 2:

$2175 Sales
×.11 Rate
——————
2175
2175
——————
$239.25 Commission

Susan earned a commission of $239.25.

► Compute each of the commissions below. The answer to Number 1 is $327.52.

	Commission Rate	Sales		Commission Rate	Sales
1)	2%	$16,376	26)	6%	$19,139
2)	3%	$17,842	27)	11%	$9,839
3)	10%	$844	28)	7%	$13,632
4)	2%	$19,634	29)	3%	$15,744
5)	2%	$19,638	30*	2%	$141,163
6)	6%	$19,702	31)	4%	$16,319
7)	16%	$6,073	32)	2%	$10,398
8)	7%	$15,137	33)	16%	$9,608
9)	2%	$17,166	34)	9%	$13,904
10*	15%	$19,502	35)	9%	$13,131
11)	3%	$16,637	36)	18%	$6,639
12)	9%	$15,296	37)	6%	$17,889
13)	3%	$10,296	38)	3%	$15,909
14)	10%	$3,713	39)	6%	$8,899
15)	5%	$1,138	40*	7%	$83,985
16)	6%	$15,177	41)	9%	$12,598
17)	6%	$10,591	42)	11%	$5,171
18)	4%	$4,571	43)	9%	$16,325
19)	5%	$4,382	44)	3%	$13,970
20*	7%	$115,940	45)	11%	$4,300
21)	6%	$15,194	46)	7%	$16,003
22)	10%	$4,268	47)	9%	$5,795
23)	15%	$7,611	48)	17%	$2,188
24)	9%	$7,750	49)	18%	$4,738
25)	7%	$2,926	50*	9%	$116,710

WAGES PLUS COMMISSION

Some stores and companies pay salespeople regular wages plus a commission. This is called total pay.

Example A:

Elaine worked 35 hours at $4.05 per hour. She earned 2% commission on her sales of $3,182. Elaine computed her total pay.

Step 1:	**Step 2:**	**Step 3:**
$4.05	$3182	$141.75
× 35	× .02	+ 63.64
20 25	$63.64	$205.39
121 5		
$141.75		

Elaine's total pay was $205.39.

Example B:

Louis worked 28 hours at $5.12 per hour. He earned 1.7% commission on his sales of $2,990. Louis computed his total pay.

Step 1:	**Step 2:**	**Step 3:**
$5.12	$2990	$143.36
× 28	× .017	+ 50.83
40 96	20 930	$194.19
102 4	29 90	
$143.36	$50.83Ø	

Louis's total pay was $194.19.

▶ Compute the total pay. Add the commission to the regular wages. The answer to Number 1 is $176.80. If necessary, round to the nearer cent.

	Hours	Rate	Commission	Sales
1)	33	$3.91	1%	$4,777
2)	34	$4.08	3%	$4,642
3)	38	$4.00	3%	$3,024
4)	26	$5.09	2%	$688
5)	30	$4.93	7%	$3,099
6)	17	$5.52	2%	$1,515
7)	32	$8.57	6%	$4,274
8)	26	$5.37	8%	$2,339
9)	25	$7.15	3%	$1,144
10*	31	$15.92	10.4%	$11,628
11)	34	$3.75	2%	$4,414
12)	19	$9.74	4%	$4,561
13)	17	$8.50	8%	$2,849
14)	38	$4.29	9%	$3,747
15)	38	$6.58	6%	$4,961
16)	20	$4.31	3%	$2,668
17)	22	$7.09	10%	$3,611
18)	27	$5.83	10%	$4,562
19)	21	$3.35	6%	$1,494
20*	32	$12.72	8.3%	$7,504
21)	36	$4.31	9%	$1,606
22)	38	$8.60	7%	$2,602
23)	15	$7.95	4%	$683
24)	30	$5.75	6%	$1,489
25)	27	$5.54	8%	$1,279

BONUS COMMISSION

Business Vocabulary:

Quota — The amount of sales that an employer expects from a salesperson.

Some salespeople earn a bonus commission when they sell more than their quota.

Example:

Sheryl sells used cars. She earns 5% commission on sales up to $8,000 each month. She earns 7% on all sales over $8,000.

Sheryl's total sales in March were $11,500. Sheryl computed her total commission.

Step 1:

$8000	Quota
× .05	Rate
$400.00	Regular commission

Step 2:

$11,500	Sales
− 8,000	Quota
$ 3,500	Excess

Step 3:

$3500	Excess
× .07	Rate
$245.00	Bonus commission

Step 4:

$400	Regular commission
+245	Bonus commission
$645	Total commission

Sheryl's commission was $645.

▶Compute the total commission for each example below. Add the bonus commission to the regular commission. The answer to Number 1 is $560.40.

	Quota	Rate	Sales	Bonus Rate
1)	$8,000	7%	$8,005	8%
2)	$3,100	11%	$4,484	14%
3)	$8,300	8%	$8,625	15%
4)	$5,500	6%	$10,804	15%
5)	$8,000	6%	$15,290	13%
6)	$1,900	4%	$3,099	12%
7)	$1,100	9%	$1,440	18%
8)	$10,200	3%	$16,604	9%
9)	$1,300	7%	$2,413	12%
10)	$2,400	4%	$2,451	11%
11)	$4,900	5%	$7,252	7%
12)	$9,900	11%	$8,975	16%
13)	$5,400	6%	$8,163	10%
14)	$7,300	3%	$14,433	8%
15)	$10,700	9%	$11,739	13%
16)	$7,000	11%	$7,308	15%
17)	$5,500	10%	$7,835	19%
18)	$2,400	7%	$3,459	9%
19)	$8,100	8%	$15,695	11%
20)	$10,600	2%	$17,459	5%
21)	$8,400	11%	$15,256	15%
22)	$8,400	8%	$13,219	10%
23)	$2,700	7%	$3,047	14%
24)	$7,500	6%	$2,180	7%
25)	$1,600	10%	$2,789	18%

PIECEWORK

Business Vocabulary:
Piecework — Work done by the piece and paid for at a set rate per unit.

Many manufacturers pay their workers on a piecework basis. This system encourages employees to work hard. The completed products are checked by an inspector. Workers are paid only for units that pass inspection.

Example A:
During the five working days last week, Bruce bound these numbers of books: 38, 45, 22, 39, and 36. He earns $.63 per book. Bruce computed his gross pay:

Step 1:		**Step 2:**	
	38		1 80
	45		× $.63
	22		5 40
	39		108 0
	+ 36		$113.40
	180		

Bruce's gross pay was $113.40.

Example B:
Joan packs boxes. Her daily totals last week were: 99, 127, 173, 154, and 153. She earns $.27 per box. Joan computed her gross pay:

Step 1:		**Step 2:**	
	99		7 06
	127		× $.27
	173		49 42
	154		141 2
	+ 153		$190.62
	706		

Joan's gross pay was $190.62.

▶ Compute the weekly earnings for these people. Add.
Then multiply. If necessary, round to the nearer cent.
The answer to Number 1 is $206.70.

	Rate per Unit	Daily Production				
		Mon.	Tues.	Wed.	Thur.	Fri.
1)	$.78	49	57	63	42	54
2)	$1.03	36	30	30	27	35
3)	$2.50	16	20	19	19	20
4)	$3.91	6	6	7	7	7
5)	$1.74	17	18	18	15	17
6)	$4.98	4	5	5	5	5
7)	$4.57	11	10	9	11	10
8)	$1.59	37	33	35	29	34
9)	$4.29	10	10	13	10	10
10*	$3.875	12	13	12	13	11
11)	$3.90	10	8	9	9	8
12)	$4.83	11	8	11	9	9
13)	$1.80	28	28	32	31	29
14)	$1.24	25	20	24	24	23
15)	$2.15	12	9	11	11	11
16)	$1.78	21	21	24	25	25
17)	$3.87	13	11	12	11	11
18)	$.52	87	95	88	82	87
19)	$4.72	7	6	6	7	7
20*	$3.364	14	13	14	11	13
21)	$1.07	51	46	43	47	39
22)	$4.23	5	5	6	6	5
23)	$.63	68	68	73	87	75
24)	$4.27	11	10	9	9	11
25)	$2.29	10	11	9	9	10

COMPUTING TOTAL PAY
With a Calculator

Some salespeople who earn commission are paid on total sales, less returns. This means that the value of the returned goods (if any) is subtracted from the total sales.

Example A:

Rona earns a commission of 7.9% on total sales, less returns. She also earns $4.48 per hour. Find her total pay for a week when she sold $2935 worth of goods, had $117 returned, and she worked 23 hours.

$2935 − $117 = $2818

$2818 × .079 = $222.622 (Round to $223)

$4.48 × 23 = $103.04 (Round to $103)

Total pay: $223 + $103 = $326

Rona's pay was $326.

Example B:

Jay earns a commission of 8.8% on total sales, less returns, plus $5.89 per hour. Find his total pay for a week when he sold $10,123 worth of goods, had $202 returned, and he worked 20 hours.

$10,123 − $202 = $9921

$9921 × .088 = $873.048 (Round to $873)

$5.89 × 20 = $117.80 (Round to $118)

Total pay: $873 + $118 = $991

Jay's pay was $991.

▶ Calculate the total pay for each of these salespeople. Round each product to the nearer dollar. The answer to Number 1 is $862.

	Total Sales	Returns	Commission Rate	Hours	Wage Rate
1)	$14,516	$566	5.3%	25	$4.93
2)	$5,081	$101	12.3%	40	$4.58
3)	$5,615	$224	9.7%	38	$6.93
4)	$15,356	$460	11.1%	25	$5.39
5)	$15,971	$638	.7%	25	$6.12
6)	$13,694	$136	10.7%	34	$5.51
7)	$14	$0	2.1%	39	$5.33
8)	$6,632	$198	10.3%	20	$6.10
9)	$9,172	$183	9.6%	39	$6.11
10)	$8,180	$327	11.6%	21	$4.74
11)	$12,631	$505	.1%	35	$4.92
12)	$19,166	$766	5.5%	33	$6.09
13)	$621	$18	8.5%	31	$4.42
14)	$5,916	$59	11.7%	28	$5.16
15)	$9,602	$192	8.9%	39	$6.15
16)	$1,868	$56	8.4%	29	$5.53
17)	$9,492	$284	1.5%	40	$5.58
18)	$19,558	$586	4.9%	29	$5.82
19)	$19,560	$195	4.7%	29	$6.42
20)	$8,494	$339	5.4%	31	$5.32
21)	$5,546	$166	6.7%	39	$4.98
22)	$19,364	$193	10.4%	20	$6.24
23)	$18,643	$745	4.6%	35	$6.07
24)	$11,476	$114	5.7%	31	$4.38
25)	$15,139	$454	4.3%	39	$6.12

BASIC SKILL REVIEW

1) Joe produced 422 units. However, 85 did not pass inspection. How many units passed inspection?

2) Sixty-five brushes can be packed into one box. How many boxes are needed for 1430 brushes?

3) The shipping charge for one package is $29. What is the shipping charge for 145 packages?

4) Last week, Colleen's sales were $1269, $954, $877, $2654, and $12,650. Find her total sales.

5) Martha earns $2.75 for each disk drive she assembles. How much will she earn if she assembles 138 disk drives?

6) During six days the returns were: $40, $36.95, $142.96, $75.25, $108, and $96.27. Find the total returns.

7) Last month, the total of the charge sales and the cash sales was $10,625.79. The charge sales totaled $1877.95. Find the total cash sales.

8) Carol earns $3.90 for each shirt she sews. If her total pay was $276.90, how many shirts did she sew?

9) Night-shift production is only $\frac{4}{5}$ of day-shift production. If day-shift production is 760 units, what is night-shift production?

10) One-fourth of an order was shipped on Monday. Two-fifths of the order was shipped on Tuesday. How much of the order was shipped on either Monday or Tuesday?

11) Each wrench weighs $2\frac{1}{4}$ kilograms. How many wrenches will go in a box that holds only 36 kg?

Computer Program: **PAYROLL**

This program can compute the total pay for a number of employees.

Type the program into a computer and run it. Use an hourly rate of $6.00 per hour. If you type the program in correctly, the computer will print the total pay for Burns as $285. Δ means to type a blank space.

```
10   REM PAYROLL PROGRAM
20   PRINT "TYPE IN THE HOURLY RATE. PRESS RETURN."
30   PRINT "FOR EXAMPLE, TYPE 5.25 FOR $5.25."
40   REM R = HOURLY RATE
50   INPUT R
60   PRINT "WAGE RATE = $";R; "/HR. UP TO 40 HOURS."
70   PRINT "TIME AND A HALF = $";1.5 * R;"/HR."
80   PRINT
90   PRINT "NAMEΔΔΔΔΔ WAGESΔΔΔ OT.Δ WAGES
            ΔΔΔΔΔTOTALΔ PAY"
100  REM N$ = NAME, H = HOURS
110  READ N$,H
120  IF N$ = "ZZZ" THEN 250
130  IF H > 40 THEN 190
140  REM W = REGULAR WAGES, OT = OVERTIME WAGES
150  LET W = R * H
160  LET OT = 0
170  GOTO 210
180  REM 40 * R = REGULAR WEEKLY WAGES, (H−40) =
            OVERTIME HOURS, 1.5 * R = TIME AND A
            HALF RATE
190  LET W = 40 * R
200  LET OT = 1.5 * R * (H−40)
210  PRINT N$;"ΔΔΔΔ$";W;"ΔΔΔΔΔ$";OT;"ΔΔΔΔ$";W+OT
220  GOTO 110
230  DATA "AARON",36,"BURNS",45,"CADEN",40
240  DATA "ZZZ",−1
250  END
```

Run the program several times. Use different rates, names, and hours. Which tool can figure a payroll faster — a calculator, or a computer?

CHAPTER REVIEW

▶ Number your paper from 1 to 11. Next to each number write the correct answer for the question mark. Round money to the nearer cent.

	Sales	Commission Rate	Commission
1)	$3,486	15%	?
2)	$54,827	4%	?

	Hours Worked	Wage Rate	Sales	Commission Rate	Total Pay
3)	25	$6.42	$ 5,963	5%	?
4)	37	$7.89	$28,977	2%	?

	Commission Rate	Sales	Bonus Rate	Total Pay
5)	7%	$12,896	9% beyond $10,000	?
6)	12%	$37,000	16% beyond $35,000	?
7)	9%	$25,706	12% beyond $30,000	?

	Acceptable Units Produced	Unit Pay	Total Pay
8)	454	$ .08	?
9)	18	$4.10	?

		Weekly Production				Unit Pay	Total Pay
	M	T	W	Th	F		
10)	9	11	10	10	8	$4.86	?
11)	87	110	108	99	120	$ .90	?

Chapter 3

Real Estate and Sales Tax

People who live all alone, on their own deserted islands, do not have to pay taxes. Taxes are only necessary to pay the expenses of a government. State and local governments require real estate and sales taxes to pay for services like...

schools,

police protection,

fire protection,

and road maintenance.

Can you name some other services provided by state and local governments?

This chapter presents ways to compute real estate and sales taxes.

REAL ESTATE TAXES

Business Vocabulary:

Real estate — Land and any buildings on it.

Tax assessor — A government worker who inspects property and places a value on it for tax purposes.

Assessment — The assessor's estimate of property value.

Local governments use real estate taxes to pay for schools, police, and other services. Real estate tax is based on property value. Property owners pay real estate (or property) tax every year.

Example:

The tax assessment on Mr. Wilson's home is $74,500. The local tax rate is $3.12 per $100 of the assessment. What is Mr. Wilson's property tax?

Step 1: Divide the assessment by $100. Move the decimal point two places to the left.

$$\$74,500 \div \$100 = 745$$

Step 2: Multiply by the rate.

```
      745
 X $3.12  Rate
    14 90
    74 5
   2235
 $2324.40
```

Mr. Wilson's property tax is $2,324.40.

▶Compute the real estate tax. Round up to the next cent if necessary. The answer to Number 1 is $232.99.

	Assessment	Rate per $100		Assessment	Rate per $100
1)	$3,770	$6.18	26)	$61,580	$6.03
2)	$57,180	$5.21	27)	$64,360	$4.62
3)	$98,020	$4.79	28)	$11,960	$2.78
4)	$82,210	$6.39	29)	$18,130	$2.72
5)	$15,110	$6.36	30*	$766,715	$4.61
6)	$86,640	$6.55	31)	$60,810	$6.03
7)	$61,190	$3.11	32)	$44,900	$2.69
8)	$43,920	$6.78	33)	$75,480	$3.71
9)	$38,830	$2.24	34)	$41,990	$3.76
10*	$330,125	$6.52	35)	$27,370	$2.28
11)	$13,560	$6.40	36)	$65,650	$7.24
12)	$59,320	$6.84	37)	$51,720	$4.39
13)	$44,700	$1.64	38)	$75,270	$5.56
14)	$14,350	$7.39	39)	$20,260	$6.20
15)	$14,840	$7.39	40*	$214,955	$5.31
16)	$72,670	$7.41	41)	$39,490	$6.38
17)	$81,490	$3.24	42)	$11,070	$4.57
18)	$73,430	$6.02	43)	$80,490	$4.32
19)	$11,100	$6.64	44)	$91,580	$5.64
20*	$855,815	$1.91	45)	$90,970	$5.40
21)	$26,690	$6.48	46)	$91,640	$3.42
22)	$91,120	$6.07	47)	$57,010	$6.86
23)	$27,680	$4.53	48)	$24,550	$6.25
24)	$45,380	$2.52	49)	$23,650	$4.11
25)	$14,930	$1.73	50*	$332,215	$3.72

SALES TAX

Business Vocabulary:

Revenue — Government income. Most revenue comes from taxes.

Many states and cities impose a retail sales tax. This tax is collected by merchants who sell goods subject to the tax. The merchants send the tax money to the local or state governments.

Example A:

Joe bought a coat for $107. He also had to pay a 4% sales tax. Compute the amount of sales tax.

Step 1: Change the percent to a decimal.

4% = .04

Step 2:

$1 07	Purchase price
× .04	Tax rate
$4.28	Sales tax

> This amount is not rounded because it has a whole number of cents.

The sales tax on the coat was $4.28.

Example B:

Evelyn bought a video cassette recorder for $295.90. She also had to pay a 7% sales tax. Compute the amount of the sales tax.

Step 1: 7% = .07

Step 2:

$295.90
× .07
$20.7130

> The normal rule for rounding (5 and above, round up) is not used in tax calculations. If the tax does not contain a whole number of cents, we round it *up* to the next cent.
>
> $20.713 rounds up to $20.72.

The sales tax on the VCR was $20.72.

▶ Compute the sales tax on these purchases. If necessary, round up the answer to the next cent. The answer to Number 1 is $6.72.

	Purchase Price	Sales Tax Rate		Purchase Price	Sales Tax Rate
1)	$ 95.89	7%	26)	$ 93.05	6%
2)	$ 83.08	3%	27)	$ 9.38	5%
3)	$ 58.15	7%	28)	$ 38.10	2%
4)	$ 19.49	7%	29)	$ 39.41	6%
5)	$ 51.78	3%	30*	$171.49	2.3%
6)	$666.27	2%	31)	$ 55.56	8%
7)	$ 5.09	7%	32)	$ 90.76	7%
8)	$ 4.81	2%	33)	$ 91.47	4%
9)	$ 93.45	6%	34)	$ 37.90	3%
10*	$ 26.19	8.1%	35)	$ 13.94	7%
11)	$ 10.74	2%	36)	$963.49	3%
12)	$ 46.42	3%	37)	$ 47.39	7%
13)	$ 84.38	4%	38)	$ 23.12	5%
14)	$ 73.49	7%	39)	$ 19.57	2%
15)	$ 89.38	6%	40*	$ 39.38	8.4%
16)	$ 27.02	4%	41)	$ 29.59	7%
17)	$ 91.13	2%	42)	$ 77.37	4%
18)	$481.91	5%	43)	$ 23.19	6%
19)	$ 73.46	2%	44)	$ 88.98	5%
20*	$ 13.96	3.2%	45)	$ 24.77	2%
21)	$ 15.89	7%	46)	$ 21.83	7%
22)	$ 14.49	5%	47)	$192.06	4%
23)	$ 83.59	5%	48)	$ 49.67	4%
24)	$757.68	3%	49)	$ 61.60	8%
25)	$101.25	8%	50*	$ 15.08	7.5%

SALES TAX CHART

In some retail stores, the sales tax is computed automatically by the cash register. In many other stores, however, the cashier uses a chart to find the amount of sales tax to charge the customer.

Here is part of a sales tax chart to be used in a state that has a 6% sales tax.

6% STATE SALES TAX

Amount of Sale	Tax	Amount of Sale	Tax	Amount of Sale	Tax
.16	.01	1.84 - 2.00	.12	3.67 - 3.83	.23
.17 - .33	.02	2.01 - 2.16	.13	3.84 - 4.00	.24
.34 - .50	.03	2.17 - 2.33	.14	4.01 - 4.16	.25
.51 - .66	.04	2.34 - 2.50	.15	4.17 - 4.33	.26
.67 - .83	.05	2.51 - 2.66	.16	4.34 - 4.50	.27
.84 - 1.00	.06	2.67 - 2.83	.17	4.51 - 4.66	.28
1.01 - 1.16	.07	2.84 - 3.00	.18	4.67 - 4.83	.29
1.17 - 1.33	.08	3.01 - 3.16	.19	4.84 - 5.00	.30
1.34 - 1.50	.09	3.17 - 3.33	.20	5.01 - 5.16	.31
1.51 - 1.66	.10	3.34 - 3.50	.21	5.17 - 5.33	.32
1.67 - 1.83	.11	3.51 - 3.66	.22	5.34 - 5.50	.33

Example A:

Sally needed a pen. The selling price was $1.59. Find the sales tax on the chart. The tax was $.10. What was the total price?

$1.59 Selling price
+ .10 Sales tax
$1.69 Total price

Example B:

Frank filled out an invoice in the billing department for $3.83. Find the sales tax on the chart. The tax was $.23. What was the total price?

$3.83 Selling price
+ .23 Sales tax
$4.06 Total price

▶ Find the sales tax for each of these amounts. Use the chart on page 40. Then find the total price. The answers to Number 1 are $.05 and $.72.

1) $ .67	26) $3.13	51) $3.37
2) $1.66	27) $4.71	52) $1.45
3) $1.12	28) $1.04	53) $2.36
4) $ .49	29) $4.10	54) $4.91
5) $4.62	30) $2.78	55) $ .47
6) $ .45	31) $1.41	56) $2.35
7) $1.25	32) $3.26	57) $2.60
8) $2.64	33) $ .27	58) $3.95
9) $1.36	34) $ .26	59) $ .76
10) $ .40	35) $4.45	60) $ .74
11) $1.32	36) $ .25	61) $2.25
12) $2.03	37) $ .50	62) $ .85
13) $4.98	38) $5.03	63) $4.68
14) $4.52	39) $3.55	64) $ .77
15) $1.88	40) $1.40	65) $2.82
16) $2.33	41) $4.72	66) $5.33
17) $5.05	42) $ .57	67) $2.65
18) $4.39	43) $ .19	68) $3.71
19) $3.98	44) $ .22	69) $1.52
20) $3.52	45) $2.42	70) $5.45
21) $2.14	46) $4.54	71) $4.92
22) $4.69	47) $1.73	72) $5.01
23) $3.89	48) $3.96	73) $3.94
24) $4.47	49) $4.50	74) $ .89
25) $ .92	50) $4.81	75) $2.44

COMPUTING SALES TAX MENTALLY

You may want to check a sales tax sometime when you don't have a pencil or paper or calculator. Try to calculate sales tax mentally. It can be surprisingly easy to work out simple percents in your head.

Example A: The selling price is $9. The tax rate is 5%. What is the sales tax?

$$5 \times 9 = 45$$
Therefore, 5% of $9 is $.45.

Example B: Selling price, $30; tax rate, 7%.

$$7 \times 30 = 210$$
Therefore, 7% of $30 is $2.10.

Example C: Selling price, $37; tax rate, 4%.

$$4 \times 30 = 120$$
$$4 \times 7 = 28$$
Therefore, 4% of $37 is $1.48.

Example D: Selling price, $704; tax rate, 6%.

$$6 \times 700 = 4200$$
$$6 \times 4 = 24$$
Therefore, 6% of $704 is $42.24.

▶ Compute these sales tax charges in your head. The selling price and the tax rate are given. Write down only the answer. The answer to Number 1 is $.07.

1) $1; 7%	26) $80; 8%
2) $6; 8%	27) $70; 4%
3) $7; 8%	28) $90; 6%
4) $8; 6%	29) $90; 3%
5) $4; 2.5%	30) $80; 5%
6) $7; 1%	31) $60; 1%
7) $8; 3%	32) $50; 9%
8) $3; 2%	33) $80; 1%
9) $9; 4%	34) $10; 8%
10) $3; 1%	35) $10; 1.5%
11) $9; 8%	36) $90; 7%
12) $5; 2%	37) $50; 4%
13) $8; 5%	38) $70; 5%
14) $6; 4%	39) $70; 2%
15) $1; 7.5%	40) $40; 7%
16) $2; 2%	41) $90; 2%
17) $6; 9%	42) $82; 7%
18) $7; 3%	43) $99; 9%
19) $3; 4%	44) $24; 9%
20) $6; 6%	45) $33; 9%
21) $1; 5%	46) $58; 5%
22) $2; 9%	47) $82; 6%
23) $4; 8%	48) $21; 7%
24) $7; 6%	49) $54; 5%
25) $90; 7.5%	50) $500; 3%

FINDING THE PROPERTY TAX RATE
With a Calculator

Business Vocabulary:

Tax base — The total assessed value of all of the taxable property in a community.

The greatest source of funding for local governments is the property tax. While some communities receive outside funding to help meet their expenses, others do not. They rely entirely on the property tax. To find the property tax rate, they divide their total budget by the tax base.

Example: Square Town has a budget of $2,500,000. Its tax base is $94,000,000. Find the tax rate.

$$2,500,000 \div 94,000,000 = .026595744$$

This rate may be expressed in different ways:

A) as a 6-place decimal (Round up to the millionths place.):

.026596

B) as a percent (Round up to the next hundredth of a percent.):

2.66%

C) as an amount per $100 of assessed value (Round up to the next higher cent.):

$2.66

D) as an amount per $1000 of assessed value (Round up to the next higher cent.):

$26.60

▶ Find the tax rate and express it in four ways: A), as a 6-place decimal; B), as a percent; C), as an amount per $100; and D), as an amount per $1000. The answers to Number 1 are: A) .031537; B) 3.16%; C) $3.16; and D) $31.54.

	Total Budget	Tax Base
1)	$648,327	$20,557,695
2)	$422,849	$18,084,938
3)	$731,304	$18,016,511
4)	$741,588	$35,378,311
5)	$928,135	$44,366,379
6)	$138,375	$6,783,579
7)	$307,079	$14,693,770
8)	$488,417	$16,926,799
9)	$546,217	$19,887,176
10)	$1,431	$45,371
11)	$34,601	$1,384,218
12)	$687,103	$26,150,084
13)	$164,300	$4,234,436
14)	$798,163	$33,424,421
15)	$837,562	$18,402,431
16)	$226,922	$6,972,573
17)	$820,350	$24,549,893
18)	$917,878	$40,234,048
19)	$633,956	$19,501,424
20)	$818,890	$28,607,248
21)	$914,589	$35,846,023
22)	$22,257	$607,122
23)	$302,077	$12,520,646
24)	$873,839	$33,390,065
25)	$418,138	$14,173,729

BASIC SKILL REVIEW

1) A town has 14,527 one-family houses, 6,428 two-family houses, 3,591 three-family houses, and 157 apartment houses. How many dwellings are there in the town?

2) A town contains 89,127 private properties. Of these, 4,825 are properties that are not taxed, such as churches and schools. How many properties are taxed?

3) Each Type A apartment house pays $45,000 in taxes. What is the total tax on 50 Type A apartment houses?

4) Martina's assessment was $2,850. Joe's assessment was 1.4 times as much. What was Joe's assessment?

5) The sales tax on radio B is $6.27. The sales tax on radio C is $4.67. How much more is the tax on radio B?

6) Jay sold six suits today. The sales tax charges on the suits were $8.59, $17.26, $12.53, $15.49, $6.24, and $9.29. What was the total sales tax?

7) The price on Chana's stereo, including 5% sales tax, was $379.05. What was the selling price of the stereo alone? (Hint: Divide $379.05 by 1.05)

8) Two-ninths of 10,404 homeowners are retired. How many are retired?

9) A piece of land contains 45 acres. How many $2\frac{1}{2}$-acre plots can be made from it?

10) Suri owns $43\frac{1}{4}$ acres of pasture, $24\frac{3}{8}$ acres of farmland, and a 3-acre lake. What is the total area?

Computer Program: REAL ESTATE TAX

This program calculates the real estate tax due on rectangularly-shaped properties.

Type the program into a computer and run it. Make up the rates and dimensions. Run the program several times with different rates and dimensions.

```
20   REM REAL ESTATE TAX PROGRAM
30   PRINT "TYPE IN THE TAX RATE/$100 ON THE BLDG."
35   INPUT TB
40   PRINT "TYPE IN THE TAX RATE/$100 ON THE OTHER"
42   PRINT "STRUCTURES (SEPARATE GARAGE, ETC.)"
45   INPUT TS
50   PRINT "TYPE IN THE (DEPTH) LENGTH OF THE LAND."
55   INPUT D
60   PRINT "TYPE IN THE (FRONTAGE) WIDTH OF THE
     LAND."
65   INPUT F
70   PRINT "TYPE IN THE LAND ASSESSMENT PER ACRE."
75   INPUT AL
80   PRINT "TYPE IN THE ASSESSMENT OF THE BUILD-
     ING."
85   INPUT AB
90   PRINT "TYPE IN THE ASSESSMENT OF THE SEPA-
     RATE" : PRINT "STRUCTURES"
95   INPUT AS
100  LET A = D * F / 43320
105  PRINT "TOTAL AREA OF LAND = "; INT (1000 *
     A + .5) / 1000;" ACRES."
110  LET TT = INT (AL * A + .5)
115  PRINT "TAX ON LAND = $"; TT
120  PRINT "TAX ON THE BUILDING = $"; TB * (AB / 100)
125  PRINT "TAX ON THE SEPARATE STRUCTURES =
     $";TS * (AS/100)
130  PRINT "TOTAL TAX BILL = $";TT + TB * (AB / 100)
     + TS * (AS / 100)
135  END
```

How could a program like this be helpful?

CHAPTER REVIEW

▶ Number your paper from 1 to 8. Next to each number write the correct answer or answers for the question marks. If necessary, round tax answers up to the next cent.

	Tax Rate	Assessed Value	Tax
1)	$4.52 per $100	$ 64,000	?
2)	$3.20 per $100	$ 75,800	?
3)	$6.27 per $100	$200,000	?
4)	$7.26 per $100	$ 47,500	?

	Selling Price	Tax Rate	Sales Tax	Total Price
5)	$6.82	6%	?	?
6)	$4.17	6%	?	?
7)	$41.82	5%	?	?
8)	$264.95	7%	?	?

▶ Find the answers.

9) Each house in a development pays $1500 in taxes. The total assessment of the development is $88,500. How many houses are in the development?

10) Harold bought $27\frac{1}{3}$ acres of farmland. $15\frac{1}{2}$ of the acres are planted with corn. How many of the acres are not planted with corn?

11) Nine percent of 27,500 property owners paid their taxes early. How many paid their taxes early?

Chapter 4

Income Taxes

Most of the money withheld from an employee's wages is for federal and state income taxes. Each taxpayer must file a personal income tax return with the federal government by April 15 every year. Taxpayers usually have to file a state income tax return, too.

By filling out the income tax form, the taxpayer finds out the amount of tax he or she is responsible for paying. Perhaps enough money was withheld from wages to pay the tax. If too little was withheld, the taxpayer must pay the balance. If too much was withheld, the taxpayer may apply for a refund.

Tax laws and tables change often. New forms and instruction booklets are sent to taxpayers each year. There are three federal income tax forms available: Form 1040EZ, Form 1040A, and Form 1040. One of the first steps a taxpayer must take is to decide which form is most appropriate for him or her.

FORM 1040A — THE SHORT FORM

Business Vocabulary:

Tax return — The form on which you list your income and all the information needed to compute your taxes.

Single — A person who is not married.

Credit — An amount subtracted from tax owed.

Deduction — An amount subtracted from taxable income.

Form 1040A can be used if your taxable income is less than $50,000, and if:

- You are married or single.
- You had dividend income.
- You are claiming a credit for political contributions, child care expenses, or the earned income credit.
- You had interest income of any amount.
- You had unemployment compensation.
- You made an IRA contribution.
- You are claiming the deduction for married couples who both work.

FORM 1040EZ

Form 1040EZ is the simplest form of all. It is designed for single taxpayers who earn less than $50,000. Other conditions for using Form 1040EZ are:

- You can claim only one personal exemption.
- All of your income is from wages, salaries, tips, and interest.
- Your interest income is $400 or less.

Example:

Kim Lane earned $12,390 in wages. She had interest income of $253.00. She gave $150 to charity. Her employer withheld $1535 for federal income tax. Kim completed Form 1040EZ. Her tax return is shown below. She is due a refund of $192.00.

Department of the Treasury - Internal Revenue Service
Form 1040EZ Income Tax Return for
Single filers with no dependents

OMB No. 1545-0675

Name & address

Use the IRS mailing label. If you don't have one, please print:

Please print your numbers like this.

1234567890

► **Kim Lane**
Print your name above (first, initial, last)

202 Adams Street
Present home address (number and street)

Chicago, Illinois 60634
City, town, or post office, State, and ZIP code

Social security number

110 75 3784

Presidential Election Campaign Fund
Check box if you want $1 of your tax to go to this fund. ► [X]

Dollars   Cents

Figure your tax

1   Total wages, salaries, and tips. This should be shown in Box 10 of your W-2 form(s). (Attach your W-2 form(s).)   **1** | 12,390.

2   Interest income of $400 or less. If the total is more than $400, you cannot use Form 1040EZ.   **2** | 253.

Attach Copy B of Form(s) W-2 here

3   Add line 1 and line 2. This is your **adjusted gross income.**   **3** | 12,643.

4   Allowable part of your charitable contributions. Complete the worksheet on page 21 of the instruction booklet.   **4** | 75.

5   Subtract line 4 from line 3.   **5** | 12,568.

6   Amount of your personal exemption.   **6** | 1,000.00

7   Subtract line 6 from line 5. This is your **taxable income.**   **7** | 11,568.

8   Enter your Federal income tax withheld. This should be shown in Box 9 of your W-2 form(s).   **8** | 1,535.

9   Use the **single** column in the tax table on pages 31-36 of the instruction booklet to find the **tax** on your taxable income on line 7. Enter the amount of tax.   **9** | 1,343.

Refund or amount you owe

10   If line 8 is larger than line 9, subtract line 9 from line 8. Enter the **amount of your refund.**   **10** | 192.

11   If line 9 is larger than line 8, subtract line 8 from line 9. Enter the **amount you owe.** Attach check or money order for the full amount, payable to "Internal Revenue Service."   **11** |

Attach tax payment here

Sign your return

I have read this return. Under penalties of perjury, I declare that to the best of my knowledge and belief, the return is true, correct, and complete.

Your signature: *Kim Lane*   Date: *april 15, 19—*

For IRS Use Only—Please do not write in boxes below.

READING A TAX TABLE

Line 9 on Kim Lane's Form 1040EZ required her to look in the tax table to find the tax on her taxable income. The tax table fills several pages of the instruction booklet.

Kim looked for the box marked $11,000, since her taxable income was $11,568. Then she looked for the line that fitted her income.

Next, she found the column for "Single" (and 1040EZ filers)." She read down that column. The amount shown where the income line and her column meet is $1,343. This is her tax.

At least	But less than	Single (and 1040EZ filers)	Married filing jointly	Married filing separately	Head of a household
					Your tax is—
11,350	11,400	1,307	1,012	1,529	1,246
11,400	11,450	1,316	1,019	1,540	1,254
11,450	11,500	1,325	1,026	1,551	1,263
11,500	11,550	1,334	1,033	1,562	1,271
11,550	11,600	(1,343)	1,040	1,573	1,280
11,600	11,650	1,352	1,047	1,584	1,288

Tax Table Based on Taxable Income

If 1040A, line 19, OR 1040EZ, line 7 is—		And you are—				If 1040A, line 19, OR 1040EZ, line 7 is—		And you are—			
At least	But less than	Single (and 1040EZ filers)	Married filing jointly	Married filing separately	Head of a household	At least	But less than	Single (and 1040EZ filers)	Married filing jointly	Married filing separately	Head of a household
		Your tax is—						Your tax is—			
11,000						**12,000**					
11,000	11,050	1,244	963	1,452	1,186	12,000	12,050	1,424	1,105	1,672	1,359
11,050	11,100	1,253	970	1,463	1,195	12,050	12,100	1,433	1,113	1,683	1,368
11,100	11,150	1,262	977	1,474	1,203	12,100	12,150	1,442	1,121	1,694	1,377
11,150	11,200	1,271	984	1,485	1,212	12,150	12,200	1,451	1,129	1,705	1,386
11,200	11,250	1,280	991	1,496	1,220	12,200	12,250	1,460	1,137	1,716	1,395
11,250	11,300	1,289	998	1,507	1,229	12,250	12,300	1,469	1,145	1,727	1,404
11,300	11,350	1,298	1,005	1,518	1,237	12,300	12,350	1,478	1,153	1,739	1,413
11,350	11,400	1,307	1,012	1,529	1,246	12,350	12,400	1,487	1,161	1,751	1,422
11,400	11,450	1,316	1,019	1,540	1,254	12,400	12,450	1,496	1,169	1,764	1,431
11,450	11,500	1,325	1,026	1,551	1,263	12,450	12,500	1,505	1,177	1,776	1,440
11,500	11,550	1,334	1,033	1,562	1,271	12,500	12,550	1,514	1,185	1,789	1,449
11,550	11,600	1,343	1,040	1,573	1,280	12,550	12,600	1,523	1,193	1,801	1,458
11,600	11,650	1,352	1,047	1,584	1,288	12,600	12,650	1,532	1,201	1,814	1,467
11,650	11,700	1,361	1,054	1,595	1,297	12,650	12,700	1,541	1,209	1,826	1,476
11,700	11,750	1,370	1,061	1,606	1,305	12,700	12,750	1,550	1,217	1,839	1,485
11,750	11,800	1,379	1,068	1,617	1,314	12,750	12,800	1,559	1,225	1,851	1,494
11,800	11,850	1,388	1,075	1,628	1,323	12,800	12,850	1,568	1,233	1,864	1,503
11,850	11,900	1,397	1,082	1,639	1,332	12,850	12,900	1,577	1,241	1,876	1,512
11,900	11,950	1,406	1,089	1,650	1,341	12,900	12,950	1,586	1,249	1,889	1,521
11,950	12,000	1,415	1,097	1,661	1,350	12,950	13,000	1,596	1,257	1,901	1,530

▶ Use the information on Form 1040EZ. Deduct one-half of the contributions. Use the tax table on page 52. Compute the refund or amount you owe for each problem below. The answer to Number 1 is: Amount owed, $222.

	Wages	Interest Income	Charitable Contributions	Income Tax Withheld
1)	$12,460	$169	$250	$1,112
2)	$13,115	$389	$ 60	$1,300
3)	$12,884	$ 90	$425	$1,509
4)	$12,090	$246	$ 50	$1,475
5)	$13,350	$365	$190	$1,150
6)	$13,140	$285	$ 60	$1,208
7)	$12,975	$ 70	$150	$1,143
8)	$13,226	$382	$ 65	$1,460
9)	$13,070	$290	$348	$1,322
10)	$12,142	$168	$125	$1,509
11)	$12,324	$350	$100	$1,078
12)	$13,307	$247	$245	$1,612
13)	$12,298	$327	$185	$1,555
14)	$12,567	$399	$325	$1,246
15)	$12,774	$234	$ 50	$1,130
16)	$13,446	$308	$ 80	$1,584
17)	$12,053	$366	$275	$1,462
18)	$12,838	$294	$ 90	$1,206
19)	$12,635	$349	$ 70	$1,438
20)	$12,285	$213	$ 55	$1,393
21)	$12,804	$164	$470	$1,160
22)	$12,321	$174	$ 65	$1,214
23)	$12,542	$269	$ 85	$1,625
24)	$13,080	$347	$290	$1,581
25)	$13,220	$290	$ 90	$1,475

USING A TAX TABLE

Business Vocabulary:

Married filing jointly — A married couple who file one tax return.

Married filing separately — A husband and wife who each file a tax return.

Head of a household — An unmarried person with dependents.

Dependent — A person who relies on another for support.

Taxpayers who use the Form 1040A also need to look at the tax tables to find their tax. They must know their filing status to use the correct column.

Example: Mark Brown is married and filing separately. His taxable income is $26,100. Find his income tax. Mark's tax will be $6,112.

Tax Table Based on Taxable Income

If 1040A, line 19, OR 1040EZ, line 7 is—		And you are—				If 1040A, line 19, OR 1040EZ, line 7 is—		And you are—			
At least	But less than	Single (and 1040EZ filers)	Married filing jointly	Married filing separately	Head of a household	At least	But less than	Single (and 1040EZ filers)	Married filing jointly	Married filing separately	Head of a household
		Your tax is—						Your tax is—			
25,000						**26,000**					
25,000	25,050	4,573	3,571	5,694	4,233	26,000	26,050	4,873	3,821	6,074	4,513
25,050	25,100	4,588	3,584	5,713	4,247	26,050	26,100	4,888	3,834	6,093	4,527
25,100	25,150	4,603	3,596	5,732	4,261	26,100	26,150	4,903	3,846	6,112	4,541
25,150	25,200	4,618	3,609	5,751	4,275	26,150	26,200	4,918	3,859	6,131	4,555
25,200	25,250	4,633	3,621	5,770	4,289	26,200	26,250	4,933	3,871	6,150	4,569
25,250	25,300	4,648	3,634	5,789	4,303	26,250	26,300	4,948	3,884	6,169	4,583
25,300	25,350	4,663	3,646	5,808	4,317	26,300	26,350	4,963	3,896	6,188	4,597
25,350	25,400	4,678	3,659	5,827	4,331	26,350	26,400	4,978	3,909	6,207	4,611
25,400	25,450	4,693	3,671	5,846	4,345	26,400	26,450	4,993	3,921	6,226	4,625
25,450	25,500	4,708	3,684	5,865	4,359	26,450	26,500	5,008	3,934	6,245	4,639
25,500	25,550	4,723	3,696	5,884	4,373	26,500	26,550	5,023	3,946	6,264	4,653
25,550	25,600	4,738	3,709	5,903	4,387	26,550	26,600	5,038	3,959	6,283	4,667
25,600	25,650	4,753	3,721	5,922	4,401	26,600	26,650	5,053	3,971	6,302	4,681
25,650	25,700	4,768	3,734	5,941	4,415	26,650	26,700	5,068	3,984	6,321	4,695
25,700	25,750	4,783	3,746	5,960	4,429	26,700	26,750	5,083	3,996	6,340	4,709
25,750	25,800	4,798	3,759	5,979	4,443	26,750	26,800	5,098	4,009	6,359	4,723
25,800	25,850	4,813	3,771	5,998	4,457	26,800	26,850	5,113	4,021	6,378	4,737
25,850	25,900	4,828	3,784	6,017	4,471	26,850	26,900	5,128	4,034	6,397	4,751
25,900	25,950	4,843	3,796	6,036	4,485	26,900	26,950	5,143	4,046	6,416	4,765
25,950	26,000	4,858	3,809	6,055	4,499	26,950	27,000	5,158	4,059	6,435	4,779

▶ Use the tax table on page 54 to determine the tax due in each case. The answer for problem Number 1 is $3,896.

	Filing Status	Taxable Income
1)	Married filing jointly	$26,300
2)	Head of a household	$26,882
3)	Married filing jointly	$26,543
4)	Married filing jointly	$26,118
5)	Single	$25,474
6)	Married filing jointly	$25,242
7)	Married filing jointly	$26,553
8)	Married filing separately	$26,792
9)	Married filing jointly	$25,370
10)	Married filing jointly	$25,727
11)	Head of a household	$26,397
12)	Single	$26,585
13)	Married filing separately	$26,466
14)	Single	$25,445
15)	Single	$26,113
16)	Married filing separately	$25,748
17)	Head of a household	$26,387
18)	Head of a household	$25,797
19)	Married filing separately	$26,301
20)	Head of a household	$26,137
21)	Single	$26,173
22)	Married filing separately	$26,477
23)	Married filing jointly	$25,921
24)	Married filing separately	$25,587
25)	Married filing separately	$26,484

USING A TAX SCHEDULE

Not all taxpayers can use the tax table. Certain people, such as those whose taxable income is over $50,000, use Tax Rate Schedules to compute their taxes.

Schedule X, for single taxpayers, is shown below.

Schedule X
Single Taxpayers

Use this Schedule if you checked **Filing Status Box 1** on Form 1040—

If the amount on Form 1040, line 37 is: Over—	But not over—	Enter on Form 1040, line 38	of the amount over—
$0	$2,300	—0—	
2,300	3,400	. . . . 11%	$2,300
3,400	4,400	$121 + 12%	3,400
4,400	6,500	241 + 14%	4,400
6,500	8,500	535 + 15%	6,500
8,500	10,800	835 + 16%	8,500
10,800	12,900	1,203 + 18%	10,800
12,900	15,000	1,581 + 20%	12,900
15,000	18,200	2,001 + 23%	15,000
18,200	23,500	2,737 + 26%	18,200
23,500	28,800	4,115 + 30%	23,500
28,800	34,100	5,705 + 34%	28,800
34,100	41,500	7,507 + 38%	34,100
41,500	55,300	10,319 + 42%	41,500
55,300	81,800	16,115 + 48%	55,300
81,800	. . . .	28,835 + 50%	81,800

Example:
Dan Dodd is filing a single return. His taxable income is $52,000. He looks at Schedule X to find the correct line. He locates "If the amount on Form 1040, line 37 is at least $41,500, but less than $55,300..." This is where his income fits. The tax is $10,319 plus 42% of the amount over $41,500. So Dan does this arithmetic:

$52,000 Taxable income $10,500 $10,319
−41,500   ×   .42 Times 42% + 4,410
$10,500 Amount over   21000 $14,729
        $41,500   42000
                         $4410.00

Dan owes $14,729 in taxes. Dan is in the 42 percent bracket.

▶ Use Schedule X to compute the income tax on these taxable incomes. The answer to Number 1 is $17,291.

1) $57,750	16) $63,753	31) $54,616
2) $48,857	17) $50,804	32) $44,420
3) $47,113	18) $61,866	33) $54,736
4) $58,673	19) $52,772	34) $47,693
5) $51,106	20* $685,924	35) $28,939
6) $53,827	21) $49,227	36) $44,703
7) $38,499	22) $52,489	37) $46,096
8) $47,961	23) $48,440	38) $51,576
9) $48,403	24) $39,467	39) $49,935
10* $530,657	25) $51,216	40) $46,323
11) $48,223	26) $54,042	41) $60,722
12) $49,603	27) $69,041	42) $51,597
13) $49,421	28) $52,785	43) $48,935
14) $50,161	29) $54,607	44) $51,266
15) $58,142	30* $8,286,573	45) $46,396

COMPUTING STATE INCOME TAX
With a Calculator

Most of the states require their citizens to pay an income tax. These taxes are regularly withheld from an employee's wages. Taxpayers file a state income tax return each year. Each state has its own way of determining the amount of taxes due. A typical state income tax is calculated from a chart like the one below:

TAX RATE SCHEDULE

Taxable Income

Over	But Not Over	Amount of Tax
$ 0	$1,000	2% of taxable income
1,000	2,000	$20 plus 3% of excess over $1,000
2,000	3,000	$50 plus 4% of excess over $2,000
3,000	—	$90 plus 5% of excess over $3,000

Example: Alex's taxable income is $4,527. Find his state income tax.

$4527	Taxable income
− 3000	
$1527	Excess over $3,000
× .05	Times 5%
$76.35	
+ 90.00	
$166.35	State income tax

Alex's tax is $166.35.

▶ Use the chart on page 58 to find the income tax owed. Round up to the next cent. The answer to Number 1 is $528.54.

1)	$11,770.75	26)	$28,765.64
2)	$43,243.82	27)	$39,211.76
3)	$32,046.07	28)	$1,186.89
4)	$33,383.54	29)	$22,190.93
5)	$2,516.27	30*	$191,335.49
6)	$22,208.93	31)	$774.59
7)	$1,681.64	32)	$48,067.65
8)	$11,087.54	33)	$2,890.74
9)	$31,223.61	34)	$35,705.93
10*	$2,106,980.70	35)	$13,719.87
11)	$752.94	36)	$22,497.85
12)	$11,652.85	37)	$9,992.91
13)	$37,096.67	38)	$40,536.88
14)	$40,978.54	39)	$36,316.76
15)	$39,084.09	40*	$2,939,385.20
16)	$39,353.12	41)	$20,007.43
17)	$1,482.67	42)	$41,751.91
18)	$45,216.99	43)	$28,688.28
19)	$17,303.74	44)	$2,735.94
20*	$2,132,395.60	45)	$1652.92
21)	$777.01	46)	$10,014.88
22)	$39,173.78	47)	$15,738.17
23)	$28,878.63	48)	$28,921.34
24)	$1,277.47	49)	$24,500.43
25)	$1,220.96	50*	$3,487,380.40

BASIC SKILL REVIEW

1) This year Stan paid $7954 in federal income tax and $2963 in state income tax. Last year he paid $6438 in federal income tax and $2419 in state income tax. What was the total of Stan's income tax payments for the past two years?

2) Marsha had $24,594 of federal tax withheld. She owed only $22,684. Find her tax overpayment.

3) Frank's federal tax withholding was $17 per week for a year. What was his total federal withholding?

4) Milton's total withholding for the year was $5076. Find the withholding per month.

5) Sally's biweekly withholding for state income tax was $11.84. Find her total withholding for 26 biweekly deductions.

6) Elliott paid $7643.21 in state income tax. He paid $18,169 in federal income tax. How much more federal income tax did he pay than state income tax?

7) The deductions on David's last paycheck were: federal income tax, $79.64; Social Security, $37.25; and state income tax, $5. What was the total of his deductions?

8) Hillel's total yearly deduction for federal income tax was $589.68. Find his weekly deduction.

9) Barry's employer withholds 1.49% of Barry's wages for state income tax. Barry's gross pay was $400. How much was withheld for state income tax?

10) Rusty made one-fourth of his charitable contributions to the Red Cross. He made two-thirds of his contributions to the United Fund. How much more did he give to the United Fund than to the Red Cross?

Computer Program: FEDERAL INCOME TAX

This program can calculate the amounts to be filled in on a Form 1040EZ.

Type the program into a computer and run it. Input the appropriate information. You may run it several times, changing the amounts you input.

```
5    REM THIS PROGRAM DOES THE ARITHMETIC FOR
     FORM 1040EZ
10   PRINT  "TYPE IN TOTAL WAGES+SALARIES+TIPS."
15   INPUT TW
20   PRINT "TYPE IN THE TOTAL INTEREST INCOME."
25   INPUT T
30   IF TW >= 50000 OR T > 400 THEN PRINT "YOU ARE
     NOT ELIGIBLE TO USE FORM 1040EZ.":GOTO 120
35   PRINT "FILL IN THIS AMOUNT ON LINE 3 -> ";TW+T
40   PRINT "TYPE IN CHARITABLE CONTRIBUTIONS."
50   INPUT CC : LET CC = .5 * CC
55   IF CC > .5 * (TW + T) THEN CC = .5 * (TW + T)
60   PRINT "FILL IN THIS AMOUNT ON LINE 4 ->";CC
65   PRINT "FILL IN THIS AMOUNT ON LINE 5 ->";TW +
          T - CC
70   PRINT "THE PERSONAL EXEMPTION = 1000."
80   IF TW + T - CC - 1000 <= 0 THEN PRINT "STOP
     HERE.  YOUR REFUND (LINE 10)=YOUR TOTAL TAX
     WITHHELD (LINE 8)": GOTO 120
85   PRINT "FILL IN THIS AMOUNT ON LINE 7 ->";TW +
          T - CC - 1000
90   PRINT "TYPE IN THE FEDERAL INCOME TAX WITH-
          HELD."
95   INPUT FT
100  PRINT "TYPE IN THE AMOUNT OF TAX."
105  INPUT TX
110  IF FT > TX THEN PRINT "FILL IN THIS AMOUNT
     (YOUR REFUND)":PRINT "ON LINE 10 ->"; FT - TX
115  IF TX >= FT THEN PRINT "FILL IN THIS AMOUNT
     (WHAT YOU OWE) ON LINE 11 ->";TX - FT
120  END
```

CHAPTER REVIEW

► Find the answer to each problem. You may look back at the tax tables and schedules in the chapter.

1) Ricky's taxable income is $12,224. He is using Form 1040EZ. What is his tax?

2) Debbie's taxable income was $12,869. Her employer withheld $1634. Debbie is using Form 1040EZ. Does she owe any tax or does she get a refund? What is the amount?

3) Last year Sid earned $14,650 in wages. His interest income was $250. He is married. Is Form 1040EZ the correct one for him to use?

4) Mark's wages were $11,500. His interest income was $380. He contributed $480 to charity. $1435 was withheld. He is using the 1040EZ form. Does Mark owe any tax or does he get a refund? What is the amount?

5) John and Alice are married and are filing jointly. Their taxable income is $25,331. What is their tax?

6) Bob is single. His taxable income is $25,972. What is his tax?

7) Denise is filing as head of a household. Her taxable income is $26,729. What is her tax?

8) Pat's taxable income is $29,840. He uses Schedule X to compute his taxes. How much income tax is he responsible to pay?

9) Jean's taxable income is $48,125. According to Schedule X, what is her tax?

10) George and Ann use the state income tax schedule on page 58. Their taxable income is $16,390. How much state income tax must they pay?

Chapter 5

Life Insurance and Health Insurance

Whether you are at home or at work, inside or out-side, asleep or awake, you are always facing a certain amount of risk. At almost any time you risk some kind of loss:

- Loss of life.
- Loss of health.
- Loss of goods by theft, accident, fire, or storm.
- Loss of earning power.

Any single loss could be a disaster if the entire financial burden were to fall upon one person or one family. However, when many people share in the cost of these losses, they don't have to fear financial disaster. The way this sharing is done is through *insurance*.

Insurance depends upon the *cooperation* of many persons in meeting losses. By paying small sums regularly, insured persons avoid a great financial burden if they suffer a loss.

This chapter will help you solve problems relating to health and life insurance.

MORTALITY TABLE

Business Vocabulary:

Mortality table — A chart that shows the probability of death at each age and the expectation of life.

For over 300 years insurance companies have been keeping records of how long people live. Such records were used to make the mortality table below.

Example: At age 34, 2 out of 1,000 persons on the average will die, but the rest can expect to live about 39 more years. At age 88, the probability of death is 193.27 out of 1,000, with a life expectancy of about 3½ years. (3.66 years)

Commissioners 1980 Standard Ordinary Table of Mortality

(1970-1975)

Age	Deaths Per 1,000	Expectation of Life (Yrs.)	Age	Deaths Per 1,000	Expectation of Life (Yrs.)	Age	Deaths Per 1,000	Expectation of Life (Yrs.)
0	4.18	70.83	34	2.00	39.54	67	30.44	12.76
1	1.07	70.13	35	2.11	38.61	68	33.19	12.14
2	.99	69.20	36	2.24	37.69	69	36.17	11.54
3	.98	68.27	37	2.40	36.78	70	39.51	10.96
4	.95	67.34	38	2.58	35.87	71	43.30	10.39
5	.90	66.40	39	2.79	34.96	72	47.65	9.84
6	.86	65.46	40	3.02	34.05	73	52.64	9.30
7	.80	64.52	41	3.29	33.16	74	58.19	8.79
8	.76	63.57	42	3.56	32.26	75	64.19	8.31
9	.74	62.62	43	3.87	31.38	76	70.53	7.84
10	.73	61.66	44	4.19	30.50	77	77.12	7.40
11	.77	60.71	45	4.55	29.62	78	83.90	6.97
12	.85	59.75	46	4.92	28.76	79	91.05	6.57
13	.99	58.80	47	5.32	27.90	80	98.84	6.18
14	1.15	57.86	48	5.74	27.04	81	107.48	5.80
15	1.33	56.93	49	6.21	26.20	82	117.25	5.44
16	1.51	56.00	50	6.71	25.36	83	128.26	5.09
17	1.67	55.09	51	7.30	24.52	84	140.25	4.77
18	1.78	54.18	52	7.96	23.70	85	152.95	4.46
19	1.86	53.27	53	8.71	22.89	86	166.09	4.18
20	1.90	52.37	54	9.56	22.08	87	179.55	3.91
21	1.91	51.47	55	10.47	21.29	88	193.27	3.66
22	1.89	50.57	56	11.46	20.51	89	207.29	3.41
23	1.86	49.66	57	12.49	19.74	90	221.77	3.18
24	1.82	48.75	58	13.59	18.99	91	236.98	2.94
25	1.77	47.84	59	14.77	18.24	92	253.45	2.70
26	1.73	46.93	60	16.08	17.51	93	272.11	2.44
27	1.71	46.01	61	17.54	16.79	94	295.90	2.17
28	1.70	45.09	62	19.19	16.08	95	329.96	1.87
29	1.71	44.16	63	21.06	15.38	96	384.55	1.54
30	1.73	43.24	64	23.14	14.70	97	480.20	1.20
31	1.78	42.31	65	25.42	14.04	98	657.98	.84
32	1.83	41.38	66	27.85	13.39	99	1,000.00	.50
33	1.91	40.46						

► Use the mortality table to answer these questions:

1) What is life expectancy at age 15?

2) At age 30, what is the life expectancy?

3) About how many 30-year-olds out of 1,000 will die before they become 31?

4) What is the probability of death at age 52?

5) How many more years can a 52-year-old person expect to live?

6) At what age do about 10 out of every 1,000 people die?

7) At what age do about 25 out of every 1,000 people die?

8) At what age can a person expect to live 50 more years?

9) What is the life expectancy at age 59?

10) At what age can a person expect to live 20 more years?

11) At what age do about 70 out of every 1,000 people die?

12) What is the life expectancy for a 2-year-old child?

13) About how many 67-year-olds out of 1,000 will die before they become 68?

14) What is the life expectancy at age 72?

15) At what age do about 98 out of every 1,000 people people die?

16) About how many years can an 18-year-old person expect to live?

TERM INSURANCE

Term insurance offers protection for a family for a specified period of time — usually one, five, 10, or 20 years, or up to age 65. A term insurance policy pays a benefit only if you die during the period covered by the policy. At the end of the term, the coverage ends.

You may be able to renew the policy, but each time it is renewed, the premium will be higher. Premiums increase with the age of the insured.

Example:
Greg is 30 years old. He bought $30,000 of coverage for one year. He paid a premium of $85.00.

WHOLE LIFE INSURANCE

Whole life is a plan of insurance for a person's entire life. It is sometimes called "straight life" insurance. At your death, the insurance company pays benefits to your dependents. You may choose to pay a premium that does not increase as you grow older.

Whole life insurance has a "cash value." This is a sum that increases over the years. You can receive it if you give up the insurance.

Example:
Tom is 30 years old. He bought $30,000 of coverage. He pays a premium of $435 every year.

In five years, the cash value of his policy will grow to $1830.

In the chart below are typical annual premium rates for term insurance and whole life insurance. The buyer pays the amount shown for each $1,000 worth of coverage. The amount is different for each age group.

Life Insurance Premiums per $1,000
(Female)

Age	Term Annual	Term Semiannual	Whole Life Annual	Whole Life Semiannual
15	—	—	$14.37	$ 7.47
20	$ 2.67	$ 1.39	14.46	7.52
25	2.71	1.41	15.39	8.00
30	2.81	1.46	17.47	9.08
35	3.05	1.59	20.70	10.76
40	3.68	1.91	25.07	13.04
45	5.21	2.71	30.54	15.88
50	7.78	4.05	37.16	19.32
60	16.85	8.76	55.80	29.02
65	25.90	13.47	70.84	36.84

Example: Jodi bought a $50,000 term policy at the age of 35. How much is her semiannual premium?

Step 1: $50,000 coverage ÷ $1,000 = 50

Step 2: $1.59 × 50 = $79.50

Jodi's semiannual premium is $79.50

▶ Find the premium for each of these policies. Use the chart above. The answer to Number 1 is $139.00.

	Age	Policy	Coverage
1)	20	Term, Semiannual	$100,000
2)	45	Whole Life, Annual	$200,000
3)	60	Term, Annual	$250,000
4)	30	Whole Life, Semiannual	$ 50,000
5)	40	Whole Life, Annual	$150,000
6)	35	Term, Semiannual	$ 75,000
7)	50	Term, Annual	$100,000
8)	25	Whole Life, Annual	$250,000
9)	65	Term, Semiannual	$125,000
10)	15	Whole Life, Semiannual	$200,000

UNIVERSAL LIFE INSURANCE

Business Vocabulary:

Market rate — The highest interest rate available to most savers.

Universal life insurance is a fairly new form of life insurance. The policies may be thought of as market rate savings accounts from which companies take premium payments for term insurance. Companies raise or lower their interest rates to keep those rates current.

The term insurance remains in force as long as the savings balance is large enough to cover the insurance charges. Policyholders have much freedom in making payments. They may pay every month, year, or whenever they wish. They may also pay more money than the premium due. They may change the amount of the coverage very easily.

Example: Kathy had $5,480 in her universal life account, earning .95% interest per month. On the first of the month, $380 was withdrawn to pay this month's premium. Compute her new savings balance and her interest for the coming month.

Step 1:

$5,480 Old balance
− 380 Premium
$5,100 New balance

Step 2:

$5,100 New balance
× .0095 Interest rate
25500
45900
$48.45ØØ This month's interest (expected)

▶ For each of these universal life policies, compute the new savings balance and the current month's interest. Round to the next lower cent. The answers to Number 1 are: New balance, $4,760. Month's interest, $43.79.

	Balance in Savings Account	Monthly Premium Due Now	Monthly Interest Rate
1)	$ 5,487	$727	.92%
2)	$ 2,392	$622	.75%
3)	$ 7,901	$321	.95%
4)	$ 8,685	$655	.82%
5)	$ 3,476	$706	1.01%
6)	$ 1,052	$702	.94%
7)	$ 9,341	$511	1.07%
8)	$ 9,294	$514	1.04%
9)	$ 9,738	$648	.93%
10)	$ 4,737	$408	.73%
11)	$ 7,577	$547	1.08%
12)	$10,846	$206	.71%
13)	$ 3,289	$859	.96%
14)	$ 7,709	$659	.87%
15)	$ 3,152	$822	.92%
16)	$ 6,522	$132	.9%
17)	$ 5,968	$158	.97%
18)	$ 5,248	$758	.9%
19)	$ 4,790	$770	.75%
20)	$10,257	$890	.93%
21)	$ 1,661	$161	.89%
22)	$ 9,057	$867	1.01%
23)	$ 9,943	$13	.95%
24)	$ 1,347	$867	1.06%
25)	$ 6,895	$615	1.06%

HEALTH INSURANCE

Business Vocabulary:

Copay — The *percent* of medical bills (over the deductible) paid by the policyholder.

Copayment — The *amount* of a bill paid by the policyholder.

Health insurance helps pay the costs of medical care. A bad injury or a long illness may cost thousands of dollars. Few people without health insurance can afford to pay such high bills. Most health insurance plans include a deductible and a copay. A copayment is always rounded up.

Example: Joe's policy had a deductible amount of $400, and a copay of 25%. His bills were $559.80, $844.21, $680.10, $831.71, and $26.51. Compute Joe's copayment and the insurance payment.

Step 1:

$ 559.80
844.21
680.10
831.71
+ 26.51
$2942.33 Total charges

Step 2:

$2942.33
− 400.00 Deductible
$2542.33

Step 3:

$2542.33 Over deductible
× .25 Times 25%
1271165
508466
$635.5825 ≈ $635.59
(Round to the next cent.)

Step 4:

$ 635.59
+ 400.00 Deductible
$1035.59 Copayment

Step 5:

$2942.33 Total charges
−1035.59 Copayment
$1906.74 Insurance payment

Joe's copayment is $1,035.59.
The insurance will pay $1,906.74.

▶ Compute the copayment and the insurance payment for each case below. The answers to Number 1 are: Copayment, $234.34.   Insurance, $309.06.

	Deduct- ible	Copay	Charges
1)	$200	10%	$322, $186.90, $7.67, $26.83
2)	$400	5%	$553.80, $962.20, $804.10
3)	$400	5%	$86.15, $270, $881, $125, $18.72
4)	$100	25%	$44.70, $4.47, $14.84, $72.67
5)	$400	20%	$753.90, $19.10, $70
6)	$100	25%	$258.80, $435.80, $18.49, $625.60
7)	$300	5%	$6.06, $519.30, $756.80
8)	$200	5%	$401.90, $255.70, $66.45, $734.70
9)	$300	5%	$14.68, $814.20, $484, $70.90
10)	$400	20%	$552.10, $243.05, $284, $985.70
11)	$300	15%	$83.25, $15.84, $200.90
12)	$300	20%	$18.92, $19.83, $19.69, $638.10
13)	$200	5%	$38.60, $237.80, $199.90, $216.10
14)	$300	5%	$68.82, $970.10, $759.80
15)	$400	20%	$248.20, $11.41, $803.70, $60.08
16)	$300	10%	$9.86, $514.10, $862, $807.20
17)	$200	5%	$493.40, $18.71, $15.90
18)	$400	5%	$935.30, $561, $14.61, $481.60
19)	$200	25%	$465.70, $700.70, $308.10
20)	$400	20%	$6.45, $177.30, $9.48
21)	$300	15%	$652.70, $749.80, $588.40, $485.54
22)	$200	20%	$484.60, $6.33, $94.68
23)	$200	10%	$12.04, $5.20, $225.80, $2.67
24)	$300	5%	$752.60, $28.35, $68.09
25)	$300	10%	$447.70, $13.99, $620.90, $98.65

COMPUTING THE NET GROUP INSURANCE PREMIUM *With a Calculator*

Business Vocabulary:

Group insurance — Low-cost insurance covering many people under one policy.

Insurance companies provide discounts to large groups. It costs less to sell one group policy to 7,500 people than to sell the identical coverage to 7,500 separate people.

A sample discount schedule is shown below.

Group Size	Discount
Less than 1,000	None
1,000 to 1,999	1%
2,000 to 2,999	2%
3,000 to 3,999	3%
4,000 to 4,999	4%
5,000 to 5,999	5%
6,000 to 6,999	6%
7,000 to 7,999	7%
8,000 to 8,999	8%
9,000 to 9,999	9%
10,000 or more	10%

Example: A group of 5,439 employees had a total premium of $754,925. Find the net premium after the group discount.

Step 1: 100% − 5% = 95%, or .95

Step 2: $754,925 × .95 = $717,178.75.
Round to the next lower dollar.

The net premium was $717,178.

► Find the net premium after the group discount for each policy below. Round down to the next lower dollar. The answer for Number 1 is $759,125.

Total Premium	Group Size	Total Premium	Group Size
1) $834,204	9,931	26) $390,845	4,295
2) $844,830	2,835	27) $1,536,710	7,570
3) $2,541,476	9,142	28) $416,936	2,743
4) $562,947	7,311	29) $137,432	838
5) $663,132	4,542	30) $365,310	1,353
6) $163,006	1,094	31) $177,429	1,207
7) $581,256	6,318	32) $530,088	3,398
8) $281,436	1,497	33) $578,272	4,252
9) $2,573,298	9,426	34) $492,232	4,733
10) $2,322,698	8,477	35) $81,024	633
11) $526,330	3,605	36) $1,045,058	8,782
12) $145,376	1,652	37) $1,760,157	8,757
13) $2,042,885	7,709	38) $1,435,200	5,200
14) $356,160	2,120	39) $455,988	2,886
15) $853,820	7,762	40) $1,376,340	7,910
16) $507,042	4,971	41) $381,016	3,928
17) $232,887	1,563	42) $385,832	2,837
18) $1,169,532	9,282	43) $539,973	2,857
19) $1,914,240	7,976	44) $919,960	8,440
20) $493,020	4,482	45) $1,611,584	5,408
21) $1,588,704	5,928	46) $527,058	1,974
22) $671,460	5,890	47) $332,652	4,377
23) $88,810	830	48) $2,121,000	7,575
24) $814,509	8,397	49) $807,196	9,386
25) $750,114	4,311	50) $836,825	4,675

BASIC SKILL REVIEW

1) Shira's four life insurance policies had face amounts of $45,000, $95,000, $150,000, and $75,000. What was Shira's total coverage?

2) Ray-Ellen has twice as much life insurance as Alice. Alice has $97,000. How much insurance does Ray-Ellen have?

3) Peter borrowed $7,700 of his $19,100 cash value. How much was left?

4) Golda spent $1,500 each for her employee's health insurance policies. She spent $105,000. How many policies did she buy?

5) Ernie's employer will allow him to buy group life insurance up to one and one-half times his annual salary. He earns $42,000. What is the most he can buy?

6) Charlotte must pay $\frac{1}{10}$ more for her insurance because she smokes. She must pay $\frac{1}{20}$ more because she is an airline pilot. How much more must she pay?

7) One-fifth of the population of Oakdale shortens their lives by eating either too much or too little. If $\frac{3}{20}$ eat too much, how many eat too little?

8) In a certain group 7 out of every 1,000 34-year-olds died last year. If 693 died, how many were in the group?

9) Dierdre's life insurance policy cost $409.70. Her health insurance policy cost $1,093.85. Her car insurance cost $627.90. Her property insurance cost $217. What was the total cost of her policies?

10) Jimmy spent $784.10 on life insurance. He spent $1,200 on health insurance. How much more was his health insurance than his life insurance?

Computer Program:
LIFE INSURANCE PREMIUMS

This program is an example of one that an insurance agent might use to calculate annual premiums. This program is for term and whole life insurance.

Type the program into a computer and run it. Input different ages and coverages.

```
10   REM LIFE INSURANCE SOFTWARE
20   PRINT "TYPE IN THE AGE OF THE PERSON." PRINT:
       "(SUBTRACT 3 YEARS FROM A WOMAN'S AGE)"
30   INPUT AG
40   PRINT "TYPE IN THE AMOUNT OF COVERAGE RE-
       QUESTED."
50   INPUT CO
60   REM LINES 61-66 CONTAIN THE FORMULAS TO COM-
       PUTE THE PERSON'S PROBABILITY OF DYING THIS
       YEAR.
61   IF AG > 33 THEN D = 0
62   IF AG < = 33 THEN D = .00030268 * (AG + 12) * (AG -
       33) ^ 2
63   LET PD = 10 ^ (.033 * (AG - 1.28))
64   LET PD = - (D + PD) / 10000
65   LET PD = 1 - 10 ^ PD
66   LET PD = INT (10000 * PD) / 100
70   PRINT "THIS PERSON'S PROBABILITY OF DYING THIS
       YEAR = ";PD;"%"
80   PRINT "THE COST TO THE COMPANY FOR $";CO;"
       WORTH OF TERM COVERAGE WOULD BE $";PD * CO/
       100
100  PRINT "QUOTE THESE ANNUAL PREMIUMS TO THE
       CUSTOMER:"
110  PRINT "CURRENT ANNUAL TERM PREMIUM = $";
       PD * CO * .013
120  PRINT "ANNUAL WHOLE LIFE PREMIUM = $ ";PD *
       CO * .04
130  END
```

CHAPTER REVIEW

▶ Solve these problems. You may use any charts from the chapter.

1) What is the life expectancy of a person who is 22 years old?

2) What is the probability of death of a 20-year-old person?

3) How many more years can a 40-year-old person expect to live?

4) Jane, 40, wants a 5-year term life insurance policy. How much more would the annual premium be for coverage of $250,000 than for $100,000?

5) Find the number of deaths per thousand and the life expectancy for 66-year-old people. Round to the nearer whole number.

6) Jean's health insurance policy has a deductible of $100 and a copay of 20%. Her medical bills were $396, $128, $144, and $605. How much of this does Jean have to pay?

7) How much will the insurance company pay on Jean's claim?

8) Betty's health insurance policy has a deductible of $300 and a copay of 10%. Her medical bills were $254, $405, $214, and $245. How much of this will the insurance company pay?

9) How much of Betty's medical expenses does she have to pay?

10) A group of 2,450 union members had a total insurance premium of $300,000. What was the net premium after a 2% discount?

11) Find the number of deaths per thousand and the life expectancy for 94-year-old people. Round to the nearer whole number.

Chapter 6

Casualty Insurance

Insurance is important for every business. Firms insure their buildings and offices against theft, fire, and flood. Many firms own cars and trucks which must be insured. Why must firms carry car and truck insurance? This chapter discusses casualty insurance — protection against losses due to damaged property.

FIRE INSURANCE

People buy insurance to share financial risk. People will spend a few dollars for fire insurance rather than risk a loss of thousands of dollars. The size of the premium depends on the amount of insurance, whether the building is made of brick or wood, and the location. The level of risk in an area depends on the number of fires and the average dollar value of losses in that area. An example of a rate chart is shown.

INSURANCE RATE CHART

COVERAGE		LOW RISK	MED. RISK	HIGH RISK
$0-9,999	Wood Frame	$20 + .27%	$20 + .31%	$20 + .39%
	Brick or Stone	20 + .21%	20 + .25%	20 + .34%
$10,000-19,999	WF	47 + .26%	51 + .30%	59 + .38%
	BS	41 + .20%	45 + .24%	54 + .33%
$20,000-29,999	WF	73 + .25%	81 + .29%	97 + .37%
	BS	61 + .19%	69 + .23%	87 + .32%
$30,000-39,999	WF	98 + .24%	110 + .28%	134 + .36%
	BS	80 + .18%	92 + .22%	119 + .31%
$40,000-49,999	WF	122 + .23%	138 + .27%	170 + .35%
	BS	98 + .17%	114 + .21%	150 + .30%
$50,000-59,999	WF	145 + .22%	165 + .26%	205 + .34%
	BS	115 + .16%	135 + .20%	180 + .29%
$60,000-69,999	WF	167 + .21%	191 + .25%	239 + .33%
	BS	131 + .15%	155 + .19%	209 + .28%
$70,000-79,999	WF	188 + .20%	216 + .24%	272 + .32%
	BS	146 + .14%	174 + .18%	237 + .27%
$80,000-89,999	WF	208 + .19%	240 + .23%	304 + .31%
	BS	160 + .13%	192 + .17%	264 + .26%
$90,000-99,999	WF	227 + .18%	263 + .22%	335 + .30%
	BS	173 + .12%	209 + .16%	290 + .25%
$100,000-109,999	WF	245 + .17%	285 + .21%	365 + .29%
	BS	185 + .11%	225 + .15%	315 + .24%
$110,000-119,999	WF	262 + .16%	306 + .20%	394 + .28%
	BS	196 + .10%	240 + .14%	339 + .23%
$120,000-129,999	WF	278 + .15%	326 + .19%	422 + .27%
	BS	206 + .09%	254 + .13%	362 + .22%
$130,000-139,999	WF	293 + .14%	345 + .18%	449 + .26%
	BS	215 + .08%	267 + .12%	384 + .21%
$140,000-149,999	WF	307 + .13%	363 + .17%	475 + .25%
	BS	223 + .07%	279 + .11%	405 + .20%
$150,000-159,999	WF	320 + .12%	380 + .16%	500 + .24%
	BS	230 + .06%	290 + .10%	425 + .19%
$160,000-169,999	WF	332 + .11%	396 + .15%	524 + .23%
	BS	236 + .05%	300 + .09%	444 + .18%
$170,000-179,999	WF	343 + .10%	411 + .14%	547 + .22%
	BS	241 + .04%	309 + .08%	462 + .17%

Example: What was Dominic's premium on an $89,000 policy for a wooden building in a high risk area?

Premium = $304 plus .31% of amount over $80,000.

Step 1:	**Step 2:**	**Step 3:**
$89,000	$9,000	$304.00
−80,000	× .0031 Times .31%	+ 27.90
$ 9,000 Amount over	9000	$331.90
$80,000	27000	
	$27.90ØØ	

Dominic's premium was $331.90.

▶ Compute the fire insurance premiums for these buildings. Use the chart on page 78. The answer to Number 1 is $388.00.

	Coverage	Construction	Risk Area
1)	$155,000	Wood Frame	Medium
2)	$8,000	Brick	Medium
3)	$112,000	Brick	Low
4)	$132,000	Brick	Low
5)	$161,000	Stone	Medium
6)	$30,000	Brick	Medium
7)	$170,000	Brick	High
8)	$120,000	Wood Frame	Medium
9)	$86,000	Brick	High
10)	$76,000	Wood Frame	Low
11)	$59,000	Brick	High
12)	$27,000	Stone	Medium
13)	$116,000	Brick	High
14)	$88,000	Wood Frame	Low
15)	$29,000	Brick	High
16)	$30,000	Brick	High
17)	$142,000	Brick	High
18)	$160,000	Wood Frame	Medium

AUTOMOBILE INSURANCE

The five major types of automobile insurance are:

1. **Liability** — Pays when you injure someone with your car.

2. **Collision** — Pays when you cause body damage to your own car.

3. **Medical payments** — Pays when you or your passengers are injured or lose time from work.

4. **Property damage** — Pays when you cause damage to someone's car or property.

5. **Comprehensive fire and theft** — Pays when your car is vandalized, damaged by a storm, burned, or stolen.

Many states require drivers to have liability insurance and property damage insurance. The other three types are optional. Many people with old cars save money by not buying either collision or comprehensive insurance.

AUTOMOBILE INSURANCE PREMIUM CHART

	1	2	3	4	5
	Liability	Collision (Deductible)	Medical Payments	Property Damage	Comprehensive Fire & Theft
A	$25K/50K $533.10	$500 $208.70	$500 $ 34.80	$10,000 $212.80	$500 Ded. $ 19.80
B	$50K/100K $607.40	$300 $281.70	$1,000 $ 53.60	$20,000 $217.90	$300 Ded. $ 56.90
C	$100K/150K $649.30	$250 $302.40	$2,000 $ 70.20	$30,000 $222.40	$250 Ded. $ 61.30
D	$100K/200K $664.90	$150 $340.80	$3,000 $ 92.90	$50,000 $229.60	$150 Ded. $127.60
E	$150K/300K $703.20	$100 $378.50	$5,000 $107.10	$75,000 $234.10	$0.00 Ded. $158.80

Rating Factors:	Age		Accidents and Moving Violations
	Under 20 = + 30%	25 - 64 = + 0%	1 = + 15%
	20 - 24 = + 10%	Over 64 = + 10%	2 = Refuse policy

Example: Denise, who is 19 years old, wants coverages 1A, 2A, 3B, and 5E. She has had one accident. Find her total premium from the chart.

Step 1: 1A = $533.10; 2A = $208.70; 3B = $53.60; 5E = $158.80

Step 2: $533.10+$208.70+$53.60+$158.80=$954.20

Step 3: Rating factors: Age = 30%; Accidents = 15%

Step 4: 30% + 15% = 45%

Step 5: $954.20 × .45 = $429.39

Step 6: $954.20 + $429.39 = $1,383.59 (Denise's annual premium)

▶ Compute the annual premium for these policies. The answer to Number 1 is $1,668.63. If necessary, round to the next higher cent.

Coverages	Age	Accidents and Moving Violations
1) 1E, 2B, 4C, 5D	20	1
2) 1E, 2A, 3A, 4D, 5D	53	0
3) 1C, 2E, 3E, 4A, 5E	66	1
4) 1C, 2B, 3C, 4E, 5C	23	1
5) 1E, 2A, 3E, 4C	41	0
6) 1A, 3A, 4E, 5E	75	3
7) 1B, 2E, 3E, 4A	61	0
8) 1B, 2E, 4D, 5B	46	1
9) 1A, 2A, 3A, 4C, 5E	53	0
10) 1A, 2B, 3A, 4B, 5E	47	0
11) 1D, 2C, 3B, 4D, 5C	39	1
12) 1B, 2A, 3D, 4E, 5C	44	2
13) 1D, 2B, 3E, 4A, 5D	38	1
14) 1A, 2D, 3E, 4C	57	0

AUTOMOBILE LIABILITY INSURANCE

All states require drivers to buy liability insurance for their cars. Suppose your liability insurance coverage is $50,000/$100,000. This means that your insurance would pay up to $50,000 to any person you injured. The insurance would pay up to $100,000 total for any accident.

If you caused $60,000 of injuries to one person, the company would only pay its $50,000 limit. You would pay the other $10,000! If you caused $40,000 of injuries to each of three people, the total would be $120,000. The insurance company would only pay its limit of $100,000. You would have to pay the other $20,000!

Example: Matthew had $50,000/$100,000 liability coverage. He injured 3 people in an accident: $20,000; $28,000; and $55,000. Find how much the insurance payment is. Find Matthew's payment.

The insurance company would pay:

Person 1: $20,000
Person 2: $28,000
Person 3: +$50,000
    Total $98,000

Matthew would pay:

Person 1: $0
Person 2: $0
Person 3: $5,000

The insurance company would pay its limit of $50,000 to Person 3. It would pay a total of $98,000. Matthew has to pay the remaining $5,000.

▶ For each case below, compute the insurance company's payment and compute the driver's payment, if any. The answers to Number 1 are: Insurance payment, $150,000. Driver's payment, $40,000.

	Coverage	Amounts Due Victims
1)	$100,000/$150,000	$30,000, $50,000, $110,000
2)	$150,000/$175,000	$153,000, $180,000
3)	$75,000/$175,000	$2,500, $79,000
4)	$50,000/$75,000	$50,000, $3,000, $3,000
5)	$50,000/$100,000	$75,000, $56,000, $30,000
6)	$150,000/$175,000	$120,000
7)	$50,000/$100,000	$58,000, $65,000
8)	$100,000/$225,000	$109,000, $109,000, $109,000
9)	$125,000/$150,000	$37,500, $25,000, $212,500
10)	$150,000/$300,000	$30,000, $135,000, $135,000
11)	$100,000/$150,000	$110,000, $110,000
12)	$75,000/$175,000	$15,000, $67,500, $60,000
13)	$50,000/$175,000	$15,000, $45,000, $30,000
14)	$100,000/$150,000	$100,000, $115,000
15)	$100,000/$200,000	$110,000, $40,000
16)	$75,000/$125,000	$75,000, $75,000, $92,000
17)	$100,000/$125,000	$118,000, $118,000, $80,000
18)	$50,000/$100,000	$10,000, $65,000, $35,000
19)	$150,000/$275,000	$150,000, $105,000
20)	$150,000/$275,000	$90,000, $195,000, $225,000
21)	$150,000/$300,000	$90,000, $195,000
22)	$150,000/$250,000	$105,000, $105,000, $180,000
23)	$100,000/$150,000	$70,000, $70,000
24)	$150,000/$175,000	$135,000
25)	$100,000/$250,000	$40,000, $50,000, $50,000

INSURANCE POLICY RIDERS

Business Vocabulary:

Rider — Any additional agreement attached to your policy which adds coverage.

Insurance policies for fire and theft have limits on the coverage for valuables. Common limits are $100 for cash, $200 for art, and $500 for jewelry. People who want more coverage buy a rider. A rider can increase coverage to $100,000 or more.

Example A: Dominic added a rider to his policy for $5,000 coverage on his diamond ring. Find the premium if the rate was 1.1%.

> **Step 1:** 1.1% = .011

> **Step 2:** $5,000 Coverage
> × .011 Rate
> 5000
> 5000
> $55.00̸0 Premium

The premium for Dominic's rider was $55 per year.

Example B: Melissa added a rider to her policy for $95,000 to cover her antique piano. Find the premium if the rate was .8%.

> **Step 1:** .8% = .008

> **Step 2:** $95,000 Coverage
> × .008 Rate
> $760.00̸0 Premium

Melissa's rider premium was $760 per year.

▶ Compute the premium for each of these riders. Round to the nearer cent. The answer to Number 1 is $63.00.

	Coverage	Rate		Coverage	Rate
1)	$9,000	.7%	26)	$2,190	1.2%
2)	$1,531	2.2%	27)	$876	.7%
3)	$8,293	.5%	28)	$8,039	1.5%
4)	$6,674	1.4%	29)	$5,699	1.6%
5)	$5,971	2.2%	30*	$39,420	.6%
6)	$8,641	1.9%	31)	$2,531	.7%
7)	$8,592	.7%	32)	$5,763	1.7%
8)	$8,915	2.0%	33)	$8,048	1.5%
9)	$3,180	1.5%	34)	$2,473	1.2%
10*	$278,640	1.2%	35)	$4,179	1.8%
11)	$1,732	1.1%	36)	$4,250	1.2%
12)	$8,863	1.0%	37)	$1,789	.9%
13)	$8,651	.7%	38)	$20,120	1.6%
14)	$18,798	1.5%	39)	$5,315	1.3%
15)	$726	1.2%	40*	$108,765	1.8%
16)	$20,626	.7%	41)	$8,328	.8%
17)	$20,630	.7%	42)	$35,000	.7%
18)	$20,696	1.7%	43)	$6,843	.8%
19)	$3,394	1.9%	44)	$8,622	1.1%
20*	$120,285	1.7%	45)	$5,601	.6%
21)	$18,108	.6%	46)	$5,198	1.9%
22)	$1,180	1.8%	47)	$7,390	2.1%
23)	$8,784	.9%	48)	$6,995	2.1%
24)	$8,100	2.1%	49)	$3,683	2.1%
25)	$5,549	.9%	50*	$282,690	1.4%

FEDERAL FLOOD INSURANCE

Hundreds of thousands of homes suffer flood damage each year. However, home insurance policies do not pay for flood damage from rain water. Companies cannot sell flood insurance at an affordable price. Therefore, the federal government began its own flood insurance program for people living in high risk areas. The chart shows an example of premiums.

Federal Flood Insurance Premium Chart

Building:

Up to $100,000	$.45 per $100
$100,000 to $200,000	$.17 per $100 + $280

Contents:

Up to $10,000	$.55 per $100
$10,000 to $60,000	$.28 per $100 + $27

Example: Mr. Ruiz bought $105,000 of coverage on a building and $12,000 on its contents. Compute the annual premium.

Step 1: Divide each coverage by $100.
Building: $105,000 ÷ $100 = 1,050.
Contents: $12,000 ÷ $100 = 120.

Step 2: Find the building premium.

```
   10 50
 X   .17 Rate
   73 50
  105 0
 $178.50
 +280.00  Additional charge
 $458.50  Premium
```

Step 3: Find the contents premium.

```
   120
 X .28 Rate
   9 60
  24 0
 $33.60
 +27.00  Additional
 $60.60  Premium
```

Step 4: Add the premiums to find the total.

```
 $458.50  Building
 + 60.60  Contents
 $519.10  Total Premium
```

▶ Compute the premium on these federal flood insurance policies. Use the chart on page 86. The answer to Number 1 is $539.90.

	Building	Contents		Building	Contents
1)	$ 81,000	$53,000	26)	$ 96,000	$35,000
2)	115,000	10,000	27)	209,000	6,000
3)	182,000	40,000	28)	78,000	1,000
4)	182,000	50,000	29)	38,000	51,000
5)	119,000	50,000	30)	51,000	7,000
6)	226,000	39,000	31)	234,000	6,000
7)	162,000	8,000	32)	197,000	54,000
8)	118,000	2,000	33)	182,000	8,000
9)	117,000	50,000	34)	79,000	2,000
10)	89,000	31,000	35)	142,000	3,000
11)	13,000	9,000	36)	193,000	34,000
12)	98,000	7,000	37)	94,000	8,000
13)	219,000	24,000	38)	69,000	5,000
14)	76,000	14,000	39)	68,000	7,000
15)	213,000	13,000	40)	141,000	8,000
16)	83,000	8,000	41)	89,000	2,000
17)	138,000	35,000	42)	178,000	41,000
18)	125,000	1,000	43)	102,000	4,000
19)	59,000	7,000	44)	105,000	6,000
20)	52,000	15,000	45)	55,000	1,000
21)	16,000	2,000	46)	132,000	7,000
22)	52,000	39,000	47)	6,000	8,000
23)	164,000	19,000	48)	40,000	59,000
24)	37,000	30,000	49)	76,000	55,000
25)	138,000	1,000	50)	165,000	28,000

FIRE INSURANCE CLAIMS
With a Calculator

Business Vocabulary:

Clause — A section of an agreement or insurance policy.

Coinsurance — A type of fire insurance under which, if property is not insured up to a certain percent of its value, the owner cannot collect the full amount of the loss.

Replacement value — The cost of reconstructing a destroyed building.

Most fire insurance policies have a coinsurance clause. This clause states that a building must be insured for a minimum amount. Often this amount is 80% of the replacement value. If the coverage is less than 80%, the company will not pay the full amount of a claim.

Example: Mr. Chavez bought $30,000 of fire insurance for a building whose replacement value was $45,000. A fire caused $8,000 worth of damage. How much will the insurance company pay? The coinsurance was 80%.

Step 1: Find 80% of $45,000. $45,000 × .80 = $36,000. Since the amount of the insurance, $30,000, was less than $36,000, the company will not pay the full amount of the loss.

Step 2: Find what part $30,000 is of $36,000. $30,000 ÷ $36,000 = .833333 (Round to 6 decimal places.)

Step 3: Multiply the loss, $8,000, by .833333. $8,000 × .833333 = $6,666 (Round to next lower dollar.)

The insurance company will pay Mr. Chavez $6,666 for his $8,000 fire.

▶ Compute the insurance payments for these fires. Use a coinsurance of 80%. Round to the next lower dollar. The answer to Number 1 is $6,187.

	Replacement Value	Coverage	Loss
1)	$ 50,000	$ 33,000	$7,500
2)	$126,000	$ 85,000	$93,240
3)	$111,000	$ 43,000	$82,140
4)	$114,000	$100,000	$62,700
5)	$ 56,000	$ 33,000	$45,360
6)	$ 66,000	$ 25,000	$17,820
7)	$113,000	$ 42,000	$84,750
8)	$ 87,000	$ 80,000	$34,800
9)	$ 32,000	$ 12,000	$28,800
10*	$420,000	$411,000	$273,000
11)	$128,000	$108,000	$35,840
12)	$101,000	$ 82,000	$10,100
13)	$115,000	$ 95,000	$9,200
14)	$ 54,000	$ 46,000	$44,280
15)	$106,000	$ 49,000	$49,820
16)	$ 73,000	$ 29,000	$9,490
17)	$ 33,000	$ 23,000	$22,770
18)	$ 92,000	$ 60,000	$9,200
19)	$ 51,000	$ 20,000	$10,200
20*	$970,000	$640,000	$523,800
21)	$105,000	$ 63,000	$19,950
22)	$103,000	$ 56,000	$38,110
23)	$ 67,000	$ 31,000	$8,710
24)	$ 93,000	$ 89,000	$42,780
25)	$ 78,000	$ 63,000	$48,360

BASIC SKILL REVIEW

1) A judge awarded $143,839 to the five people Joyce injured in a car accident. Joyce's insurance policy has an accident limit of $125,000. Joyce will have to pay at least how much of her own money to the victims?

2) Jerome's Delivery Service must pay $647 car insurance for each of its eight vans. What is Jerome's total car insurance premium?

3) A jury awarded these amounts to the three people Mark injured with his car: $42,823; $69,398; and $106,350. What was the total award?

4) Chaya's Jewelry Store has nine rings insured for $5,000 each. The total premium is $8,829. Find the premium for one ring.

5) An insurance company must pay $\frac{5}{17}$ of Max's fire loss of $340,000. How much must they pay?

6) One insurance company must pay $\frac{9}{14}$ of a fire loss. Another company must pay $\frac{2}{7}$ of that loss. What part of the loss is covered by these two companies?

7) Bruce purchased a $5\frac{1}{2}$-month insurance policy for $220. How much is that per month?

8) Walter bought a policy for ten months. He canceled it after $5\frac{1}{4}$ months. How much time was left on the policy when he canceled it?

9) The separate premiums for Dot's policies were $246.95, $329.50, $19.82, and $409. How much did Dot spend on these policies?

10) Steve's total premium was $386.10. He canceled the policy and got a refund of $159.95. What was his net payment?

Computer Program:
FIRE INSURANCE PAYMENTS

Some buildings carry more than one fire insurance policy. This is called coverage by multiple carriers. These buildings, like all others, must carry insurance equal to at least 80% of the replacement value. When a fire loss occurs, the insurance companies share the reimbursement according to their share of the total coverage. This program computes the payment share for each insurance company.

```
10   REM FIRE INSURANCE PAYMENT OF MULTIPLE CARRIERS
20   DIM C(10): REM MAXIMUM NO. OF CARRIERS = 10
30   LET TC=0: REM TC=TOTAL COVERAGE OF ALL POLICIES
40   PRINT "TYPE IN THE NUMBER OF INSURANCE COMPANIES
         WITH POLICIES ON THIS BUILDING."
50   INPUT N: REM N=NUMBER OF POLICIES
60   FOR P=1 TO N: REM P=POLICY
70   PRINT "TYPE IN THE COVERAGE OF POLICY ";P
80   INPUT C(P): REM C(P)=COVERAGE OF POLICY NO. P
90   LET TC = TC + C(P)
100  NEXT P
110  PRINT "TYPE IN THE REPLACEMENT VALUE OF THIS
         BUILDING."
120  INPUT RV: REM RV=REPLACEMENT VALUE
130  PRINT "TYPE IN THE AMOUNT OF THE LOSS."
140  INPUT LO: REM LO=LOSS
150  IF TC < .80 * RV THEN 200
160  PRINT "THE LOSS WILL BE FULLY COVERED."
170  REM PC=1 MEANS 100% COVERAGE OF LOSS. PC<1
         MEANS < 100% COVERAGE OF LOSS.
180  LET PC = 1
190  GOTO 220
200  PRINT "THE BUILDING WAS UNDERINSURED.  ONLY
         ABOUT "; INT (100 * TC/(.80 * RV));"% OF THE
         LOSS WILL BE COVERED."
210  LET PC = TC/(.80 * RV)
220  PRINT "TO THE NEARER DOLLAR:"
230  FOR P = 1 TO N
240  PRINT "COMPANY ";P;" WILL PAY $"; INT (.5 + LO * C(P)/
         TC * PC)
250  NEXT P
260  END
```

CHAPTER REVIEW

▶ Solve these problems. Use any charts from this chapter.

1) Brian wants to buy $62,000 of fire insurance coverage on his brick building, which is in a medium risk area. What will his premium be?

2) Maria needs $108,000 fire insurance coverage on her wood frame building, which is in a low risk area. What will her premium be?

3) Joyce, who is 25, needs car insurance. According to the chart on page 80, what would her premium be for coverage of 1A, 2C, 3D, and 4B? She has had no accidents or moving violations.

4) Gary, age 36, wants car insurance coverage of 1B, 2D, 3C, 4C, and 5B. He has had no accidents or moving violations. What would his premium be?

5) Marvin has auto liability coverage of $75,000/$150,000. He injured four people in an accident: $40,000, $80,000, $60,000, and $39,000. How much does Marvin have to pay?

6) LaShanda has auto liability coverage of $50,000/$125,000. She caused these injuries to three people: $25,000, $36,000, and $47,000. How much does she have to pay?

7) Kevin added a rider to his insurance policy for coverage of $92,000 on his business equipment. If the rate was 2.1%, what was the premium?

8) Amy added a rider to her policy for $54,000 extra coverage. If the rate was 1.7%, what was the premium?

9) Joann got flood insurance coverage of $54,000 for her house at the rate of $.47 per $100. Coverage for the contents was $27,000 at the rate of $.22 per $100. What was her total premium?

Chapter 7

Investing
In Stocks

Millions of people invest money in stocks. Stocks are bought and sold through salespeople called brokers. Brokers place the buy and sell orders in a stock exchange.

I can invest my $8,000 in the stock market and get dividends up to 8% or 10%. If my stock doubles in price, it will be worth $16,000.

BUYING STOCKS

Business Vocabulary:

Stock — Shares of ownership in a corporation.
Stockholder — One who owns shares of a corporation.

People buy stock to increase their wealth. If the price of a stock increases, it may be sold at a profit. However, a fall in price may result in a loss of money for the stockholder. Sometimes, stockholders will sell a stock at a loss to avoid losing more money! Stocks are priced in fractions of a dollar.

Fractions Expressed As Decimals		
$\frac{1}{8}$ = .125	$\frac{1}{2}$ = .5	$\frac{3}{4}$ = .75
$\frac{1}{4}$ = .25	$\frac{5}{8}$ = .625	$\frac{7}{8}$ = .875
$\frac{3}{8}$ = .375		

Example: Jim bought 300 shares of stock at $76 \frac{5}{8}$. How much did he pay?

Step 1: Convert the fraction to a decimal.

$$\frac{5}{8} = \frac{.625}{8\overline{)5.000}}$$

Step 2: Add the decimal to the whole number. Write the number as dollars and cents.

$76.625

Step 3: Multiply the price by the number of shares.

$$\begin{array}{r} \$76.625 \\ \times \quad 300 \\ \hline \$22,987.50\cancel{0} \end{array}$$

Jim paid $22,987.50 for the 300 shares.

▶ Compute the total price for these stock shares. The answer for Number 1 is $10,841.25.

	Price	Number of Shares		Price	Number of Shares
1)	$154 \frac{7}{8}$	70	21)	$197 \frac{3}{8}$	70
2)	$4 \frac{1}{2}$	80	22)	$189 \frac{1}{8}$	90
3)	$193 \frac{3}{4}$	60	23)	$104 \frac{5}{8}$	20
4)	$84 \frac{1}{4}$	90	24)	$80 \frac{3}{4}$	30
5)	$57 \frac{1}{8}$	90	25)	$105 \frac{7}{8}$	70
6)	$115 \frac{7}{8}$	90	26)	$92 \frac{1}{8}$	40
7)	$25 \frac{1}{8}$	100	27)	$48 \frac{5}{8}$	60
8)	$142 \frac{7}{8}$	100	28)	$43 \frac{3}{8}$	80
9)	$87 \frac{5}{8}$	20	29)	$175 \frac{1}{8}$	70
10*	$1,080 \frac{1}{8}$	80	30*	$1,197 \frac{7}{8}$	80
11)	$20 \frac{3}{4}$	30	31)	$33 \frac{1}{8}$	50
12)	$136 \frac{1}{8}$	60	32)	$192 \frac{3}{4}$	60
13)	$86 \frac{3}{4}$	20	33)	$122 \frac{1}{4}$	10
14)	$80 \frac{1}{4}$	40	34)	$103 \frac{5}{8}$	60
15)	$128 \frac{1}{8}$	100	35)	$47 \frac{1}{8}$	50
16)	$147 \frac{3}{4}$	70	36)	$168 \frac{1}{8}$	90
17)	$36 \frac{7}{8}$	70	37)	$23 \frac{7}{8}$	100
18)	$19 \frac{7}{8}$	60	38)	$82 \frac{1}{4}$	30
19)	$130 \frac{3}{4}$	90	39)	$96 \frac{7}{8}$	30
20*	$1,611 \frac{5}{8}$	30	40*	$1,260 \frac{3}{8}$	40

STOCKBROKER'S COMMISSION

Business Vocabulary:

Corporation — A company whose ownership is divided into shares of stock.

Stock exchange — A place where stocks are bought and sold for investors.

Transaction — A purchase or sale of stock.

People buy stock as an investment. Stockbrokers earn their income from commissions. Investors pay the commission when they buy and sell their stock.

A Typical Commission Schedule	
Transaction	**Commission**
Less than $3,000	1.2% + $18.00
$3,000 to $7,000	.6% + $36.00
More than $7,000	.3% + $57.00

Example: Elaine bought $300 of stock. Find the commission charge.

Step 1: Multiply.

$300 Purchase price
× .012 Times 1.2%
600
300
$3.60Ø

Step 2: Add

$ 18.00
+ 3.60
$ 21.60 Commission

Elaine paid a commission of $21.60.

► Find the commission on these stock transactions. Use the commission schedule on page 96. If necessary, round up to the next cent. The answer to Number 1 is $25.01.

	Transaction			Transaction
1)	$584		26)	$942
2)	$5,515		27)	$6,269
3)	$113		28)	$263
4)	$134		29)	$39,078
5)	$5,831		30)	$15,510
6)	$33,528		31)	$2,394
7)	$1,469		32)	$68
8)	$5,206		33)	$3,843
9)	$2,736		34)	$1,982
10)	$48,450		35)	$2,358
11)	$808		36)	$4,344
12)	$402		37)	$5,682
13)	$28,627		38)	$334
14)	$1,798		39)	$2,024
15)	$5,192		40)	$7,320
16)	$799		41)	$7,628
17)	$3,325		42)	$6,414
18)	$2,023		43)	$6,514
19)	$12,612		44)	$730
20)	$24,960		45)	$48,026
21)	$5,369		46)	$138
22)	$4,188		47)	$18,679
23)	$20,619		48)	$1,936
24)	$2,140		49)	$42,371
25)	$3,658		50)	$35,040

STOCK PRICE CHANGES

If a company is earning a good profit, many people will want to buy its stock. The price of that stock will then increase. If a company loses money, many people who own that stock will try to sell it. The price of that stock will then fall. Stock prices are expressed in fractions of a dollar.

Example A: Norm bought some stock at $154\frac{3}{8}$.

When the price rose to $207\frac{7}{8}$, he sold it. How much did the price increase?

$207\frac{7}{8}$ Selling price

$- \ 154\frac{3}{8}$ Purchase price

$53\frac{4}{8}$ or $53\frac{1}{2}$ Change

The price increased $53\frac{1}{2}$.
This means $53.50.

Example B: Randy bought some stock at $79\frac{1}{2}$. When the price fell to $58\frac{1}{4}$, he sold it. How much did the price decrease?

$79\frac{1}{2} \ = \qquad 79\frac{2}{4}$ Purchase price

$- \ 58\frac{1}{4} \ = \quad - \ 58\frac{1}{4}$ Selling price

$21\frac{1}{4}$ Change

The price decreased $21\frac{1}{4}$.
This means $21.25.

▶ Compute the price changes for these stocks. Subtract the smaller price from the larger price. Leave your answers in fractional form. The answer to Number 1 is $18\frac{5}{8}$.

Price Then	Price Now		Price Then	Price Now
1) $151\frac{7}{8}$	$133\frac{1}{4}$	21)	$62\frac{5}{8}$	$31\frac{1}{2}$
2) $199\frac{5}{8}$	$62\frac{1}{4}$	22)	$106\frac{7}{8}$	$20\frac{1}{2}$
3) $129\frac{5}{8}$	$27\frac{3}{8}$	23)	$196\frac{5}{8}$	$92\frac{3}{8}$
4) $157\frac{1}{2}$	$194\frac{3}{4}$	24)	$8\frac{5}{8}$	$164\frac{3}{4}$
5) $123\frac{3}{8}$	$108\frac{1}{8}$	25)	$139\frac{5}{8}$	$35\frac{1}{4}$
6) $114\frac{3}{4}$	$40\frac{1}{8}$	26)	$88\frac{5}{8}$	$76\frac{3}{8}$
7) $91\frac{3}{8}$	$57\frac{1}{8}$	27)	$96\frac{1}{2}$	$77\frac{1}{8}$
8) $155\frac{3}{8}$	$32\frac{3}{8}$	28)	$121\frac{7}{8}$	$156\frac{7}{8}$
9) $184\frac{3}{4}$	$100\frac{3}{8}$	29)	$111\frac{1}{2}$	$92\frac{3}{8}$
10* $50\frac{1}{4}$	$738\frac{7}{8}$	30*	$184\frac{7}{8}$	$225\frac{3}{4}$
11) $183\frac{3}{4}$	$154\frac{1}{2}$	31)	$196\frac{3}{4}$	$188\frac{5}{8}$
12) $62\frac{1}{4}$	$83\frac{7}{8}$	32)	$181\frac{1}{8}$	$190\frac{3}{4}$
13) $56\frac{5}{8}$	$94\frac{7}{8}$	33)	$65\frac{3}{4}$	$151\frac{7}{8}$
14) $75\frac{1}{4}$	$176\frac{3}{8}$	34)	$151\frac{5}{8}$	$160\frac{3}{4}$
15) $89\frac{1}{2}$	$137\frac{3}{4}$	35)	$151\frac{1}{2}$	$53\frac{1}{4}$
16) $146\frac{7}{8}$	$4\frac{1}{4}$	36)	$35\frac{1}{8}$	$145\frac{1}{2}$
17) $58\frac{3}{4}$	$166\frac{7}{8}$	37)	$117\frac{5}{8}$	$80\frac{1}{8}$
18) $142\frac{3}{8}$	$135\frac{1}{4}$	38)	$26\frac{3}{4}$	$74\frac{7}{8}$
19) $147\frac{3}{8}$	$141\frac{1}{4}$	39)	$116\frac{3}{4}$	$62\frac{5}{8}$
20* $19\frac{1}{2}$	$1,151\frac{5}{8}$	40*	$82\frac{1}{2}$	$801\frac{5}{8}$

STOCK DIVIDENDS

Business Vocabulary:

Board of directors — A group of people who vote dividends, set policy, and oversee the job performance of the top executives.

Stockholders — Those who own stock in a company.

Dividends — The part of a company's profit which is divided among the stockholders.

There are two ways that investors make money in the stock market. If the price of a stock increases, they may sell the stock for a profit. Investors also make money while they own stocks. A few times a year, the board of directors votes to divide some or all of the company's net profit among the stockholders. This net profit per share is called the *dividend.*

Example: The XYZ Corporation's board of directors voted to distribute a $9,000,000 net profit among 4,000,000 shares. Compute the dividend.

Step 1: $9,000,000 net profit divided by 4,000,000 shares.

$$\frac{\$9,000,000}{4,000,000} = \frac{\$9}{4}$$

Step 2:

$$\begin{array}{r} \$2.25 \\ 4\overline{)\$9.00} \\ \underline{8} \\ 10 \\ \underline{8} \\ 20 \\ \underline{20} \end{array}$$

The dividend was $2.25 per share.

▶ Compute the dividend on each of these stocks. Round to the nearer cent. The answer to Number 1 is $2.37.

	Net Profit	Shares
1)	$7,095,000	3,000,000
2)	$6,760,000	2,000,000
3)	$14,820,000	2,000,000
4)	$61,840,000	8,000,000
5)	$78,720,000	8,000,000
6)	$9,210,000	3,000,000
7)	$34,160,000	7,000,000
8)	$21,560,000	11,000,000
9)	$5,460,000	1,000,000
10)	$50,220,000	6,000,000
11)	$34,350,000	5,000,000
12)	$31,980,000	6,000,000
13)	$22,020,000	3,000,000
14)	$4,320,000	6,000,000
15)	$68,070,000	3,000,000
16)	$330,880,000	8,000,000
17)	$21,540,000	3,000,000
18)	$14,400,000	2,000,000
19)	$818,800,000	10,000,000
20)	$806,500,000	10,000,000
21)	$171,440,000	2,000,000
22)	$7,260,000	3,000,000
23)	$73,260,000	9,000,000
24)	$167,240,000	4,000,000
25)	$42,620,000	2,000,000

INVESTOR'S BREAK-EVEN POINT

Business Vocabulary:

Break-even point — Total amount paid per share, including purchase price, commissions, and fees. If a stock is sold at this amount, there is neither a profit nor a loss.

Many investors use the break-even point to decide when to sell a stock. Some investors will not sell a stock until its price has climbed above the break-even point. Investors make a profit when they sell a stock above the break-even point.

Example: Donna bought 200 shares of DEF stock at $43 per share. The commission was $29. When Donna sold the stock, the commission was also $29. The fees came to $2.00. What was the break-even point?

Step 1:

$43.00 Purchase price
× 200 Number of shares
$8,600.00 Total purchase price

Step 2:

$8,600 Total purchase price
29 Buying commission
29 Selling commission
+ 2 Fees
$8,660 Total expense

Step 3: Find the amount per share. Divide $8,660 by 200.

```
        $   43.30
200)$8,660.00
      8 00
        660
        600
         60 0
         60 0
```

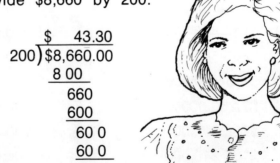

The break-even point was $43.30.

▶Compute the break-even point for these stocks. Round up to the next cent. The answer to Number 1 is $55.38.

	Total Purchase Price	Number of Shares	Buying Commission	Selling Commission	Fees
1)	$ 8,100	150	$106.50	$ 97.35	$2.10
2)	1,097	700	61.19	60.58	2.99
3)	5,502	700	107.78	106.91	1.57
4)	2,885	100	78.85	78.30	2.07
5)	3,468	300	81.56	81.40	2.75
6)	10,455	200	165.01	165.17	2.28
7)	2,782	600	76.99	76.22	1.88
8)	2,712	100	78.75	78.36	2.05
9)	8,097	100	128.55	128.55	1.08
10*	17,774	200	245.52	244.54	2.24
11)	6,065	200	116.72	115.67	2.88
12)	10,039	200	149.39	149.54	2.64
13)	7,348	200	124.22	124.72	2.46
14)	8,490	200	132.36	133.28	1.09
15)	2,729	400	78.11	77.96	1.28
16)	2,491	600	76.66	76.51	1.00
17)	3,993	500	91.13	92.04	1.15
18)	7,639	100	118.76	117.57	1.00
19)	2,068	100	68.62	68.55	1.15
20*	17,138	200	214.53	216.46	2.54
21)	6,299	300	106.70	106.16	2.66
22)	7,578	600	126.54	125.91	1.62
23)	3,040	400	82.53	83.36	1.39
24)	3,307	600	86.38	87.07	2.95
25)	8,178	500	135.87	135.19	1.92

COMPUTING THE PRICE-EARNINGS RATIO
With a Calculator

Business Vocabulary:

Preferred Stock — Those shares which are paid a fixed dividend before shares of common stock are paid a dividend.

Price-earnings ratio — Market price per share divided by the earnings per share.

Corporations with preferred stock pay part of their net profit to holders of that stock. The board of directors then votes to distribute the remaining net profit. They may decide to re-invest in facilities and equipment. Or, they may decide to re-invest some of it and pay the remaining part as dividends to holders of common stock.

Investors base many decisions on the price-earnings ratio. It measures how profitable a company has been during the past year. To compute the price-earnings ratio:

Step 1: Subtract the total preferred dividend from the net profit. (= Earnings available for common stock)

Step 2: Divide the earnings available for common stock by the number of shares. (= Earnings per share)

Step 3: Divide the market price by the earnings per share. (= Price-earnings ratio)

Example: XYZ Corporation earned a net profit of $5,638,491. Their total dividend for preferred stock was $281,924. Find the earnings available for common stock.

$5,638,491 − $281,924 = $5,356,567

XYZ has issued 2,099,200 shares of common stock. Find the earnings per share.

$5,356,567 divided by 2,099,200 = $2.551 ≈ $2.55

Round to the next lower cent.

The market price is $42. Find the price-earnings ratio. Round to the nearer tenth.

$42 divided by $2.55 = 16.47 ≈ 16.5

▶ Compute the earnings available for common stock, the earnings per share, and the price-earnings ratio. Round to the next lower cent. The answers for Number 1 are: $505,000, $1.68, and 14.9.

	Net Profit for Year	Dividend for Preferred Stock	Number of Shares	Earnings per Share	Market Price
1)	$ 535,000	$ 30,000	300,000	?	$25
2)	$ 3,472,316	$104,169	2,505,200	?	$24
3)	$10,460,715	$627,642	2,154,700	?	$33
4)	$ 3,757,095	$112,712	231,900	?	$158
5)	$ 9,062,417	$453,120	637,700	?	$136
6)	$ 7,027,692	$421,661	2,698,900	?	$33
7)	$ 8,184,969	$163,699	812,900	?	$112
8)	$ 4,521,320	$271,279	2,130,300	?	$30
9)	$10,219,485	$919,753	3,152,900	?	$40
10)	$10,651,818	$426,072	1,121,200	?	$159
11)	$ 2,355,640	$117,782	900,800	?	$28
12)	$ 7,933,168	$634,653	656,700	?	$104
13)	$ 8,882,501	$ 88,825	426,600	?	$157
14)	$ 7,047,646	$211,429	2,771,600	?	$33
15)	$ 9,846,541	$886,188	2,333,300	?	$31

BASIC SKILL REVIEW

1) Jeff owned 210 shares of stock. He sold 45 shares. How many did he have left?

2) Jason bought stock five times last year. He bought 150 shares, 425 shares, 350 shares, 220 shares, and 590 shares. How many shares did he buy in all?

3) Ginnie bought 970 shares of stock at $73 each. How much did she pay?

4) Sharonda bought $2,700 worth of shares at $18 each. How many shares did she buy?

5) George bought 60 shares at $20\frac{1}{4}$. How much did he pay?

6) Isidore's math class bought one share of stock at $48\frac{5}{8}$, and another at $29\frac{3}{4}$. How much did the class pay?

7) Ellen spent $230 on stock that cost $2\frac{7}{8}$ per share. How many shares did she buy?

8) Mrs. Brown bought some stock at $40\frac{3}{8}$. The price dropped $4\frac{1}{2}$. What was the new price?

9) Nina's four commissions this morning were $38.25, $69.50, $25.00, and $54.95. What was her total commission?

10) Milton bought 20 shares of stock at $20.75 each. How much did he pay?

11) Judy bought $3,150 worth of stock at $4.50 per share. How many shares did she buy?

12) Mendel's total bill for a stock purchase was $948.53. The stock itself cost $920.75. How much was the extra charge?

Computer Program:
STOCK MARKET TRANSACTIONS

This program calculates the net gain or net loss from a stock transaction. Type it into a computer. Run the program several times with different sets of data.

```
10   REM STOCK PROGRAM
20   PRINT "THIS PROGRAM COMPUTES THE NET GAIN
     OR NET LOSS FROM A STOCK TRANSACTION."
30   PRINT "TYPE IN THE NUMBER OF SHARES."
40   INPUT NS
50   PRINT "TYPE IN THE PURCHASE PRICE.   TYPE IN
     FRACTIONS AS DECIMALS."
60   PRINT "   1/8  =  .125   5/8  =  .625"
70   PRINT "   1/4  =  .25    3/4  =   .75"
80   PRINT "   3/8  =  .375   7/8  =  .875"
90   PRINT "   1/2  =  .5"
100  INPUT PP
110  PRINT "TYPE IN THE TOTAL PURCHASE COMMIS-
           SION AND FEES."
120  INPUT PC
130  LET TP = PP * NS + PC: REM TP=TOTAL PURCHASE
140  PRINT "TYPE IN THE SALE PRICE.   TYPE IN FRAC-
     TIONS AS DECIMALS."
150  INPUT SP
160  PRINT "TYPE IN THE TOTAL SALES COMMISSION
     AND FEES."
170  INPUT SC
180  LET TS = SP * NS + SC: REM TS=TOTAL SALE
190  PRINT "THE TOTAL PURCHASE PRICE PLUS COM-
     MISSION AND FEES = $";TP
200  PRINT "THE TOTAL SALE PRICE PLUS COMMISSION
     AND FEES = $";TS
210  IF TS − TP >= 0 THEN PRINT "THE NET GAIN ON
     THE ";NS;" SHARES OF STOCK WAS $";TS − TP
220  IF TS − TP < 0 THEN PRINT "THE NET LOSS ON
     THE ";NS;" SHARES OF STOCK WAS $";TP − TS
230  END
```

CHAPTER REVIEW

1) John bought 50 shares at $73\frac{1}{2}$ each. What was the total price?

2) Sue bought 200 shares at $24\frac{5}{8}$ each. What was the total price?

3) The amount of a stock transaction was $820. What was the commission? Use the schedule on page 96.

4) The amount of a stock transaction was $3500. What was the commission? Use the schedule on page 96.

5) The new price of a share is $164\frac{5}{8}$. The old price was $159\frac{1}{2}$. What is the price change?

6) The new price of a share is $99\frac{1}{8}$. The old price was $174\frac{1}{2}$. What is the price change?

7) The new price of a share is $28\frac{1}{4}$. The old price was $19\frac{5}{8}$. What is the price change?

8) The new price of a share is $138\frac{1}{4}$. The old price was $183\frac{3}{8}$. What is the price change?

9) The net profit of the GB Company was $4,161,000. There were 3,000,000 shares. What was the dividend?

10) The net profit of FA, Inc. was $7,096,000. There were 8,000,000 shares. What was the dividend?

11) What is the break-even point? The purchase price was $3,112.50 for 300 shares. The buying commission was $81.62; the selling commission was $82.36; and fees were $2.37.

12) What is the break-even point? The purchase price was $5,200 for 1,300 shares. The buying commission was $98.45; the selling commission was $99.14; and fees were $2.18.

Chapter **8**

Compound and Simple Interest

People save money in banks for safety and invest-ment. Money is always safer in a bank than hidden at home. Also, banks pay interest to encourage people to open and maintain savings accounts. This payment of interest makes people with savings accounts investors.

In this chapter you will find out about simple and compound interest.

SECOND FEDERAL

8% Interest
Compounded Quarterly

SIMPLE INTEREST

Business Vocabulary:

Interest — Money paid to individuals for the use of their money.

Principal — The amount of a loan or initial deposit.

The amount of simple interest on a loan or savings account is the same each year. Simple interest is computed on the original principal only. The formula for simple interest is:

$$I = PRT$$

This means interest (I) = principal (P) × rate (R) × time (T). The time is always expressed in years or in the equivalent of years.

Example: Donald borrowed $1,200 at 15% simple interest for two years. How much interest did he have to pay?

Step 1: Multiply the principal times the rate.

$$
\begin{array}{r}
\$1200 \text{ Principal} \\
\times \quad .15 \text{ Rate} \\
\hline
6000 \\
1200 \\
\hline
\$180.00
\end{array}
$$

Step 2: Multiply that product by the time.

$$
\begin{array}{r}
\$180.00 \\
\times \quad 2 \text{ Time} \\
\hline
\$360.00
\end{array}
$$

The interest on Donald's loan was $360.00.

▶ Compute the simple interest for each of these loans. Round fractions of a cent up to the next higher cent. The answer to Number 1 is $108.00.

	Principal	Rate	Time in Years		Principal	Rate	Time in Years
1)	$ 900	4%	3	26)	$ 1,400	11%	5
2)	$ 800	13%	3	27)	$ 600	13%	5.5
3)	$ 2,600	8%	5	28)	$ 1,900	4%	2
4)	$ 2,800	7%	4	29)	$ 2,800	9%	5
5)	$ 1,600	7%	6	30*	$25,500	8%	2
6)	$ 1,000	15%	3	31)	$ 2,200	13%	4.25
7)	$ 200	10%	3	32)	$ 1,200	11%	4
8)	$ 1,400	8%	5	33)	$ 1,600	10%	4
9)	$ 1,900	4%	5	34)	$ 2,500	7%	2
10*	$28,600	9%	4	35)	$ 1,100	6%	2
11)	$ 2,600	12%	3	36)	$ 2,200	13%	2
12)	$ 1,300	5%	3.5	37)	$ 1,400	11%	4
13)	$ 1,400	10%	6	38)	$ 1,600	12%	1.5
14)	$ 1,200	14%	6	39)	$ 2,000	10%	1
15)	$ 1,500	10%	2	40*	$36,350	12%	2.75
16)	$ 3,000	5%	6	41)	$ 2,000	7%	2
17)	$ 1,000	9%	1	42)	$ 1,800	15%	4.5
18)	$ 2,400	5%	1	43)	$ 2,900	10%	5
19)	$ 2,100	13%	4	44)	$ 3,000	7%	3
20*	$44,100	11%	6.5	45)	$ 1,000	14%	6
21)	$ 2,700	11%	3	46)	$ 2,400	12%	2
22)	$ 1,400	5%	6	47)	$ 2,300	7%	5.25
23)	$ 2,100	15%	2	48)	$ 2,500	3%	2
24)	$ 200	8%	6	49)	$ 1,200	8%	6.25
25)	$ 2,600	14%	4	50*	$16,200	3%	1.5

SIMPLE INTEREST WITH TIME IN MONTHS

The formula for simple interest is:

Interest = Principal × Rate × Time

The amount of time must be expressed in years. Therefore, a term measured in months is expressed as a fraction of a year.

Example: Sam borrowed $16,560 at 10% simple interest for 5 months. Find the interest.

Step 1: Multiply the principal by the rate.

$$\begin{array}{r} \$16{,}560 \text{ Principal} \\ \times \quad .10 \text{ Rate} \\ \hline \$1656.00 \end{array}$$

Step 2: Multiply that product by the time.

$$5 \text{ months} = \frac{5}{12} \begin{array}{l} \text{Months} \\ \text{Number of months in a year} \end{array}$$

$$\frac{\$1656}{1} \times \frac{5}{12} = \frac{\$8280}{12}$$

$$\begin{array}{r} \$\,690 \\ 12\overline{)\$8280} \\ 72 \\ \hline 108 \\ 108 \\ \hline 00 \end{array}$$

Sam had to pay $690 in interest.

▶ Compute the simple interest on these loans. Round to the nearer cent. The answer to Number 1 is $24.96.

	Principal	Rate	Time in Months		Principal	Rate	Time in Months
1)	$416	12%	6	26)	$21,960	20%	5
2)	$3,840	23%	1	27)	$18,480	19%	9
3)	$16,080	25%	5	28)	$14,160	13%	12
4)	$15,960	24%	10	29)	$17,760	16%	6
5)	$19,200	15%	6	30*	$126,000	21%	4
6)	$6,000	17%	2	31)	$11,640	13%	2
7)	$15,480	25%	10	32)	$19,320	14%	12
8)	$14,040	15%	7	33)	$16,320	11%	5
9)	$14,640	16%	1	34)	$12,120	12%	1
10*	$235,200	19%	7	35)	$8,400	14%	3
11)	$20,760	22%	5	36)	$840	10%	8
12)	$8,280	13%	1	37)	$2,520	22%	9
13)	$11,400	13%	6	38)	$23,640	24%	4
14)	$20,160	12%	11	39)	$15,960	15%	8
15)	$21,720	25%	2	40*	$205,200	17%	10
16)	$18,600	16%	12	41)	$4,680	19%	8
17)	$13,440	16%	3	42)	$7,560	12%	4
18)	$5,880	22%	2	43)	$14,880	25%	12
19)	$11,520	24%	4	44)	$17,040	16%	1
20*	$105,600	17%	6	45)	$18,240	14%	5
21)	$8,760	15%	9	46)	$8,160	13%	4
22)	$7,440	21%	10	47)	$19,320	21%	4
23)	$1,800	13%	3	48)	$6,840	15%	11
24)	$13,440	10%	3	49)	$7,320	10%	10
25)	$9,000	16%	9	50*	$208,800	17%	5

COMPOUND INTEREST FOR TWO YEARS

The money you earn in savings account interest is yours. You may withdraw it or leave it in the account to earn more interest. Interest that you earn on interest is called *compound interest*.

The four steps in computing compound interest for two years are: Multiply, Add, Multiply, Add. Think of the word MAMA to help you remember the steps.

Example: Louis left $900 on deposit at 5% compound interest. Find his balance after two years.

Step 1: Multiply $ 900 Principal
                            × .05 Rate
                         $45.00 First year interest

Step 2: Add   +$900.00 Principal
                         $945.00 Balance after first year

Step 3: Multiply   ×   .05
                         $47.2500 Second year interest

Step 4: Add   +$945.00
                         $992.25̸0̸0̸ Balance after second year

Louis's balance after two years was $992.25. He earned $92.25 in interest. ($992.25 − $900 = $92.25)

▶ Each of these savings accounts earns compound interest. Find the balance after two years. Find the total interest earned. Use the MAMA method. Round answers to the next lower cent. The answers to Number 1 are: Balance, $699.84; Interest, $99.84.

	Principal	Rate		Principal	Rate
1)	$ 600	8%	26)	$ 7,000	10.5%
2)	$ 900	5%	27)	$ 1,000	6.2%
3)	$ 100	12%	28)	$ 2,000	11.5%
4)	$ 500	10%	29)	$ 6,000	12.4%
5)	$ 900	10%	30*	$20,000	12.4%
6)	$ 800	12%	31)	$ 4,000	8.3%
7)	$ 200	12%	32)	$ 2,000	11.9%
8)	$ 800	13%	33)	$ 5,000	9.7%
9)	$ 600	6%	34)	$ 7,000	6.8%
10*	$4,000	13%	35)	$ 2,000	10.4%
11)	$ 400	5%	36)	$ 8,000	4.5%
12)	$ 300	13%	37)	$ 8,000	9.9%
13)	$ 200	12%	38)	$ 7,000	13.6%
14)	$ 600	13%	39)	$ 9,000	7.5%
15)	$ 400	4%	40*	$90,000	6.8%
16)	$ 200	14%	41)	$ 2,000	8.3%
17)	$ 300	9%	42)	$ 4,000	14.6%
18)	$ 700	14%	43)	$ 5,000	6.9%
19)	$ 800	7%	44)	$ 8,000	6.7%
20*	$7,000	12%	45)	$ 5,000	6.7%
21)	$1,000	13.7%	46)	$ 8,000	8.3%
22)	$1,000	6.8%	47)	$ 8,000	5.9%
23)	$9,000	12.3%	48)	$ 2,000	13.5%
24)	$5,000	8.2%	49)	$ 5,000	7.1%
25)	$2,000	4.6%	50*	$60,000	8.1%

COMPARING SIMPLE INTEREST AND COMPOUND INTEREST

If the rates are equal and the time is more than one year, the amount of compound interest will always be greater than the amount of simple interest.

Example: Joe deposited $700 for two years at 5% simple interest in Bank ABC. At Bank DEF, he deposited another $700 for two years at 5% compound interest. Find the total interest from each account.

Step 1: Simple Interest. (I = PRT)

$$
\begin{array}{rl}
\$700 & \text{Principal} \\
\times\ .05 & \text{Rate} \\
\hline
\$35.00 & \\
\times\quad 2 & \text{Time (2 years)} \\
\hline
\$70.00 &
\end{array}
$$

Step 2: Compound Interest. (MAMA)

$$
\begin{array}{rl}
\$700 & \text{Principal} \\
\times\ .05 & \text{Rate} \\
\hline
\$35.00 & \text{First year interest} \\
+\$700.00 & \\
\hline
\$735.00 & \text{Balance after first year} \\
\times\quad .05 & \\
\hline
\$36.7500 & \text{Second year interest} \\
+\$735.0000 & \\
\hline
\$771.75\cancel{0}\cancel{0} & \text{Balance after second year}
\end{array}
$$

Subtract the original principal to find the interest.
$771.75 − $700 = $71.75.

The compound interest of $71.75 was greater than the simple interest of $70.00.

▶ Compute the simple interest and the compound interest for each account. Round to the nearer cent. The answers to Number 1 are: Simple interest, $90.00; compound interest, $92.70.

Principal	Rate	Time in Years		Principal	Rate	Time in Years
1) $750	6%	2	26)	$1,400	5%	2
2) $3,000	4%	2	27)	$500	3%	2
3) $200	13%	2	28)	$1,900	8%	2
4) $1,800	11%	2	29)	$2,000	9%	2
5) $2,900	10%	2	30*	$9,400	5%	2
6) $2,500	13%	2	31)	$600	5%	2
7) $500	13%	2	32)	$2,100	9%	2
8) $2,600	13%	2	33)	$1,900	12%	2
9) $1,900	6%	2	34)	$1,400	8%	2
10* $20,400	14%	2	35)	$2,300	7%	2
11) $1,200	4%	2	36)	$1,300	7%	2
12) $1,000	13%	2	37)	$900	4%	2
13) $1,500	13%	2	38)	$2,000	15%	2
14) $1,800	14%	2	39)	$1,600	9%	2
15) $1,400	3%	2	40*	$30,300	11%	2
16) $500	15%	2	41)	$700	13%	2
17) $600	15%	2	42)	$800	13%	2
18) $2,200	15%	2	43)	$700	11%	2
19) $2,500	6%	2	44)	$1,200	13%	2
20* $29,200	12%	2	45)	$400	9%	2
21) $400	14%	2	46)	$2,400	9%	2
22) $2,300	3%	2	47)	$2,700	11%	2
23) $900	13%	2	48)	$2,700	10%	2
24) $2,700	12%	2	49)	$2,700	7%	2
25) $900	9%	2	50	$23,700	14%	2

THE COMPOUND INTEREST TABLE

The compound interest table was created to shorten problems. If you use the table, a 25-year compound interest problem takes only two steps instead of 50! Look at the table. It shows that $1 will grow to $3.3863 in 25 years at 5% compound interest. Therefore, $70 will grow to $237.04 ($\approx$ $3.3863 $\times$ 70).

	Amounts for $1.00 Compounded Annually			
Years	5%	8%	10%	15%
1	1.0500	1.0800	1.1000	1.1500
2	1.1025	1.1664	1.2100	1.3225
3	1.1576	1.2597	1.3310	1.5208
4	1.2155	1.3604	1.4641	1.7490
5	1.2762	1.4693	1.6105	2.0113
6	1.3400	1.5868	1.7715	2.3130
7	1.4071	1.7138	1.9487	2.6600
8	1.4774	1.8509	2.1435	3.0590
9	1.5513	1.9990	2.3579	3.5178
10	1.6288	2.1589	2.5937	4.0455
11	1.7103	2.3316	2.8531	4.6523
12	1.7958	2.5181	3.1384	5.3502
13	1.8856	2.7196	3.4522	6.1527
14	1.9799	2.9371	3.7974	7.0757
15	2.0789	3.1721	4.1772	8.1370
16	2.1828	3.4259	4.5949	9.3576
17	2.2920	3.7000	5.0544	10.7612
18	2.4066	3.9960	5.5599	12.3754
19	2.5269	4.3157	6.1159	14.2317
20	2.6532	4.6609	6.7275	16.3665
21	2.7859	5.0338	7.4002	18.8215
22	2.9252	5.4365	8.1402	21.6447
23	3.0715	5.8714	8.9543	24.8914
24	3.2250	6.3411	9.8497	28.6251
25	3.3863	6.8484	10.8347	32.9189
26	3.5556	7.3963	11.9181	37.8567
27	3.7334	7.9880	13.1099	43.5353
28	3.9201	8.6271	14.4209	50.0656
29	4.1161	9.3172	15.8630	57.5754
30	4.3219	10.0626	17.4494	66.2117

Example: John left $400 on deposit at 8% compound interest for three years. Find the balance after the three years.

Step 1: Look in the table under 8% for 3 years. Find $1.2597.

Step 2: Multiply $1.2597 by 400.

$$\begin{array}{r} \$\ 1.2597 \\ \times\ \ \ \ \ \ 400 \\ \hline \$503.88\cancel{00} \end{array}$$

After three years, John's balance was $503.88.

▶ Compute each balance below. Round down to the next lower cent. The answer to Number 1 is $779.48.

	Principal	Rate	Years		Principal	Rate	Years
1)	$400	10%	7	16)	$500	10%	28
2)	$900	5%	3	17)	$200	10%	15
3)	$500	10%	9	18)	$400	8%	7
4)	$800	15%	7	19)	$900	8%	19
5)	$800	15%	23	20)	$700	5%	21
6)	$400	15%	11	21)	$400	15%	6
7)	$800	5%	30	22)	$800	8%	22
8)	$900	8%	13	23)	$900	10%	24
9)	$200	15%	27	24)	$500	15%	10
10)	$800	8%	27	25)	$200	8%	12
11)	$100	15%	16	26)	$900	10%	8
12)	$800	15%	28	27)	$800	5%	26
13)	$500	8%	17	28)	$200	10%	30
14)	$600	15%	24	29)	$300	15%	6
15)	$100	5%	18	30)	$200	15%	20

PRESENT VALUE

Business Vocabulary:

Present value — The amount of money one must invest today to yield a specific amount in the future.

Worth of money — A current interest rate for "safe" investments.

In business it is often necessary to determine the value today of some payment in the future. For example, someone may promise to pay you $10,000 for a piece of land. However, the person cannot pay you today. Instead, he will pay you the $10,000 in one year. If money is worth 11%, what is the real value (today) of his offer?

The value of his offer is only $9,009. He can invest $9,009 at 11% interest today and have $10,000 in one year. Therefore, his offer to pay $10,000 in one year is only worth $9,009 today. This is the idea behind present value.

	Chart of the Present Value of $1.00					
Years	8%	9%	10%	11%	12%	13%
1	.9259	.9174	.9090	.9009	.8928	.8849
2	.8573	.8416	.8264	.8116	.7971	.7831
3	.7938	.7721	.7513	.7311	.7117	.6930
4	.7350	.7084	.6830	.6587	.6355	.6133
5	.6805	.6499	.6209	.5934	.5674	.5427
6	.6301	.5962	.5644	.5346	.5066	.4803
7	.5834	.5470	.5131	.4816	.4523	.4250
8	.5402	.5018	.4665	.4339	.4038	.3761
9	.5002	.4604	.4240	.3909	.3606	.3328
10	.4631	.4224	.3855	.3521	.3219	.2945
11	.4288	.3875	.3504	.3172	.2874	.2606
12	.3971	.3555	.3186	.2858	.2566	.2307
13	.3676	.3261	.2896	.2575	.2291	.2041
14	.3404	.2992	.2633	.2319	.2046	.1806
15	.3152	.2745	.2393	.2090	.1826	.1598
16	.2918	.2518	.2176	.1882	.1631	.1414
17	.2702	.2310	.1978	.1696	.1456	.1252
18	.2502	.2119	.1798	.1528	.1300	.1108

Example: Someone just offered to buy Sharon's house for $80,000 two years from now. What is the value of that offer today if money is worth 11%?

According to the table, at 11%, each dollar promised two years from now is worth only $.8116 today.

Multiply. $.8116
         ×   80,000
         $64,928.00∅∅

The present value of the offer is only $64,928.

▶ Compute the present value of these future payments. The answer to Number 1 is $19,868.80.

	Amount	Years in Future To Be Paid	Money Is Worth
1)	$32,000	5	10%
2)	$20,000	2	8%
3)	$75,000	18	9%
4)	$30,000	8	9%
5)	$20,000	13	13%
6)	$40,000	5	9%
7)	$95,000	17	11%
8)	$70,000	7	11%
9)	$79,000	10	10%
10)	$10,000	8	14%
11)	$52,000	15	12%
12)	$50,000	2	10%
13)	$24,000	7	11%
14)	$30,000	6	12%
15)	$90,000	14	12%

SEMIANNUAL, QUARTERLY, AND MONTHLY COMPOUNDING

Business Vocabulary:

Semiannual — Two times per year (every six months)
Quarterly — Four times per year (every three months)
Monthly — Twelve times per year (every month)
Interest period — Amount of time between compounding.

Most banks compound savings account interest several times per year. With semiannual compounding, the bank computes and pays one-half the interest every six months. With quarterly compounding, the bank computes and pays one-fourth the interest every three months. With monthly compounding, the bank computes and pays one-twelfth the interest each month.

Example: Jessica's savings account paid 8% interest, compounded quarterly, for 18 years. Find the rate per interest period, and the number of periods.

Step 1: Rate per period.
Divide the yearly rate by the number of periods per year.

8% divided by 4 = 2%

Step 2: Number of periods.
Multiply the number of years times the number of periods per year.

    18 Years
  × 4 Periods per year
    72 Total periods

Jessica's account paid 2% per period for 72 periods.

▶ Find the rate per period and the number of interest periods. Round interest rates to the nearer one-hundredth percent. The answers to Number 1 are .42% for 72 periods.

1) 5% compounded monthly for 6 years

2) 12% compounded semiannually for 4 years

3) 10% compounded quarterly for 17 years

4) 12% compounded monthly for 17 years

5) 9% compounded monthly for 4 years

6) 8% compounded quarterly for 26 years

7) 9% compounded monthly for 13 years

8) 11% compounded semiannually for 4 years

9) 7% compounded monthly for 13 years

10* 16.9% compounded semiannually for 13 years

11) 6% compounded semiannually for 30 years

12) 12% compounded monthly for 22 years

13) 10% compounded monthly for 9 years

14) 8% compounded quarterly for 3 years

15) 19% compounded semiannually for 3 years

16) 11% compounded monthly for 27 years

17) 9% compounded quarterly for 16 years

18) 7% compounded semiannually for 4 years

19) 16% compounded quarterly for 23 years

20* 14.1% compounded semiannually for 7 years

21) 8% compounded quarterly for 21 years

22) 13% compounded monthly for 6 years

23) 8% compounded quarterly for 23 years

24) 12% compounded semiannually for 12 years

25) 6% compounded monthly for 20 years

USING A COMPOUND INTEREST TABLE
WITH PERIODIC RATES

When interest is compounded several times a year, only a portion of the interest rate is used. The table below helps to make calculations easier.

	Amounts for $1.00 Compounded Periodically						
Periods	1%	1.5%	2%	3%	4%	6%	12%
2	1.02	1.03	1.04	1.06	1.08	1.12	1.25
4	1.04	1.06	1.08	1.12	1.16	1.26	1.57
6	.06	1.09	1.12	1.19	1.26	1.41	1.97
8	1.08	1.12	1.17	1.26	1.36	1.59	2.47
10	1.10	1.16	1.21	1.34	1.48	1.79	3.10
12	1.12	1.19	1.26	1.42	1.60	2.01	3.89
14	1.14	1.23	1.31	1.51	1.73	2.26	4.88
16	1.17	1.26	1.37	1.60	1.87	2.54	6.13
18	1.19	1.30	1.42	1.70	2.02	2.85	7.68
20	1.22	1.34	1.48	1.80	2.19	3.20	9.64
22	1.24	1.38	1.54	1.91	2.36	3.60	12.10
24	1.26	1.42	1.60	2.03	2.56	4.04	15.17
26	1.29	1.47	1.67	2.15	2.77	4.54	19.04
28	1.32	1.51	1.74	2.28	2.99	5.11	23.88
30	1.34	1.56	1.81	2.42	3.24	5.74	29.95
32	1.37	1.61	1.88	2.57	3.50	6.45	37.58
34	1.40	1.65	1.96	2.73	3.79	7.25	47.14
36	1.43	1.70	2.03	2.89	4.10	8.14	59.13
38	1.45	1.76	2.12	3.07	4.43	9.15	74.17
40	1.48	1.81	2.20	3.26	4.80	10.28	93.05
42	1.51	1.86	2.29	3.46	5.19	11.55	116.72
44	1.54	1.92	2.39	3.67	5.61	12.98	146.41
46	1.58	1.98	2.48	3.89	6.07	14.59	183.66
48	1.61	2.04	2.58	4.13	6.57	16.39	230.39
50	1.64	2.10	2.69	4.38	7.10	18.42	289.00
52	1.67	2.16	2.80	4.65	7.68	20.69	362.52
54	1.71	2.23	2.91	4.93	8.31	23.25	454.75
56	1.74	2.30	3.03	5.23	8.99	26.12	570.43
58	1.78	2.37	3.15	5.55	9.72	29.35	715.55
60	1.81	2.44	3.28	5.89	10.51	32.98	897.59

Example: Morris deposited $500 at 6% interest, compounded quarterly, for 14 years. Find the amount to which the $500 grew in 14 years.

Step 1: Find the rate per period.
Divide the yearly rate by the number of periods per year. 6% divided by 4 = 1.5%

Step 2: Find the number of periods.
Multiply the number of years by the number of periods per year.

14 × 4 = 56 periods

Step 3: Look in the table for 56 periods at 1.5%.
The table shows that $1.00 grows to $2.30.

Multiply $2.30 by 500.

$$\begin{array}{r} \$2.30 \\ \times \quad 500 \\ \hline \$1,150.00 \end{array}$$

Morris's $500 grew to $1,150 in 14 years.

▶ For each principal below, compute the amount to which it grew. Use the table on page 124. The answer to Number 1 is $888.

1) $600 at 8% for 5 years, compounded quarterly
2) $900 at 6% for 1 year, compounded quarterly
3) $200 at 6% for 12 years, compounded quarterly
4) $500 at 24% for 3 years, compounded monthly
5) $800 at 24% for 5 years, compounded monthly
6) $300 at 8% for 18 years, compounded semiannually
7) $400 at 6% for 6 years, compounded quarterly
8) $200 at 6% for 5 years, compounded semiannually
9) $600 at 24% for 1 year, compounded quarterly
10) $200 at 6% for 3 years, compounded quarterly
11) $400 at 6% for 15 years, compounded semiannually
12) $300 at 12% for 2 years, compounded monthly
13) $800 at 24% for 5 years, compounded semiannually
14) $200 at 24% for 13 years, compounded quarterly
15) $500 at 8% for 4 years, compounded semiannually

CALCULATING SIMPLE INTEREST WITH A TERM IN DAYS
With a Calculator

The formula for simple interest is:

Interest = Principal × Rate × Time

The amount of time must be expressed in terms of one year. Therefore, a term measured in days is expressed as a fraction of a year. In this exercise, we will use a year of 365 days.

Example A: Mike borrowed $12,317 at 25% simple interest for 226 days. Find the interest. Round to the nearer cent.

25% = .25   226 days $= \dfrac{226}{365}$ year

Simple interest equals:

$12,317 × .25 × 226 ÷ 365 = $1906.6041

$1906.6041 is rounded to $1906.60.

Mike paid $1906.60 in interest.

Example B: Bob borrowed $8,012 at 16% simple interest for 277 days. Find the interest.

16% = .16   277 days $= \dfrac{277}{365}$ year

Simple interest equals:

$8,012 × .16 × 277 ÷ 365 = $972.85435

$972.85435 is rounded to $972.85.

Bob paid $972.85 in interest.

▶ Use a calculator to compute the simple interest on these loans. Round to the nearer cent. The answer to Number 1 is $20.55.

	Principal	Rate	Number of Days		Principal	Rate	Number of Days
1)	$2,500	10%	30	26)	$8,161	13%	204
2)	$4,968	23%	344	27)	$8,292	11%	89
3)	$5,044	18%	253	28)	$15,634	14%	175
4)	$4,079	22%	248	29)	$18,027	17%	68
5)	$8,014	23%	101	30*	$153,750	21.31%	133
6)	$1,924	13%	325	31)	$6,222	21%	289
7)	$17,793	20%	190	32)	$1,500	13%	69
8)	$8,509	17%	5	33)	$11,237	10%	64
9)	$6,757	19%	14	34)	$7,583	16%	253
10*	$108,160	13.46%	201	35)	$18,317	20%	146
11)	$4,383	12%	255	36)	$15,485	19%	273
12)	$1,129	20%	318	37)	$11,829	13%	343
13)	$8,090	20%	353	38)	$14,878	16%	168
14)	$15,257	22%	327	39)	$5,567	21%	107
15)	$8,830	13%	133	40*	$157,530	13.8%	40
16)	$3,348	20%	172	41)	$18,636	20%	107
17)	$16,134	19%	349	42)	$4,263	15%	293
18)	$11,162	19%	116	43)	$6,943	18%	32
19)	$1,566	21%	144	44)	$1,506	15%	59
20*	$163,420	23.35%	218	45)	$4,577	10%	105
21)	$16,205	11%	126	46)	$12,339	11%	7
22)	$4,798	17%	173	47)	$14,461	25%	274
23)	$4,567	23%	305	48)	$5,371	20%	336
24)	$2,880	11%	328	49)	$12,022	19%	117
25)	$18,925	24%	281	50*	$215,590	13.59%	163

BASIC SKILL REVIEW

1) Joe deposited $37,100 in an account in Bank A. He deposited twice as much in an account in Bank B. How much did he deposit in Bank B?

2) May borrowed $82,000. So far, she has repaid $49,654. How much does she still owe?

3) Ellen's will stated that her bank account of $120,972 should be left in equal shares to her eight children. How much will each child receive?

4) Jill has five separate savings accounts. Their current balances are: $679; $8.00; $19,729; $2,664; and $92. Find the total of these five accounts.

5) Sam had $1,600 in his savings account. He withdrew $249.67. How much did he have left?

6) Steve has $4,649.94 more in his savings account now than when he was seventeen. He had $1,635.65 in the account when he was seventeen. What is Steve's balance now?

7) Sandra spent $4,689.96 to buy eleven gold coins. How much did each one cost?

8) Tom made monthly savings deposits of $25.59 for 48 months. What was the total of his deposits?

9) Lew's paycheck was $1,213.84. He spent half and deposited the rest. How much did he deposit?

10) Gerri spends half of her paycheck on food and a third on rent. What part of her paycheck is left for other things?

11) George borrowed $4,000 for one year at 9.9% simple interest. What was George's total interest payment?

Computer Program:
COMPOUND INTEREST

Business Vocabulary:

Nominal rate — The stated annual rate of interest.

Effective rate — The rate of simple interest that yields the same amount of interest as the nominal rate.

This program will calculate the growth of a deposit that earns compound interest.

Type the program into a computer. Run it several times with different data.

```
10   REM COMPOUND INTEREST SOFTWARE
20   PRINT "TYPE IN THE AMOUNT OF MONEY INVESTED."
30   INPUT M
40   PRINT "TYPE IN THE NUMBER OF YEARS THAT THE":
     PRINT "MONEY WILL BE INVESTED."
50   INPUT Y
60   PRINT "TYPE IN THE NUMBER OF INTEREST PERIODS":
     PRINT "PER YEAR."
70   INPUT P
80   PRINT "TYPE IN THE NOMINAL RATE OF INTEREST
     AS A DECIMAL."
90   INPUT R
100  LET C = M * (1 + R/P) ^ (Y * P)
110  PRINT "AFTER ";Y;" YEARS, $";M;" WILL GROW TO":
     PRINT "$";C;" AT ";R * 100;"% INTEREST":PRINT
     "COMPOUNDED ";P; "TIMES PER YEAR."
120  PRINT
130  PRINT "THE EFFECTIVE RATE OF INTEREST WILL
     BE ":PRINT "((1 + R / P) ^ P - 1) * 100;"%"
140  END
```

CHAPTER REVIEW

▶ Find the simple interest.

1) $800 at 5% for one year

2) $1,250 at 8% for $2\frac{1}{2}$ years

3) $900 at 10% for six months

4) $2,400 at 11% for 11 months

5) $900 at 6% for two years

6) $1,100 at 9% for two years

▶ Find the compound interest.

7) $1,100 at 9% for two years

8) $900 at 6% for two years

▶ Use the table on page 118 for the compound interest.

9) $600 at 5% for 8 years

10) $1,200 at 15% for 10 years

▶ Find the balance after one year with simple interest.

11) $622 at 6%   12) $1,873 at 9%

▶ Find the rate per period and the number of interest periods.

13) 17% compounded quarterly for 5 years

14) 18% compounded monthly for 7 years

▶ Find the amount for each principal.
Use the table on page 124.

15) $800 at 8% for 5 years, compounded quarterly

16) $1,000 at 12% for 10 years, compounded semi-annually.

Chapter **9**

Interest in Banking And Commerce

Interest is the most important concept in the world of finance. Open a newspaper to the financial section. You will find many advertisements that mention a rate of interest. Interest plays a part in nearly every loan, savings account, and installment purchase.

In this chapter you will find out more about how interest is computed on loans and installment purchases.

FIRST STATE SAVINGS and LOAN

LOAN OFFICER

LOAN TERM AND TOTAL INTEREST

Business Vocabulary:

Term — The amount of time agreed upon for repaying a loan.

Borrowing money is like "renting" the money. The longer you have someone else's money, the more interest you must pay. Two loans of the same amount of money and the same interest rate could have two different amounts of total interest, depending on the term for each loan.

The chart below shows monthly payments for a $1,000 loan for four different terms.

Monthly Payments for a $1,000 Loan				
Rate	24 Mo.	36 Mo.	48 Mo.	60 Mo.
12%	$47.08	$33.22	$26.34	$22.25
13%	$47.55	$33.70	$26.83	$22.76
14%	$48.02	$34.18	$27.33	$23.27
15%	$48.49	$34.67	$27.84	$23.79
16%	$48.97	$35.16	$28.35	$24.32
17%	$49.45	$35.66	$28.86	$24.86
18%	$49.93	$36.16	$29.38	$25.40
19%	$50.41	$36.66	$29.91	$25.95
20%	$50.90	$37.17	$30.44	$26.50
21%	$51.39	$37.68	$30.97	$27.06
22%	$51.88	$38.20	$31.51	$27.62
23%	$52.38	$38.71	$32.06	$28.20
24%	$52.88	$39.24	$32.61	$28.77

Example: Desiree priced two loans. They were both for $5,000 at 19% interest. Loan 1 had a term of 60 months. Loan 2 had a term of 36 months. What was the difference between the two amounts of interest?

Step 1: Look in the chart for the payment for Loan 1. 19% for 60 months is $25.95.

$25.95 Payment for $1,000

× 5

$129.75 Payment for $5,000

$129.75 Payment for 1 month

× 60 Months

$7785.00 Payment for 60 months

Step 2: Look in the chart for the payment for Loan 2. 19% for 36 months is $36.66.

$36.66 Payment for $1,000

× 5

$183.30 Payment for $5,000

$183.30 Payment for 1 mo.

× 36 Months

109980

54990

$6598.80 Payment for 36 mos.

Step 3: Subtract to find the difference.

$7,785.00 Loan 1

−6,598.80 Loan 2

$1,186.20 Difference

Loan 1 required $1,186.20 more interest. This is because Loan 1 was for a greater term.

▶ Compute the interest difference for each pair of loans. The answer to Number 1 is $413.76.

		Term of Loan 1	Term of Loan 2
1)	$4,000 at 18%	24 months	36 months
2)	$8,000 at 15%	60 months	48 months
3)	$3,000 at 24%	36 months	60 months
4)	$5,000 at 12%	24 months	36 months
5)	$9,000 at 21%	48 months	60 months
6)	$2,000 at 17%	60 months	24 months
7)	$6,000 at 20%	48 months	36 months
8)	$1,000 at 13%	36 months	60 months
9)	$4,000 at 14%	24 months	48 months
10*	$66,000 at 19%	24 months	36 months
11)	$7,000 at 16%	24 months	48 months

FIXED-RATE MORTGAGES

Business Vocabulary:

Mortgage — A loan to buy a home or other property.

Fixed-Rate Mortgage — Fixed interest rate, usually for a term of 20 to 30 years. Equal monthly payments of principal and interest until debt is paid in full.

People who want to buy a home shop around for a mortgage that is right for them. They know that a small difference in interest rates means hundreds of dollars in interest payments. They also know that mortgages with longer terms require greater total interest payments.

Example A: Jo has a mortgage for $55,000 at 13.75% for 30 years. What is her total payment?

Step 1: Look in the table. Find the payment for 13.75% and 30 years. The monthly payment is $11.66.

Monthly Payment to Amortize (Repay) a Loan of $1,000			
	Term		
Rate	20 Years	25 Years	30 Years
12.50%	$11.37	$10.91	$10.68
12.75%	11.54	11.10	10.87
13.00%	11.72	11.28	11.07
13.25%	11.90	11.47	11.26
13.50%	12.08	11.66	11.46
13.75%	12.26	11.85	11.66
14.00%	12.44	12.04	11.85
14.25%	12.62	12.23	12.05
14.50%	12.80	12.43	12.25
14.75%	12.99	12.62	12.45

Step 2: Multiply. $11.66 Monthly payment for $1,000
× 55 (Loan is $55,000)
$641.30 Monthly payment for $55,000

12 Months in 1 year $641.30 Payment for 1 month
×30 Years   × 360 Months
360 Months in 30 years   3847800
                             192390
                             $230868.00 Total payment

Jo's total payment was $230,868.

Example B: Bo has a mortgage for $55,000 at 14% for 30 years. What is his total payment?

Step 1: Look in the table. The payment at 14% for 30 years is $11.85.

Step 2: Multiply. $11.85 × 55 × 360 = $234,630

Compare: Bo's total payment: $234,630
Jo's total payment: −230,868
$ 3,762 Difference

Bo's mortgage was just .25% higher than Jo's. This made his total payment $3,762 more than Jo's!

▶ Compute the total payment for each of these mortgage loans. Compare each set of answers. The answer to Number 1 is $230,688.

Mortgage	Rate	Term	Mortgage	Rate	Term
1) $60,000	12.5%	30	6) $100,000	13%	25
2) $60,000	12.75%	30	7) $70,000	14.5%	25
3) $92,000	14.75%	25	8) $70,000	14.75%	25
4) $92,000	14.5%	25	9 * $737,000	13%	30
5) $100,000	12.75%	25	10 * $737,000	13.25%	30

BALLOON MORTGAGES

Business Vocabulary:

Balloon mortgage — Mortgage in which monthly payments are based on a fixed interest rate, usually for a three-to-five-year term. Principal is due in full at end of term.

Balloon payment — The tremendous, last payment of a balloon mortgage.

Balloon mortgages have the same size monthly payments as fixed-rate mortgages. They were created to protect lenders against quickly rising interest rates. It is important for borrowers to realize that during the first few years of a balloon mortgage, they pay very little principal. Look at the chart below.

Percentage of Mortgage Principal Left After 5 Years		
	Term	
Rate	20 Yrs.	30 Yrs.
10%	89.8%	96.6%
10.5%	90.3%	96.9%
11%	90.8%	97.2%
11.5%	91.3%	97.4%
12%	91.7%	97.7%
12.5%	92.2%	97.9%
13%	92.6%	98.1%
13.5%	93.1%	98.3%
14%	93.4%	98.4%
14.5%	93.7%	98.6%
15%	94.1%	98.7%
15.5%	94.4%	98.8%
16%	94.7%	99%

Example:

Renee obtained a $92,000, 30-year balloon mortgage at 13.5% for 5 years. How much did Renee still owe after five years?

Step 1:

Look in the table. Find the percentage at 13.5% for 30 years. The percentage is 98.3%.

Step 2: Multiply $92,000 by 98.3%.

$$98.3\% = .983$$

$$
\begin{array}{r}
\$92,000 \\
\times\ \ .983 \\
\hline
276\,000 \\
736\,000 \\
828\,000 \\
\hline
\$90,436.00\cancel{0}
\end{array}
$$

After five years, when the balloon payment was due, Renee still owed $90,436.

▶ Compute the amount of the balloon payment for each 5-year balloon mortgage. The answer to Number 1 is $82,572.

	Mortgage	Rate	Term in Years
1)	$84,000	13.5%	30
2)	$54,000	14.5%	30
3)	$99,000	13.5%	20
4)	$63,000	15.5%	20
5)	$44,000	10%	30
6)	$39,000	10.5%	20
7)	$41,000	15.5%	20
8)	$70,000	15%	20
9)	$83,000	11.5%	30
10*	$1,111,000	15.5%	30
11)	$35,000	12.5%	20
12)	$37,000	12%	30
13)	$40,000	10.5%	30
14)	$103,000	15.5%	30
15)	$101,000	12%	20
16)	$41,000	10.5%	30
17)	$98,000	11%	20
18)	$90,000	11%	20

USING AN AMORTIZATION TABLE

Business Vocabulary:

Amortization table — A chart that shows the monthly payment for a given interest rate, term, and amount financed.

Amount financed — The part of a bill paid over time.

Many stores allow customers to finance their purchases and to pay on an installment plan. These stores use an amortization table to compute the monthly payment. The amount of the monthly payment depends on three things: The interest rate, the term, and the amount financed.

Monthly Payments for Each $100 Financed

Rate	12 Mo.	18 Mo.	24 Mo.	30 Mo.	36 Mo.	42 Mo.
4%	$8.52	$5.74	$4.35	$3.51	$2.96	$2.56
5%	$8.57	$5.78	$4.39	$3.56	$3.00	$2.61
6%	$8.61	$5.83	$4.44	$3.60	$3.05	$2.65
7%	$8.66	$5.87	$4.48	$3.65	$3.09	$2.70
8%	$8.70	$5.92	$4.53	$3.69	$3.14	$2.74
9%	$8.75	$5.96	$4.57	$3.74	$3.18	$2.79
10%	$8.80	$6.01	$4.62	$3.79	$3.23	$2.84
11%	$8.84	$6.06	$4.67	$3.83	$3.28	$2.88
12%	$8.89	$6.10	$4.71	$3.88	$3.33	$2.93
13%	$8.94	$6.15	$4.76	$3.93	$3.37	$2.98
14%	$8.98	$6.20	$4.81	$3.97	$3.42	$3.03
15%	$9.03	$6.24	$4.85	$4.02	$3.47	$3.08
16%	$9.08	$6.29	$4.90	$4.07	$3.52	$3.13
17%	$9.13	$6.34	$4.95	$4.12	$3.57	$3.18
18%	$9.17	$6.39	$5.00	$4.17	$3.62	$3.23
19%	$9.22	$6.43	$5.05	$4.22	$3.67	$3.28
20%	$9.27	$6.48	$5.09	$4.27	$3.72	$3.33
21%	$9.32	$6.53	$5.14	$4.32	$3.77	$3.39
22%	$9.36	$6.58	$5.19	$4.37	$3.82	$3.44
23%	$9.41	$6.63	$5.24	$4.42	$3.88	$3.49
24%	$9.46	$6.68	$5.29	$4.47	$3.93	$3.55
25%	$9.51	$6.72	$5.34	$4.52	$3.98	$3.60

Example: Eleanor financed $5,000 worth of furniture at 21% interest for 18 months. Find the total amount that Eleanor paid.

Step 1: Look in the table. Find the payment at 21% for 18 months. The payment is $6.53.

Step 2: The payment of $6.53 is for just $100. Eleanor financed $5,000. How many $100s are in $5,000?

$$\$5,000 \div \$100 = 50$$

Step 3: Multiply.

$6.53 Payment for $100	
× 50 $100s in $5,000	
$326.50 Payment for $5,000	

$326.50 Monthly payment	
× 18 Months	
261200	
32650	
$5877.00 Total payment	

Eleanor paid a total of $5,877 for the furniture.

▶ Find the total amount paid for each of the purchases below. Use the amortization table. The answer to Number 1 is $8,807.82.

	Amount	Rate	Months		Amount	Rate	Months
1)	$6,700	16%	42	11)	$6,400	22%	36
2)	$9,800	12%	42	12)	$6,200	14%	24
3)	$6,600	22%	18	13)	$4,100	23%	30
4)	$4,600	8%	36	14)	$6,500	6%	18
5)	$2,000	22%	30	15)	$6,900	16%	12
6)	$8,000	17%	24	16)	$6,900	24%	42
7)	$7,100	4%	24	17)	$ 800	18%	12
8)	$7,600	16%	18	18)	$5,600	17%	12
9)	$3,400	12%	18	19)	$6,800	6%	36
10)	$8,000	13%	36	20)	$3,100	12%	12

SIMPLE DISCOUNT NOTES

Business Vocabulary:

Note — A written promise to pay a specified amount of money at a definite time.

Discount interest — Interest on a loan that is paid in advance, when the loan is taken out, instead of when the loan is due.

Net proceeds — The amount actually lent to the borrower.

Many banks use the discount note for their loans of one year or less. This method allows the bank to collect its interest at the beginning of the loan.

Example: Judy borrowed $7,800 at 19% interest for 5 months. Compute the net proceeds.

Step 1: Find the interest for one year.

$7,800   Principal
× .19   Rate of 19%
70200
7800
$1,482.00   Interest for one year

Step 2: Find the interest for 5 months.

5 months = $\frac{5}{12}$ of a year.

$$\frac{\$1,482}{1} \times \frac{5}{12} = \frac{\$7,410}{12} = \$617.50$$

Step 3: Subtract the interest from the principal.

$7,800.00   Principal
−   617.50   Interest
$7,182.50   Net proceeds

The bank lent Judy $7,182.50. At the end of five months, Judy paid the bank $7,800.

▶ Compute the net proceeds for each of these simple discount notes. Round to the nearer cent. The answer to Number 1 is $800.25.

Amount	Rate	Months		Amount	Rate	Months
1) $ 900	19%	7	26)	$5,000	19%	9
2) $9,700	16%	1	27)	$6,700	16%	10
3) $7,800	20%	8	28)	$1,800	21%	5
4) $9,600	20%	10	29)	$8,100	15%	7
5) $8,100	16%	10	30*	$7,800	19.69%	11
6) $8,400	23%	8	31)	$8,900	21%	11
7) $2,700	19%	11	32)	$3,200	20%	11
8) $3,700	16%	4	33)	$2,300	22%	3
9) $8,300	16%	10	34)	$4,300	17%	5
10* $5,700	23.03%	6	35)	$9,800	21%	6
11) $1,300	24%	2	36)	$2,500	24%	10
12) $9,800	22%	12	37)	$2,500	21%	7
13) $7,900	17%	9	38)	$2,000	21%	10
14) $7,500	15%	11	39)	$4,000	17%	11
15) $7,600	15%	3	40*	$1,000	23.88%	3
16) $8,300	23%	10	41)	$5,200	21%	6
17) $2,600	20%	6	42)	$ 200	19%	4
18) $1,700	16%	1	43)	$ 400	21%	3
19) $5,900	22%	8	44)	$5,500	16%	6
20* $5,200	15.16%	3	45)	$2,200	22%	2
21) $2,100	21%	7	46)	$ 600	23%	9
22) $5,900	22%	6	47)	$4,000	24%	8
23) $2,000	22%	5	48)	$7,600	23%	10
24) $4,000	18%	4	49)	$4,700	21%	10
25) $1,300	21%	12	50*	$4,400	18.17%	3

COMPUTING PAYMENTS OF ADJUSTABLE RATE MORTGAGES
With a Calculator

Business Vocabulary:

Adjustable rate mortgage — A loan whose interest rate is fixed for only a short time, often just a year or two. The rate may go up or down each year or so after that. Usually there are limits to how much the rate can change.

Adjustable rate mortgages were invented to protect borrowers and lenders against both rising and falling interest rates. They often have lower initial interest rates than fixed-rate mortgages. When the interest rate on the loan is changed, the remaining principal is refinanced at the new rate.

Monthly Payment to Amortize (Repay) a Loan of $1,000			
	Term		
Rate	20 Years	25 Years	30 Years
12.50%	$11.37	$10.91	$10.68
12.75%	11.54	11.10	10.87
13.00%	11.72	11.28	11.07
13.25%	11.90	11.47	11.26
13.50%	12.08	11.66	11.46
13.75%	12.26	11.85	11.66
14.00%	12.44	12.04	11.85
14.25%	12.62	12.23	12.05
14.50%	12.80	12.43	12.25
14.75%	12.99	12.62	12.45

Example: Jay obtained an adjustable rate mortgage with an initial interest rate of 13.75%. When the rate rose .5%, he still owed $65,597.30. He had 25 years left to pay. Find his new monthly payment.

Step 1: Find Jay's new rate of interest.
13.75% + .5% = 14.25%

Step 2: Look in the table at 14.25% for 25 years.
The payment is $12.23 for each $1,000.

Step 3: Find the number of $1,000s in $65,597.30.
$65,597.30 ÷ $1,000 = 65.5973

Step 4: Multiply the payment for $1,000 by 65.5973.
$12.23 × 65.5973 = $802.25497, or $802.26.

Jay's new monthly payment is $802.26.

▶ Compute the new monthly payment for each of these adjustable rate mortgages. Round to the next higher cent. The answer to Number 1 is $876.74.

	Current Amount	Old Rate	Rate Change	Years Left
1)	$ 76,436.97	13.75%	−.5%	25
2)	$118,119.58	12.75%	+.25%	30
3)	$ 88,628.41	14.5%	−.5%	30
4)	$109,251.30	14.5%	−1.5%	25
5)	$ 79,345.19	14.5%	−1%	25
6)	$ 69,607.78	14.5%	−.5%	30
7)	$ 90,127.76	14.5%	−1%	25
8)	$ 58,651.31	14.75%	−.5%	30
9)	$ 99,472.06	14.75%	−2%	25
10)	$100,006.55	14.25%	+.25%	30
11)	$103,063.08	12.5%	+.75%	30
12)	$112,389.89	14.25%	−.75%	30
13)	$ 80,367.06	12.75%	+.5%	25
14)	$ 91,708.34	14.25%	−1.5%	30
15)	$ 56,974.35	13%	+.5%	25
16)	$ 97,393.15	14.25%	−1%	25
17)	$101,436.72	13.25%	+1%	25
18)	$ 67,764.05	12.75%	+1.5%	30

BASIC SKILL REVIEW

1) Stephanie took out five separate loans this year for her clothing store. The loans were $5,000; $40,000; $35,000; $80,000; and $39,000. Find the total of the loans.

2) Lee borrowed $19,500. He paid back $8,764. How much did he still owe?

3) The monthly payment for a $10,000 loan at 9% for 42 months is $279. Find the monthly payment for a $500,000 loan. (Hint: $500,000 = 50 × $10,000.)

4) The monthly payment on a loan is $87 per $1,000. Dwayne's monthly payment is $3,915. How much did he borrow?

5) Marion has paid back $\frac{3}{5}$ of his $24,000 loan. How much has he paid back?

6) Roderick repaid $\frac{1}{2}$ of his loan last year. He repaid $\frac{1}{8}$ of the loan this year. How much has he paid back?

7) Susie has repaid $\frac{3}{10}$ of her loan. How much does she still owe?

8) Johanna borrows money every $\frac{2}{3}$ of a year. How many times will she borrow money in 6 years?

9) Jim agreed to repay $24.93 per week for 104 weeks. What will be his total payment?

10) By April, Carla hopes to repay $926.59 of her $4,300 loan. How much will she still owe?

11) Angela's four monthly payments are: mortgage, $437.65; car, $96.52; TV, $42.87; and credit card, $104.96. What is the total of her monthly payments?

Computer Program:
LOAN REPAYMENT

This program prints out a chart or schedule that shows the breakdown of monthly loan payments. Type this program into a computer. Run it several times with different information. Δ = Type a space.

```
10   REM LOAN REPAYMENT PROGRAM
20   REM LB=LOAN BALANCE, AR=INTEREST RATE, MP=
     MONTHLY PAYMENT
30   PRINT "TYPE IN LOAN AMOUNT.   TYPE $500 AS 500."
40   INPUT LB
50   PRINT "TYPE IN ANN. INT. RATE.   TYPE 12% AS .12"
60   INPUT AR
70   PRINT "TYPE IN MONTHLY PAYMENT."
80   INPUT MP
90   IF MP > LB * AR / 12 THEN 120
100  PRINT "MONTHLY PAYMENT TOO SMALL."
110  GOTO 280
120  PRINT "AMOUNT = $";LB;" RATE=";100 * AR;"%";" MON.
     PAYMENT = $";MP
130  PRINT
135  PRINT "ΔΔΔΔΔΔΔ BALANCE"
140  PRINT "PAYM. ΔΔ BEFORE ΔΔΔΔ INT. ΔΔΔ PRIN. ΔΔΔ
     AMOUNT"
150  PRINT "NUM. ΔΔΔ PAYMENT ΔΔΔ PAID ΔΔΔ PAID ΔΔΔΔΔ
     DUE"
160  REM PN=PAYMENT NUMBER, LB=LOAN BALANCE,
     TP=INTEREST PAID
170  REM PP=PRINCIPAL PAID, AD=AMOUNT DUE
180  LET PN = PN+1
190  LET TP = INT ((LB * AR / 12 + .0099) * 100) / 100: REM
     ROUNDS CENTS UP
200  LET LB = INT (100 * (LB + TP) + .0099) / 100: REM
     ROUNDS CENTS UP
210  IF LB < MP THEN AD = LB
220  IF LB >= MP THEN AD = MP
230  LET PP = AD - TP
240  PRINT PN;"ΔΔΔΔΔ$";LB;" Δ$";TP;"ΔΔ$";PP;"ΔΔΔ$";AD
250  LET LB = LB - AD
260  IF LB = 0 THEN 280
270  GOTO 180
280  END
```

CHAPTER REVIEW

1) Lisa has a $5,000 loan at 19% for 24 months. What is her total payment? Use the chart on page 132.

2) Andy has a $5,000 loan at 19% for 48 months. What is his total payment? Use the chart on page 132.

3) Ellyn has a $9,500 loan at 24% for 48 months. What is her total payment? Use chart on page 132.

4) Billy has a $9,500 loan at 24% for 60 months. What is his total payment? Use chart on page 132.

5) Larry has a mortgage for $80,000 at 13.75% for 25 years. What is his total payment? Use the chart on page 134.

6) Mary has a mortgage for $80,000 at 14% for 25 years. What is her total payment? Use the chart on page 134.

7) Dot had a $77,000, 30-year balloon mortgage at 12.5% for 5 years. How much did she still owe at the end of 5 years? Use the chart on page 136.

8) Bernie had a $77,000, 20-year balloon mortgage at 12.5% for 5 years. How much did he still owe at the end of 5 years? Use the chart on page 136.

9) Jean financed a purchase for $6,300 at 24% interest for 18 months. What was the total amount Jean paid? Use the chart on page 139.

10) Alan financed a purchase for $8,500 at 19% interest for 30 months. What was the total amount Alan paid? Use the chart on page 139.

11) Mitzi used a simple discount note to borrow $800 at 15% for 2 months. What were the net proceeds?

12) Ted used a simple discount note to borrow $1,200 at 19% for 5 months. What were the net proceeds?

Chapter 10

Calculating Investment Interest

Banks offer higher rates of interest on certificates of deposit and IRA accounts than on regular savings accounts. This higher rate encourages savers to keep their money on deposit for long periods of time.

Some people invest their money by lending it to large companies. This is done when investors buy bonds issued by the companies. Bonds pay interest like savings certificates.

In this chapter you will work with applications of interest in long term bank accounts, bonds, and other investments.

FOREST TRUST BANK

CURRENT RATES

Regular Savings	5%
6-month CD	7.5%
12-month CD	7.7%
18-month CD	7.95%
24-month CD	8.02%
36-month CD	8.47%
48-month CD	9%
60-month CD	9.3%
72-month CD	9.95%
I.R.A.	10.27%

$60,000,000 OFFERING OF
XYZ CO. *$1,000 BONDS*
OFFERED AT PAR
Maturity Date: July 1, 2015
RATE: 12.17%
Interest Paid Semiannually

$25,000,000 OFFERING OF
GENERAL ROTORS CO.
100 UNITS OFFERED AT $95
Maturity Date: Jan. 2, 1998
RATE: 15.45%
Interest Paid Quarterly

CERTIFICATES OF DEPOSIT

Business Vocabulary:

Certificate of deposit — A high interest savings account for a fixed number of months. It permits only a single, large deposit. Principal and interest are paid back at the end of the term. (Abbreviation: CD)

Roll-over — To reinvest in a new certificate when one matures, without withdrawing the savings.

Certificates of deposit pay a high rate of interest. Most certificates have a term of 3 months to 12 years. Their main drawback is that early withdrawal brings a heavy penalty. The penalty can be loss of all interest for 3, 6, or 12 months. Sometimes the penalty exceeds the total interest earned. In this case, depositors lose part of their principal.

Example A: Beverly cashed in her $2,000 CD after only 8 months. It was earning 9% interest. The penalty was loss of one year's interest. Compute the amount of the penalty.

Step 1: Determine the number of months' interest lost.

$$12 \text{ Months penalized}$$
$$- 8 \text{ Months earned}$$
$$\overline{4} \text{ Net loss to principal of 4 months' interest}$$

4 months = $\frac{4}{12}$ or $\frac{1}{3}$ of a year.

Step 2: Find $\frac{1}{3}$ of the interest rate. $\frac{1}{3} \times 9\% = 3\%$

Step 3: Find 3% of the principal.

$$\begin{array}{r} \$2,000 \\ \times\ .03 \\ \hline \$60.00 \end{array}$$

Beverly's penalty was loss of all interest plus $60 of principal.

Example B: Ike cashed in his $5,000 CD that was earning 10% interest after only 11 months. The penalty was loss of 3 months' interest. Compute the amount of the penalty.

Step 1: Determine the number of months' interest lost.

11 months earned. 3 months penalized.

Since 11 months is greater than 3 months, there is no loss of principal

3 months = $\frac{3}{12}$ or $\frac{1}{4}$ of a year.

Step 2: Find $\frac{1}{4}$ of the interest rate.

$\frac{1}{4} \times 10\% = \frac{10\%}{4} = 2.5\%$

Step 3: Find 2.5% of the principal.

$$\begin{array}{r} \$5,000 \\ \times\ .025 \\ \hline 25000 \\ 10000 \\ \hline \$125.00\cancel{0} \end{array}$$

Ike's penalty was loss of $125 of the interest that had been earned.

▶ Compute the early withdrawal penalties. The answer to Number 1 is: All interest plus $260 of principal. Round to the nearer cent.

	Principal	Rate	Actual Term	Penalty Loss of Interest
1)	$ 8,000	13%	3 months	6 months
2)	$49,000	8%	6 months	12 months
3)	$28,000	12%	59 months	9 months
4)	$41,000	14%	3 months	12 months
5)	$21,000	15%	23 months	3 months
6)	$15,000	14%	8 months	12 months
7)	$29,000	15%	27 months	3 months
8)	$ 7,000	15%	8 months	12 months
9)	$36,000	15%	49 months	6 months

INDIVIDUAL RETIREMENT ACCOUNTS

Business Vocabulary:

Individual Retirement Account — A long-term investment account with great tax advantages. Deposits and earned interest are taxed in the year of withdrawal (near retirement age). (Abbreviation: IRA)

IRA's were created to encourage people to save for their retirement. IRA funds grow quickly because no portion is lost to taxes in the year the interest is earned. None of the interest is lost to taxes until that interest is withdrawn. People who withdraw IRA funds prematurely must pay heavy penalties of principal and interest.

	Growth of $1.00 Deposited Each Year With Interest Compounded Annually				
Year	10%	11%	12%	13%	14%
1	$ 1.10	$ 1.11	$ 1.12	$ 1.13	$ 1.14
2	2.31	2.34	2.37	2.40	2.44
3	3.64	3.70	3.77	3.84	3.92
4	5.10	5.21	5.34	5.47	5.61
5	6.71	6.89	7.10	7.31	7.53
6	8.48	8.75	9.07	9.39	9.72
7	10.42	10.82	11.28	11.74	12.22
8	12.56	13.12	13.75	14.40	15.07
9	14.91	15.67	16.52	17.40	18.32
10	17.50	18.50	19.62	20.79	22.03
11	20.35	21.64	23.09	24.62	26.26
12	23.48	25.13	26.98	28.95	31.08
13	26.92	29.00	31.34	33.85	36.58
14	30.71	33.30	36.22	39.39	42.85
15	34.88	38.07	41.69	45.65	50.00
16	39.46	43.37	47.82	52.72	58.16
17	44.50	49.25	54.68	60.71	67.46
18	50.05	55.78	62.37	69.75	78.07
19	56.15	63.03	70.98	79.96	90.17
20	62.86	71.07	80.63	91.50	103.97
21	70.24	80.00	91.44	104.55	119.70
22	78.36	89.91	103.55	119.30	137.64
23	87.29	100.91	117.11	135.97	158.10
24	97.11	113.13	132.30	154.81	181.43
25	107.92	126.69	149.32	176.11	208.04

Example: Lorrie and her husband deposited $4000 per year for 25 years into their IRA account. The account paid 14% per year compounded annually. Find the amount after 25 years.

Step 1: Look in the table for 25 years at 14%. The amount is $208.04 for each $1.00.

Step 2: Multiply. $208.04 Growth of $1.00 per year

$$\begin{array}{r} \$208.04 \\ \times \quad 4000 \\ \hline \$832,160.00 \end{array}$$ Growth of $4,000 per year

Lorrie and her husband's account grew to $832,160.00.

▶ Compute the amounts in these IRA accounts. The answer to Number 1 is $10,936.

	Annual Deposit	Years	Rate
1)	$200	17	12%
2)	$1,000	1	14%
3)	$600	19	13%
4)	$900	6	14%
5)	$900	24	11%
6)	$500	15	10%
7)	$300	5	14%
8)	$600	18	10%
9)	$4,000	6	12%
10)	$4,000	22	11%
11)	$800	4	10%
12)	$800	10	14%
13)	$900	11	13%
14)	$500	6	10%
15)	$600	25	13%
16)	$100	7	11%
17)	$700	24	14%
18)	$500	20	12%

MUNICIPAL BONDS

Business Vocabulary:

Municipal bonds — Bonds issued by cities, counties, or states to raise money.

Nominal rate — The stated annual rate of interest.

Net yield — The percentage of interest left after paying income taxes.

Tax bracket — The highest rate of income tax you have to pay.

Municipal bonds have an important advantage over other bonds. The interest paid on municipal bonds is "tax-free." You do not pay federal income tax on this interest income. Therefore, the net yield for a municipal bond is higher than the net yield for a corporate bond that pays the same nominal interest rate.

Example: Andrew is in the 40% tax bracket. For him, a 9% municipal bond has what equivalent taxable yield?

Step 1: Subtract 40% from 100%.

100% − 40% = 60%, or .60

Step 2: Divide 9% by .60

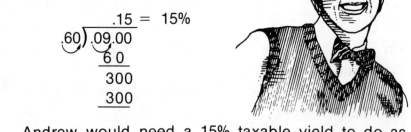

$$
\begin{array}{r}
.15 = 15\% \\
.60\overline{)\,.09.00} \\
\underline{6\,0} \\
300 \\
\underline{300}
\end{array}
$$

Andrew would need a 15% taxable yield to do as well.

▶ Find the equivalent taxable yields for each of these municipal bonds. Round to the nearer one hundredth percent (fourth decimal place). The answer to Number 1 is 25.30%.

	Tax Bracket	Nominal Rate		Tax Bracket	Nominal Rate
1)	34%	16.7%	26)	60%	12.9%
2)	61%	7.1%	27)	51%	13.2%
3)	55%	12.5%	28)	38%	7.9%
4)	52%	16.6%	29)	38%	8.6%
5)	63%	15%	30)	51%	14.3%
6)	63%	8.3%	31)	47%	14.5%
7)	64%	15.4%	32)	60%	8.9%
8)	40%	12.9%	33)	46%	10.6%
9)	66%	11.1%	34)	40%	10.7%
10)	35%	10.9%	35)	56%	8.2%
11)	34%	15.3%	36)	50%	16.5%
12)	53%	15.1%	37)	60%	11.8%
13)	47%	15.8%	38)	37%	13.7%
14)	35%	7.2%	39)	37%	14.8%
15)	35%	16.8%	40)	45%	14.2%
16)	58%	16.8%	41)	50%	7.9%
17)	62%	16.8%	42)	49%	14.8%
18)	59%	9.8%	43)	58%	15.9%
19)	33%	14.5%	44)	56%	15.8%
20)	61%	15.6%	45)	43%	15.9%
21)	63%	9.4%	46)	66%	12.5%
22)	61%	15.9%	47)	62%	9.2%
23)	50%	9.5%	48)	47%	9.1%
24)	36%	11.3%	49)	45%	9.8%
25)	31%	8.2%	50)	55%	17.3%

CORPORATE BONDS

Business Vocabulary:

Bond — A bond is a written agreement that the borrower will pay back the lender on a set date. The bond clearly states the amount of the loan and the interest rate. The yield of the bond is the amount of interest paid annually.

Some people invest their money by lending it to large corporations. This practice is called buying corporate bonds. Corporate bonds pay higher rates of interest than savings accounts. However, corporate bonds are almost always sold in multiples of $1,000.

Example A: Sharon used her lifeguard salary to buy a $3,000 corporate bond paying 8.2% interest. What was the yield?

$$\begin{array}{r} \$3,000 \\ \times \quad .082 \\ \hline 6000 \\ 24000 \\ \hline \$246.00\emptyset \end{array}$$

The yield was $246 per year.

Example B: Larry used his income from a band to buy a $2,000 corporate bond paying 11.7% interest. What was the yield?

$$\begin{array}{r} \$2,000 \\ \times \quad .117 \\ \hline 14000 \\ 2000 \\ 2000 \\ \hline \$234.00\emptyset \end{array}$$

The yield was $234 per year.

▶ Compute the yield on each of these corporate bonds. The answer to Number 1 is $182.

	Amount	Interest Rate		Amount	Interest Rate
1)	$2,000	9.1%	26)	$9,000	9.8%
2)	$2,000	11.8%	27)	$4,000	10.1%
3)	$9,000	9.1%	28)	$1,000	14.6%
4)	$3,000	16.2%	29)	$4,000	13.1%
5)	$4,000	13.7%	30*	$800,000	11.9%
6)	$6,000	7.8%	31)	$7,000	16.5%
7)	$2,000	7.7%	32)	$1,000	13.5%
8)	$3,000	10.4%	33)	$7,000	8.7%
9)	$1,000	9.8%	34)	$1,000	11.1%
10*	$100,000	13.1%	35)	$7,000	13.9%
11)	$8,000	8%	36)	$8,000	15.4%
12)	$10,000	14.5%	37)	$9,000	14.9%
13)	$10,000	9.6%	38)	$5,000	12.6%
14)	$6,000	13.6%	39)	$7,000	8.4%
15)	$7,000	10.2%	40*	$900,000	7.9%
16)	$5,000	14.7%	41)	$3,000	10.1%
17)	$6,000	8.9%	42)	$10,000	8.6%
18)	$7,000	13.1%	43)	$4,000	10.4%
19)	$10,000	16.8%	44)	$10,000	7.1%
20*	$100,000	14%	45)	$5,000	15.2%
21)	$8,000	10.9%	46)	$8,000	8.4%
22)	$3,000	11%	47)	$6,000	13.3%
23)	$3,000	10.3%	48)	$1,000	15.3%
24)	$9,000	9%	49)	$2,000	14.4%
25)	$8,000	10.1%	50*	$700,000	9%

ZERO COUPON BONDS

Most bonds make monthly or semiannual interest payments to their owners. Zero coupon bonds are sold at a discount and make no interest payments before maturity. The interest earned accumulates as compound interest. Under current law, however, interest from zero coupon bonds is taxable in the year earned — not at maturity. This law makes zero coupon bonds undesirable for some investment goals.

Zero Coupon Bond Chart					
Nominal Interest Rate	9%	10%	11%	12%	13%
Years to Double the Principal (Monthly Compounding)	7.8	7	6.3	5.8	5.4

Example: Morris bought $2,700 of zero coupon bonds at 11% interest. Find the maturity value for 18.9 years if the funds are reinvested at the same rate.

The chart shows that 11% bonds double the principal every 6.3 years.

Step 1: Find how many times the principal doubles in 18.9 years. Divide 18.9 by 6.3.

$$\begin{array}{r} 3 \\ 6.3{\overline{)18.9}} \end{array}$$ The principal doubles 3 times.

Step 2: Multiply. Double the principal three times.

$$
\begin{array}{r}
\$2{,}700 \\
\times \quad 2 \\
\hline
\$5{,}400 \\
\end{array}
$$ after 6.3 years

$$
\begin{array}{r}
\times \quad 2 \\
\hline
\$10{,}800 \\
\end{array}
$$ after 12.6 years

$$
\begin{array}{r}
\times \quad 2 \\
\hline
\$21{,}600 \\
\end{array}
$$ after 18.9 years

Morris's investment of $2,700 grew to $21,600 in 18.9 years.

▶ Compute the maturity value of each of these zero coupon bonds. Assume that the funds are reinvested at the same rate at maturity. The answer to Number 1 is $53,600.

Amount of Bonds	Interest Rate (Compounded Monthly)	Years
1) $6,700	12%	17.4
2) $9,700	9%	7.8
3) $8,000	11%	18.9
4) $9,600	11%	25.2
5) $8,300	9%	31.2
6) $8,600	13%	16.2
7) $3,400	11%	25.2
8) $4,300	9%	15.6
9) $8,500	9%	31.2
10* $67,100	13%	10.8
11) $1,200	9%	31.2
12) $2,100	13%	16.2
13) $9,800	12%	11.6
14) $7,400	12%	5.8
15) $8,600	12%	5.8
16) $3,200	13%	21.6
17) $7,800	10%	21
18) $4,900	9%	7.8
19) $1,300	11%	25.2
20* $72,600	11%	6.3
21) $2,900	9%	7.8
22) $7,000	11%	18.9
23) $7,700	11%	6.3

SINGLE PAYMENT ANNUITIES

Business Vocabulary:

Annuity — A series of equal payments made at equal intervals of time.

Many working people plan for their retirement years. In order to provide themselves with a regular income after they retire, they buy annuities from insurance companies and other organizations. An annuity solves the problem of a person outliving his or her savings. In return for a person's large single deposit or regular small deposits, the company agrees to send a series of monthly checks as long as the person lives.

Example: Gerald bought a single payment, $30,000 annuity at age 25.

Find out how much he will receive in each monthly check starting at age 70.

	Single Payment Annuity Monthly Income Purchased with $1,000					
	Age at Maturity					
Age at	Male			Female		
Purchase	60	65	70	60	65	70
20	$15.10	$20.05	$25.00	$13.48	$17.16	$22.30
25	13.17	16.89	21.80	11.75	15.10	19.49
30	11.60	14.85	19.05	10.28	13.19	16.99
35	10.01	12.90	16.61	8.95	11.50	14.84
40	8.77	11.33	14.52	7.85	10.04	12.97
45	7.62	9.82	12.67	6.83	8.75	11.40
50	6.64	8.65	11.08	5.95	7.63	9.89
55	5.79	7.47	9.61	5.20	6.64	8.69
60		6.59	8.40		5.86	7.45
65						6.61

Step 1: Look in the chart for 25 years for a male with

the age at maturity of 70 years. Age at maturity means the age at which the first check is received. Gerald will receive $21.80 each month for each $1,000 he deposited.

Step 2: Since Gerald deposited $30,000, multiply $21.80 by 30.

$21.80 Monthly payment for each $1,000
×   30
$654.00 Monthly payment for $30,000

Beginning at age 70, Gerald will receive $654 each month for as long as he lives.

▶ Compute the monthly retirement annuity check for each of these people. The answer to Number 1 is $137.48.

	Amount of Deposit	Age at Purchase	Age at Maturity	Sex
1)	$14,000	45	65	Male
2)	$18,000	60	70	Female
3)	$ 6,000	35	70	Male
4)	$ 5,000	50	65	Female
5)	$33,000	50	65	Female
6)	$30,000	35	70	Male
7)	$22,000	20	65	Male
8)	$14,000	60	70	Female
9)	$12,000	20	60	Male
10)	$10,000	40	70	Female
11)	$33,000	35	60	Female
12)	$29,000	30	60	Female
13)	$31,000	60	70	Female
14)	$ 7,000	60	70	Male
15)	$ 4,300	60	70	Female

ANNUAL PAYMENT ANNUITIES

Many people buy annuities with regular deposits every year.

Example: Ellen bought an annuity by making deposits of $300 per year from age 25 to age 70. At age 70 she started to receive monthly annuity checks. Find out how much she receives each month.

Annual Payment Annuity Monthly Income Purchased with $100 per Year (10 Years Guaranteed*)						
Age at	Age at Maturity					
First Payment	Male			Female		
	60	65	70	60	65	70
20	$35.72	$49.05	$66.65	$31.95	$43.75	$59.06
25	28.85	40.15	55.00	25.79	35.70	48.90
30	22.86	32.41	45.05	20.41	28.84	40.10
35	17.61	25.65	36.24	15.70	22.90	32.41
40	12.99	19.84	28.75	11.64	17.64	25.81
45	9.03	14.71	22.16	8.15	13.24	19.84
50	5.57	10.04	16.37	4.92	9.09	14.63
55	2.47	6.17	11.44	2.20	5.51	10.15
60		2.80	7.00		2.43	6.21
65			3.14			2.75

* "10 Years Guaranteed" means that the company will send either you or your beneficiary (if you live less than 10 years) at least 120 monthly checks.

Step 1: Look in the chart at 25 years for a female with the age at maturity of 70 years. Ellen receives $48.90 each month for each $100 annual deposit.

Step 2: Since Ellen deposited $300 per year, multiply $48.90 by 3.

$48.90 Monthly payment for each $100

×   3

$146.70 Monthly payment for $300

    Beginning at age 70, Ellen will receive a monthly check for $146.70 for as long as she lives. If she does not live 10 years, her beneficiary will receive the remaining checks for 10 years.

▶ Compute the monthly retirement annuity check for each of these people. The answer to Number 1 is $392.00.

	Amount of Annual Payment	Age at First Payment	Age at Maturity	Sex
1)	$5,600	60	70	Male
2)	$2,400	25	60	Male
3)	$500	30	60	Female
4)	$5,500	55	70	Female
5)	$3,700	50	70	Female
6)	$3,400	20	70	Male
7)	$6,000	60	65	Female
8)	$2,800	60	65	Female
9)	$2,500	35	70	Female
10)	$3,500	45	65	Male
11)	$2,400	25	65	Female
12)	$2,500	35	60	Female
13)	$1,600	45	60	Female
14)	$4,700	25	65	Male
15)	$4,700	25	60	Male
16)	$4,600	25	60	Male

SETTING RENTS

Business Vocabulary:
Rate of return — The rate of interest on an investment.

Many people buy property as an investment. Apartments and stores can be rented out. The rents are used to pay off the mortgage. When the mortgage is paid off, the profits can be very good. Landlords set their rents to achieve a certain rate of return.

Example: Cindy bought a property for $68,000 and wanted a rate of return of 15%. If her annual expenses were $4005, find the needed monthly rent.

Step 1: Find 15% of the purchase price.

$68,000 Purchase price
× .15 Rate of return
340000
68000
$10,200.00 Return wanted

Step 2: Add the expenses.

$10,200 Return wanted
+ 4,005 Annual expenses
$14,205 Total return needed

Step 3: Divide the sum by 12 to find the monthly rent.

$$12\overline{)\frac{\$\ 1,183.75}{\$14,205.00}}$$

Cindy's total monthly rent (rounded to the nearer dollar) should be set at $1,184.00.

▶ Compute the needed monthly rents. Round to the nearest dollar. The answer to Number 1 is $1,226.00.

	Cost of Property	Required Rate of Return	Annual Expenses
1)	$58,000	18%	$4,273
2)	$56,000	18%	$3,977
3)	$11,000	17%	$ 733
4)	$13,000	18%	$ 803
5)	$59,000	16%	$4,315
6)	$29,000	19%	$1,676
7)	$14,000	20%	$1,167
8)	$45,000	20%	$3,739
9)	$78,000	20%	$7,014
10*	$539,000	17.2%	$3,053
11)	$52,000	18%	$4,684
12)	$96,000	18%	$7,454
13)	$38,000	18%	$2,039
14)	$45,000	19%	$3,402
15)	$63,000	20%	$4,280
16)	$82,000	17%	$4,406
17)	$31,000	17%	$2,311
18)	$30,000	20%	$2,762
19)	$22,000	20%	$1,225
20*	$1,034,000	19.4%	$9,086
21)	$60,000	16%	$4,228
22)	$31,000	15%	$2,753
23)	$53,000	16%	$5,025
24)	$26,000	17%	$1,902
25)	$42,000	19%	$2,767

COMPUTING BOND YIELDS
With a Calculator

Business Vocabulary:

Bondholder — The purchaser of a bond.

Issuer — The company or government body that sells bonds to borrow money.

Term — The amount of time before a bond becomes due.

Yield — The percent of the purchase price paid annually as interest.

Face amount — The amount of money borrowed, or the amount printed on the bond.

When you buy a bond, the issuer promises to pay you interest for the term of the bond. The issuer also promises to repay the full amount of the loan at the end of the term. However, a bondholder may choose to sell the bond to someone else before the end of the term.

When interest rates drop, bond values increase. When interest rates rise, bond values decrease.

Example: Charles bought an $8,000 bond with 12% interest. The interest rate rose, and Charles sold the bond for $6,500. Compute the yield for the buyer.

Step 1: Find 12% of $8,000. $8,000 × .12 = $960

Step 2: Divide $960 by the new selling price.
$960 ÷ $6,500 = .14769231

(Change to a percent. Round to the nearer hundredth.)

14.77%

At $6,500, the yield was 14.77%.

▶ Compute the yield on each bond. Round the answers to the nearer hundredth percent. The answer to Number 1 is 15.26%.

	Face Value	Rate	Price
1)	$5,000	8.1%	$2,654
2)	$8,000	10%	$4,765
3)	$16,000	11.4%	$25,458
4)	$24,000	14.9%	$49,572
5)	$18,000	11.6%	$31,699
6)	$18,000	14.7%	$28,935
7)	$7,000	15.3%	$20,651
8)	$23,000	8.4%	$12,463
9)	$78,000	12.9%	$19,078
10*	$150,000	11%	$198,130
11)	$1,000	12.7%	$1,797
12)	$14,000	8.1%	$11,319
13)	$6,000	13.7%	$13,637
14)	$2,000	15.5%	$2,443
15)	$10,000	16.6%	$13,167
16)	$19,000	15.8%	$20,875
17)	$11,000	10%	$15,273
18)	$5,000	11.1%	$4,488
19)	$21,000	16.5%	$29,995
20*	$210,000	9.5%	$167,414
21)	$2,000	10.3%	$1,528
22)	$13,000	12.5%	$10,704
23)	$9,000	14.8%	$15,730
24)	$2,000	8.5%	$1,673
25)	$13,000	8.4%	$7,345

BASIC SKILL REVIEW

1) Linda owned $191,000 worth of bonds. She sold $29,000 of the bonds. How much did she have left?

2) Wanda willed her $272,000 worth of bonds to her eight children. The children received equal amounts. How much did each child receive?

3) Carlos bought $2,500 worth of bonds per year for 40 years. Compute his total bond purchase.

4) Darryl made five bond purchases: $42,000; $79,000; $83,000; $27,000; and $64,000. Find the total of his five purchases.

5) Three-fifths of Tara's bond holdings are corporate bonds. She has $375,000 worth of bonds. What is the value of Tara's corporate bonds?

6) Two-fifths of Tara's bonds are municipal bonds. She wants half of her bonds to be municipals. One-half is how much more than two-fifths?

7) Cara willed $\frac{3}{5}$ of her bonds to Ellen and $\frac{1}{4}$ of her bonds to Jeff. What part of the bonds were willed to either Ellen or Jeff?

8) When Michael retired, his IRA account contained $465,000. This is $7\frac{1}{2}$ times the money he put in. How much money did he put in?

9) The regular rate for IRA accounts at First Bank is 14.872%. Jason's account earned an extra 1.2% because it contained over $300,000. What interest rate did Jason's account earn?

10) Darnella's savings certificate had been earning 12.168%. The rate was lowered to 5.5% because Darnella withdrew her money early. How many percentage points was the penalty?

Computer Program:
INSTALLMENT PLAN PAYMENTS

This program computes the amount of a monthly payment for an installment plan purchase. Type the program into a computer and run it. Run the program several times with different sets of data.

```
10  REM THIS PROGRAM COMPUTES MONTHLY PAY-
    MENTS.
20  PRINT "TYPE IN THE AMOUNT FINANCED."
30  INPUT A
40  PRINT "TYPE IN THE INTEREST RATE AS A DECIMAL."
50  INPUT R
60  PRINT "TYPE IN THE NUMBER OF MONTHLY PAY-
    MENTS."
70  INPUT P
80  REM N = NUMERATOR OF FORMULA, D = DENOMINA-
    TOR OF FORMULA
90  N = (A * R / 12) * (1 + R / 12) ^ P
100  D = (1 + R / 12) ^ P - 1
110  REM M = MONTHLY PAYMENT ROUNDED UP TO THE
    NEXT CENT
120  M = INT (100 * N / D + .999) / 100
130  PRINT "THE MONTHLY PAYMENT WOULD BE $";M;
    " FOR ";P;" MONTHS."
140  PRINT "THE TOTAL PAYMENT WOULD BE $";M;
    " TIMES ";P;" = $";M * P
150  END
```

CHAPTER REVIEW

1) Karen cashed in her $9,000 CD after 42 months. It was earning 12% interest. The penalty was loss of 6 months' interest. How much was her penalty?

2) Walt cashed in his $3,000 CD after 5 months. It was earning 10% interest. The penalty was one year's interest. How much was the penalty?

3) Mary deposited $700 every year into an IRA account, which paid 12% compounded annually. What was the amount after 25 years?

4) Jim deposited $700 every year into his IRA account, which paid 14% compounded annually. What was the amount after 25 years?

5) Joe is in the 35% tax bracket. For him, what would be the equivalent taxable yield of a 13% municipal bond?

6) Anita is in the 20% tax bracket. For her, what would be the equivalent taxable yield of a 16% municipal bond?

7) Denise bought a $6,000 corporate bond paying 6.4% interest. What is the annual interest paid?

8) Don bought a $10,000 corporate bond paying 8.7% interest. What is the annual interest paid?

9) Vicki bought a property for $74,000 and wanted a rate of return of 18%. If her annual expenses were $4,826, what monthly rent is needed?

10) Terry bought a property for $87,000 and wanted a rate of return of 20%. If his annual expenses were $5,914, what monthly rent is needed?

11) Alex bought a $6,000 bond paying 15% interest. He sold the bond for $9,000. What was the buyer's yield?

Chapter 11

Using Percents In Business

The most important mathematics concept in business is percent. Percents are used in pricing goods. They are used in buying merchandise. They are used in preparing payrolls and paying taxes. They are even used in paying bills.

This chapter shows different uses of percent in running a business.

At what price shall I sell the new luggage so I can make 33% profit?

SINGLE SALES DISCOUNT

Business Vocabulary:

Sale price — The amount that a customer pays for an item.

Sales discount — The amount of money or the percentage of the list price that you save when you buy merchandise.

Businesses offer sales discounts for many reasons. Discounts encourage customers to buy more goods. Discounts encourage people to pay their bills promptly. Discounts also attract new customers and maintain the loyalty of old customers.

Example: Joe bought a $34.49 pair of slacks at a 6% discount. How much did he pay? Round to the next lower cent.

Step 1: Find the amount of discount. 6% = .06

$34.49   List price
×   .06   Discount rate
$2.0694   Amount of discount

Step 2: Subtract discount from list price.

$34.49   List price
− 2.06   Discount
$32.43   Sale price

Joe paid $32.43.

▶ Compute each sale price. Round discounts to the next lower cent. The answer to Number 1 is $44.93.

	List Price	Discount		List Price	Discount
1)	$48.31	7%	26)	$23.30	9%
2)	$30.63	13%	27)	$37.06	17%
3)	$22.86	40%	28)	$21.99	17%
4)	$20.57	6%	29)	$15.41	6%
5)	$16.60	38%	30*	$359.04	44.4%
6)	$ 9.20	37%	31)	$25.67	33%
7)	$29.79	41%	32)	$34.68	9%
8)	$23.21	2%	33)	$39.22	8%
9)	$ 9.56	45%	34)	$32.54	17%
10*	$107.58	45.6%	35)	$40.55	5%
11)	$48.31	36%	36)	$26.95	36%
12)	$17.02	33%	37)	$25.14	41%
13)	$37.83	5%	38)	$35.00	41%
14)	$42.49	35%	39)	$33.23	41%
15)	$ 7.06	12%	40*	$201.52	25.8%
16)	$41.27	41%	41)	$14.15	36%
17)	$38.20	12%	42)	$13.74	20%
18)	$26.72	20%	43)	$16.69	17%
19)	$11.60	6%	44)	$48.26	29%
20*	$62.59	27.7%	45)	$26.25	11%
21)	$32.06	24%	46)	$46.45	37%
22)	$ 8.48	10%	47)	$15.12	32%
23)	$11.26	10%	48)	$27.20	9%
24)	$34.46	24%	49)	$16.38	39%
25)	$30.46	34%	50*	$380.93	36.4%

MULTIPLE DISCOUNTS

Business Vocabulary:

Multiple discount — Two or more price reductions on one purchase.

A person can receive more than one discount.

Example A: Kim owns a sporting goods store. She ordered a shipment of baseball gloves at a 28% discount. The bill said, "$590 less 28%, less 5%, if paid in 10 days." How much would Kim pay for the gloves with the multiple discount?

Step 1: Subtract the discount rates from 100% to find out the percents to be paid.

100% − 28% = 72% = .72

100% − 5% = 95% = .95

Step 2: Multiply these two decimals.

```
        .72  Part to be paid
     ×  .95  Part to be paid
        360
        648
       .6840 Part of list price
             to be paid
```

Step 3: Multiply the list price by the part to be paid.

```
     $ 590   List price
     × .684  Part to be paid
       2360
       4720
       3540
    $ 403.56Ø Sale price
```

Kim would pay $403.56 for the gloves if she paid the bill within ten days.

Example B: Suppose Bob's $600 order carried a multiple discount of 32%, 11%, and 2%. How much would Bob pay?

Step 1: Subtract each discount rate from 100%.

100% − 32% = 68% = .68

100% − 11% = 89% = .89

100% − 2% = 98% = .98

Step 2: Multiply these decimals.

```
     .68              .6052
  ×  .89           ×   .98
     612             48416
     544             54468
    .6052           .593096  Part to be paid
```

Step 3: Multiply the list price by the part to be paid.

```
              .593096  Part to be paid
         ×      $600   List price
     $355.857600 (≈ $355.86 ) Sale price
```

Bob would pay $355.86.

▶ Compute the sale price after the multiple discount. Round to the next higher cent. The answer to Number 1 is $43.17.

	List Price	Discounts		List Price	Discounts
1)	$90	38%, 15%, 9%	9)	$70	8%, 10%, 4%
2)	$70	9%, 13%	10)	$70	18%, 18%, 6%
3)	$60	17%, 16%	11)	$70	41%, 26%
4)	$50	36%, 18%, 8%	12)	$40	12%, 10%
5)	$70	41%, 23%, 8%	13)	$660	37%, 27%, 8%
6)	$30	25%, 21%	14)	$30	28%, 11%
7)	$80	10%, 12%	15)	$70	24%, 17%, 6%
8)	$40	45%, 24%	16)	$40	37%, 16%

MARKUP BASED ON COST

Business Vocabulary:
Overhead — The total operating expenses of a business (often expressed as a percentage).
Markup on cost — A percentage equal to the overhead percentage plus the profit percentage.

A business must be profitable to remain open. Products must be sold for more than their cost. Business owners use a markup to set the prices of their products. The markup percentage tells how much extra money to charge in order to cover the overhead and profit.

Example A: Ellen owns a bookstore. Her overhead is 33%, and she wants a profit of 15%. Find Ellen's selling price on a book that cost her $8.54.

Step 1: Combine the percentages for overhead and for profit.

      33% Overhead
    +15% Profit
      48% Markup percent

Step 2: Multiply the cost by the percentage.

Step 3: Add the cost and the markup.

      $8.54 Cost $8.54 Cost
    ×   .48   + 4.10 Markup
       6832 $12.64 Selling price
       3416
    $4.0992 (Round to the next higher cent.)

    $4.10 Markup

Ellen's selling price would be $12.64.

Example B: Roger owns a meat market. His overhead is 28%, and he wants a profit of 13%. Find Roger's selling price on a frozen turkey that cost him $13.35. Round up to the next higher cent.

Step 1: Add the percentages for overhead and for profit.

$$\begin{array}{r} 28\% \text{ Overhead} \\ +13\% \text{ Profit} \\ \hline 41\% \text{ Markup percent} \end{array}$$

Step 2: Multiply the cost by the percentage.

$$\begin{array}{r} \$13.35 \\ \times\ \ .41 \\ \hline 13\,35 \\ 534\,0 \\ \hline \$5.47\,35 \end{array}$$ ≈ $5.48 Markup

Step 3: Add the cost and the markup.

$$\begin{array}{r} \$13.35 \text{ Cost} \\ +\ 5.48 \text{ Markup} \\ \hline \$18.83 \text{ Selling price} \end{array}$$

Roger's selling price would be $18.83.

▶ Compute the selling price for each of these products. Round fractions of a cent to the next higher cent. The answer to Number 1 is $32.06.

	Cost	Overhead	Profit
1)	$25.04	18%	10%
2)	$ 9.64	26%	23%
3)	$15.93	25%	17%
4)	$15.21	15%	26%
5)	$14.23	15%	13%
6)	$ 4.55	5%	23%
7)	$12.20	11%	23%
8)	$11.33	41%	22%
9)	$14.11	12%	11%
10*	$487.50	38.7%	26%

MARKUP BASED ON SELLING PRICE

Markup may be based on either the cost or the selling price. The markup based on selling price will yield a higher price than a markup based on cost.

Example A: Lynnette's overhead is 18%, and her profit is 22%. She is using a markup based on the selling price of a coat that costs her $120. Find the selling price.

Step 1: Combine the percentages for overhead and
for profit.

18% Overhead
+22% Profit
40% Markup percent

Step 2: Subtract the markup
percent from 100%.

100% Selling price
− 40% Markup percent
60% Cost percent

Step 3: Divide the cost by the cost percent.

$120.00 ÷ 60%

$$\begin{array}{r} \$\ \ 2\ 00. \\ .60\overline{)\$120.00} \\ \underline{120} \\ 00 \end{array}$$

Selling price

Lynnette's selling price is $200.00.

Example B: Joe's overhead is 25%, and his profit is 19%. He is using a markup based on the selling price of a hammer that cost him $11.76. Find the selling price.

Step 1: Combine the percentages for overhead and for profit.

25% Overhead
+19% Profit
44% Markup percent

Step 2: Subtract the markup percent from 100%.

100% Selling price
− 44% Markup percent
56% Cost percent

Step 3: Divide the cost by the cost percent.

$11.76 ÷ 56%

$$.56)\overline{\$11.76}$$ $ 21. Selling price
11 2
56
56
0

Joe's selling price is $21.00.

▶ Compute each of these selling prices. Round up fractions of a cent to the next higher cent. The answer to Number 1 is $67.

	Cost	Overhead	Profit
1)	$38.19	20%	23%
2)	$ 5.61	15%	34%
3)	$19.74	32%	26%
4)	$29.58	36%	13%
5)	$33.63	15%	28%
6)	$15.18	47%	20%
7)	$39.69	18%	19%
8)	$20.25	13%	12%
9)	$33.04	15%	29%
10*	$ 4.18	39%	23.4%

PRO RATA REFUNDS AND CREDITS

Business Vocabulary:

Pro rata refund — A partial refund. Part of the purchase price is returned because the item broke or failed prematurely.

A person gets a pro rata refund in proportion to the loss of the use that was guaranteed. Some businesses give pro rata credits instead of refunds. With a pro rata credit, a person receives a reduced price on a new item.

Example A: Keith bought a $46 tire that had a 30,000 mile pro rata guarantee. The tire lasted only 22,500 miles. Keith's refund will be less than $46 because he did get some use out of the tire. What was his refund?

Step 1: Reduce. $\dfrac{22,500}{30,000} = \dfrac{225}{300} = \dfrac{45}{60} = \dfrac{3}{4}$

Step 2: Multiply. $\dfrac{\$46}{1} \times \dfrac{3}{4} = \dfrac{\$138}{4} = \$34.50$

Step 3: Subtract.

$\begin{array}{ll} \$46.00 & \text{Purchase price} \\ -34.50 & \text{Value received} \\ \hline \$11.50 & \text{Refund due} \end{array}$

Keith's refund was $11.50.

Example B: Nancy's 60-month car battery lasted only 36 months. She paid $63 for it. What was her pro rata credit?

Step 1: Reduce. $\dfrac{36}{60} = \dfrac{6}{10} = \dfrac{3}{5}$

Step 2: Multiply. $\dfrac{\$63}{1} \times \dfrac{3}{5} = \dfrac{\$189}{5} = \$37.80$

Step 3: Subtract.

$63.00   Purchase price
−37.80   Value received
$25.20   Credit due

Nancy's credit was $25.20.

▶ Compute each of these pro rata refunds or credits. The answer to Number 1 is $30.00.

	Guarantee	Actual Life of Product	Purchase Price
1)	45,000 miles	35,000 miles	$135
2)	48 months	22 months	$336
3)	40,000 miles	20,000 miles	$ 28
4)	66 months	24 months	$594
5)	5 years	4 years	$ 40
6)	12 years	7 years	$120
7)	20,000 miles	15,000 miles	$ 12
8)	72 months	32 months	$720
9)	5 years	1 year	$ 55
10)	40,000 miles	25,000 miles	$ 40
11)	36 months	29 months	$144
12)	13 years	8 years	$ 78
13)	30 months	15 months	$300
14)	6 months	2 months	$ 60
15)	11 years	2 years	$ 66
16)	20,000 miles	10,000 miles	$ 18
17)	18 months	2 months	$162
18)	8 years	3 years	$ 88
19)	10,000 miles	5,000 miles	$ 11
20)	4 years	3 years	$ 24

CASH DISCOUNTS FOR PROMPT PAYMENT

Many wholesalers and manufacturers give their retail customers a discount for prompt payment. The sooner the retailer pays the wholesaler, the sooner the wholesaler can pay his employees and his bills. A common discount is "1/10, n/30." This means that retailers can take a 1% discount if they pay within 10 days of the invoice date. If the bill is not paid within 30 days, it is overdue.

Example A: Barney's Sporting Goods received a bill for $69.85 marked "2/10, n/30." Find the discount if the invoice was dated December 26, and Barney paid it on December 31.

Barney paid within the 10-day discount period. Therefore he took a 2% discount.

2% = .02. $69.85   Amount owed
$$\begin{array}{r} \times \quad .02 \\ \hline \$1.3970 \end{array}$$ Discount rate
$1.3970   Discount
$1.40   Rounded to the nearer cent

Barney's discount was $1.40.

Example B: Leona's Stationery Store received a bill for $951.44 marked "1/10, n/30." The bill was dated October 2, and Leona paid it on October 14. Find the discount.

Leona paid the bill in 12 days. She missed the 10-day discount period. Therefore, there was no discount.

Number of Days in the Months		
January .. 31	May.... 31	September .. 30
February . 28	June ... 30	October 31
March ... 31	July.... 31	November .. 30
April 30	August . 31	December .. 31

▶ Compute the cash discount on each of these bills. If a bill is overdue, write "Overdue." Round to the nearest cent. The answer to Number 1 is "No discount" because the bill was paid in 25 days.

	Invoice Amount	Sales Terms	Invoice Date	Payment Date
1)	$782.00	1/10, n/30	Apr. 20	May 15
2)	$476.00	1/10, n/30	June 20	July 5
3)	$872.40	1.5/10, n/30	Aug. 11	Aug. 15
4)	$ 69.58	1.5/10, n/30	July 19	July 28
5)	$315.33	1.5/10, n/30	Dec. 20	Jan. 11
6)	$449.03	2/10, n/30	Sept. 26	Sept. 30
7)	$894.19	1.5/10, n/30	Oct. 20	Nov. 9
8)	$758.15	1/10, n/30	Apr. 14	May 15
9)	$697.47	2/10, n/30	Apr. 1	Apr. 16
10)	$596.62	1.25/10, n/30	Sept. 1	Sept. 5
11)	$706.71	1.5/10, n/30	May 12	May 13
12)	$483.84	2/10, n/30	July 15	July 17
13)	$552.61	2/10, n/30	Dec. 6	Dec. 23
14)	$591.60	2/10, n/30	Sept. 22	Sept. 24
15)	$325.94	2/10, n/30	May 18	May 22
16)	$848.38	1/10, n/30	May 6	May 8
17)	$551.25	1.5/10, n/30	Jan. 15	Feb. 18
18)	$801.82	1.5/10, n/30	Aug. 26	Sept. 13
19)	$428.98	2/10, n/30	Sept. 21	Sept. 23
20)	$358.07	1.25/10, n/30	June 26	July 1

COMPUTING LATE CHARGES
With a Calculator

Wholesalers and manufacturers expect their retail customers to pay their bills on time. Some firms print a penalty on their invoices for overdue payment. In this lesson, we will use a penalty of .07123% per day. (= .0007123)

Example: Leon's bill of $127.98 was due on April 20. He paid it on December 18. Find the late charge and the amount due. Look in the chart for the two days.

Day of Month	Number of Each Day of the Year												Day of Month
	Jan.	Feb.	Mar.	Apr.	May	June	July	Aug.	Sept.	Oct.	Nov.	Dec.	
1	1	32	60	91	121	152	182	213	244	274	305	335	1
2	2	33	61	92	122	153	183	214	245	275	306	336	2
3	3	34	62	93	123	154	184	215	246	276	307	337	3
4	4	35	63	94	124	155	185	216	247	277	308	338	4
5	5	36	64	95	125	156	186	217	248	278	309	339	5
6	6	37	65	96	126	157	187	218	249	279	310	340	6
7	7	38	66	97	127	158	188	219	250	280	311	341	7
8	8	39	67	98	128	159	189	220	251	281	312	342	8
9	9	40	68	99	129	160	190	221	252	282	313	343	9
10	10	41	69	100	130	161	191	222	253	283	314	344	10
11	11	42	70	101	131	162	192	223	254	284	315	345	11
12	12	43	71	102	132	163	193	224	255	285	316	346	12
13	13	44	72	103	133	164	194	225	256	286	317	347	13
14	14	45	73	104	134	165	195	226	257	287	318	348	14
15	15	46	74	105	135	166	196	227	258	288	319	349	15
16	16	47	75	106	136	167	197	228	259	289	320	350	16
17	17	48	76	107	137	168	198	229	260	290	321	351	17
18	18	49	77	108	138	169	199	230	261	291	322	352	18
19	19	50	78	109	139	170	200	231	262	292	323	353	19
20	20	51	79	110	140	171	201	232	263	293	324	354	20
21	21	52	80	111	141	172	202	233	264	294	325	355	21
22	22	53	81	112	142	173	203	234	265	295	326	356	22
23	23	54	82	113	143	174	204	235	266	296	327	357	23
24	24	55	83	114	144	175	205	236	267	297	328	358	24
25	25	56	84	115	145	176	206	237	268	298	329	359	25
26	26	57	85	116	146	177	207	238	269	299	330	360	26
27	27	58	86	117	147	178	208	239	270	300	331	361	27
28	28	59	87	118	148	179	209	240	271	301	332	362	28
29	29		88	119	149	180	210	241	272	302	333	363	29
30	30		89	120	150	181	211	242	273	303	334	364	30
31	31		90		151		212	243		304		365	31

Step 1:
December 18   = Day   352
April 20   = Day −110   (Subtract)
                     242   Days

Step 2:
242 × .0007123 × $127.98 = $22.060757 (Penalty)
Round up to the next cent.

Leon's late charge was $22.07.
The amount due was $127.98 + $22.07, or $150.05.

▶ Use a calculator and the chart. Compute the late charge and the amount due for each bill below. Assume 365 days per year. Round fractions of a cent up to the next cent. The answers to Number 1 are: Late charge, $123.65; Amount due, $1,061.94.

	Invoice Amount	Date Due	Date Paid
1)	$938.29	May 7	November 8
2)	$657.14	March 15	March 2
3)	$2,269.22	April 28	October 10
4)	$4,136.89	November 24	August 19
5)	$3,587.16	October 22	September 5
6)	$5,615.62	October 6	September 15
7)	$2,440.31	July 1	January 24
8)	$281.59	January 28	August 8
9)	$8,572.14	January 1	December 16
10)	$8,238.20	April 22	September 26
11)	$6,070.25	March 13	October 2
12)	$4,181.38	June 22	February 6
13)	$1,389.23	October 4	June 24
14)	$4,722.82	August 8	November 26
15)	$9,105.27	August 3	May 11

BASIC SKILL REVIEW

1) Patrice bought 9 kg of sweeping compound for $58.50. What was the price per kilogram?

2) Ronald ordered $63,117 worth of bulbs. He returned $9,289 of the order. How much did he keep?

3) Find the cost of 55 fixtures at $498 each.

4) Manny's five pieces of office furniture cost $582, $97, $233, $300, and $654. Find the total cost of the furniture.

5) Dino ordered 1.25 tons of rock salt for $200. What was the price per ton?

6) The extended prices on Marian's invoice were $206.70, $54, $698.23, $1091.62, and $426.53. What was the invoice total?

7) Julio bought $3000 worth of goods. He sold $926.34 of the goods to his brother. What was the value of the remaining goods?

8) At he end of the day, Miguela's register contained 94 $5 bills. What was the value of those $5 bills?

9) One-fourth of a group of employees have individual health coverage. Another two-thirds of the group have family health coverage. What part of the group have either family or individual coverage?

10) Fran was scheduled to work $20\frac{1}{8}$ days on a project. Three and one-half of those days she was out sick. How many days did she actually work?

Computer Program: MULTIPLE DISCOUNTS

Many people think that a multiple discount is the same as one single discount — the sum of those discounts. This is never true. In fact, the sum of the discounts always inflates the answer. For example, a discount of 40% followed by a second discount of 40% is not equal to a single discount of 80%. It is equal to a single discount of just 64%.

Type in the computer program below. Run the program with several sets of discounts. How might this program be helpful to a buyer for a retail store?

```
10   REM THIS PROGRAM FINDS THE SINGLE DISCOUNT
     EQUAL TO A MULTIPLE DISCOUNT.
20   LET SD = 1
30   LET N = 1
40   PRINT "TYPE IN DISCOUNT NUMBER ";N
45   PRINT "TYPE IN 12% AS 12, 6.5% AS 6.5, ETC.":PRINT
50   PRINT "IF YOU HAVE TYPED IN ALL OF THE DIS-
     COUNTS, TYPE IN 0 (ZERO)."
60   INPUT D
70   IF D = 0 THEN 110
80   LET SD = SD * (100 − D) / 100
90   LET N = N + 1
100  GOTO 40
110  PRINT "THE SINGLE DISCOUNT EQUAL TO THE ";
     N − 1;" MULTIPLE DISCOUNT  IS "; 100 − SD * 100;
     "%"
120  END
```

CHAPTER REVIEW

▶ Find the sale price for each item below.

	List Price	Discount
1)	$ 38	9%
2)	$210	43%
3)	$398	5%
4)	$ 75	16%
5)	$840	5%, 10%, 20%
6)	$1,200	15%, 16%, 10%

▶ Find the selling price if the markup is based on cost. Round to the next higher cent.

	Cost	Overhead	Profit
7)	$14.55	10%	18%
8)	$ 6.15	24%	26%

▶ Find the selling price if the markup is based on selling price.

	Cost	Overhead	Profit
9)	$29.25	17%	18%
10)	$36.58	17%	21%

▶ Find the pro rata refund.

	Guarantee	Actual Life	Purchase Price
11)	30 months	6 months	$50
12)	40,000 miles	20,000 miles	$70.80

▶ Find the cash discount, if any

	Invoice Amount	Sales Terms	Invoice Date	Payment Date
13)	$ 87.35	2/10, n/30	March 12	March 21
14)	$176.90	1.5/10, n/30	Jan. 10	Feb. 15

Chapter 12

Transportation

Many businesses depend on transportation. Some service companies have employees who travel from customer to customer. Often firms rent cars and trucks for a few weeks at a time. Some companies have sales people and consultants who must fly all over the country to meet with customers.

In this chapter you will work with problems concerning business transportation.

AIR FARES

Business Vocabulary:

Coach — A class of airline transportation that entitles the passenger to average service.

First class — A class that entitles the passenger to a larger, more comfortable seat and better service than coach.

Airlines have a variety of different fares between cities. First class tickets usually cost the most. Coach tickets are less expensive. There are other rates for special plans.

The chart below shows sample fares for first class and coach between several cities. The first class fare is shown above the coach fare.

Example A: Jim flew from New York City to Phoenix, first class. What was the fare? Jim's fare was $551.

New York City						
Wash.D.C.	$164 109	Wash.D.C.				
Atlanta	372 286	320 247	Atlanta			
Chicago	405 270	375 250	262 200	Chicago		
St. Louis	435 290	325 250	208 166	245 163	St. Louis	
Houston	451 347	429 232	280 115	435 290	325 250	Houston
Phoenix	551 424	559 430	436 195	555 370	555 370	415 319	Phoenix
Los Angeles	735 490	735 490	475 195	615 410	600 400	375 135	134 89

▶ Compute the air fare for each of these trips. The answer to Number 1 is $166.

1) Coach, Atlanta to St. Louis
2) First class, Phoenix to Chicago
3) Coach, St. Louis to Los Angeles
4) First class, Houston to New York City
5) First class, Phoenix to Atlanta
6) First class, Washington, D.C. to Phoenix
7) Coach, Houston to Atlanta
8) Coach, Phoenix to New York City
9) Coach, Atlanta to Chicago
10) Coach, Los Angeles to St. Louis
11) Coach, New York to Atlanta to Chicago to New York
12) Coach, Washington, D.C. to Atlanta to Houston
13) First class, St. Louis to Atlanta to New York City
14) First class, Washington, D.C. to Los Angeles
15) Coach, Los Angeles to Phoenix to St. Louis
16) Coach, Houston to Chicago to New York City
17) First class, Phoenix to Atlanta to Washington, D.C.
18) Coach, Chicago to St. Louis to Houston
19) First class, Washington, D.C. to Chicago
20) Coach, St. Louis to New York City
21) First class, Houston to Los Angeles to Houston
22) Coach, two people, New York to Chicago
23) First class, three people, Atlanta to Houston
24) Coach, two people, Chicago to Phoenix
25) First class, three people, New York City to Chicago

COST PER MILE

Cars, trucks, and vans are very costly to run. Major expenses include insurance, maintenance, gas and oil, loan interest, and depreciation. The total cost is often expressed as "cost per mile." To compute cost per mile, divide the total cost by the annual mileage.

Example: Last year, Steven drove 14,000 miles. His car expenses were:

Insurance	$ 676
Maintenance, gas, oil	1374
Interest	530
Depreciation (10% of $12,000)	+ 1200
	$3780

Divide the total cost by the mileage.

$$14000\overline{)\,3780}\quad =\quad 14\overline{)\begin{array}{l}\$\ .27\\ \$3.78\\ \underline{2\ 8}\\ 98\\ \underline{98}\end{array}}$$

Steven's cost per mile was $.27.

▶ Compute the cost per mile for each case below. Add the expenses. Then divide by the mileage. The answer to Number 1 is $.21.

	Insurance	Maintenance	Interest	Depreciation	Mileage
1)	$582	$1417	$372	19% of $ 4,100	15,000
2)	$639	$1984	$468	17% of $12,700	25,000
3)	$411	$2653	$504	16% of $13,700	24,000
4)	$674	$ 451	$495	10% of $ 9,400	16,000
5)	$513	$ 669	$489	11% of $ 5,900	8,000
6)	$318	$1752	$336	17% of $10,200	23,000
7)	$584	$2536	$272	18% of $13,100	25,000
8)	$490	$ 211	$302	17% of $ 6,100	12,000
9)	$340	$ 213	$359	11% of $12,700	11,000
10)	$422	$1079	$483	11% of $ 5,600	13,000
11)	$649	$2033	$386	19% of $10,800	16,000
12)	$664	$ 733	$533	15% of $10,600	11,000
13)	$521	$ 326	$469	18% of $ 9,800	11,000
14)	$321	$ 216	$445	14% of $ 6,700	12,000
15)	$313	$ 336	$528	17% of $11,900	20,000
16)	$590	$1477	$333	15% of $ 4,400	9,000
17)	$528	$1683	$449	10% of $ 7,400	10,000
18)	$484	$ 551	$500	13% of $ 6,500	7,000
19)	$583	$1452	$455	10% of $ 6,600	21,000
20)	$300	$1096	$304	17% of $ 9,000	17,000
21)	$592	$1397	$439	14% of $ 7,300	23,000
22)	$685	$2807	$524	14% of $ 8,600	18,000
23)	$336	$ 105	$324	19% of $11,600	11,000
24)	$308	$1752	$481	11% of $ 6,900	15,000
25)	$656	$ 802	$532	14% of $ 6,500	10,000

RENTING CARS AND TRUCKS

Often, businesses and individuals rent cars and trucks. The rental charge depends on the number of days and the miles driven.

Example A: Sara's Catering Co. rented a van for $32 per day and $.25 per mile. Find the rental charge for two days and 47 miles.

$32 Per day $ .25 Per mile $64.00 Day charge
× 2 Days   × 47 Miles   +11.75 Mile charge
$64 Day charge   175 $75.75 Total
    100
    $11.75 Mile charge

Sara's rental charge was $75.75.

Example B: Evan rented a car after his accident. He paid $21 per day and $.15 per mile. Find the rental charge for six days and 536 miles.

$21 Per day   536 Miles $126.00 Day charge
× 6 Days   ×$ .15 Per mile   + 80.40 Mile charge
$126 Day charge   2680 $206.40 Total charges
    536
    $80.40 Mile charge

Evan's rental charge was $206.40.

▶ Find the rental charge for each item below. The answer to Number 1 is $179.08.

	Days	Cost Per Day	Cost Per Mile	Miles Driven
1)	5	$27	$.19	232
2)	2	$31	$.14	76
3)	4	$24	$.24	524
4)	2	$32	$.29	332
5)	5	$23	$.18	90
6)	1	$27	$.14	91
7)	1	$33	$.28	115
8)	5	$21	$.18	706
9)	1	$30	$.28	52
10*	24	$30	$.24	171
11)	3	$17	$.19	114
12)	6	$30	$.26	283
13)	3	$26	$.28	130
14)	4	$16	$.15	171
15)	5	$23	$.21	150
16)	3	$29	$.23	93
17)	2	$16	$.20	150
18)	1	$17	$.18	166
19)	2	$23	$.18	155
20*	29	$15	$.26	118
21)	6	$32	$.23	258
22)	4	$20	$.19	577
23)	5	$22	$.14	391
24)	2	$20	$.22	130
25)	5	$25	$.30	188

COMPUTING MILES PER GALLON
With a Calculator

Miles per gallon (MPG) measures how far a vehicle can travel on a gallon of gasoline. A low figure can suggest that the car needs to be repaired or tuned up. A high figure often means that the car is running well. The metric system uses liters instead of gallons, and kilometers instead of miles. Kilometers per liter (KPL) and MPG are computed in the same way:

Distance ÷ Amount of gasoline

Example A: Sheryl drove a truck 849.9 miles on 139.2 gallons of gasoline. Find the miles per gallon. Round the answer to the nearest tenth.

MPG = 849.9 ÷ 139.2 = 6.1056034

6.1 (rounded)

Sheryl's truck got 6.1 miles per gallon.

Example B: Sandy drove a car 955.4 kilometers on 120.9 liters of gasoline. Find the KPL.

KPL = 955.4 ÷ 120.9 = 7.9023986

7.9 (rounded)

Sandy's car got 7.9 kilometers per liter.

▶ Compute the MPG or KPL. Use a calculator. Round to the nearer tenth. The answer to Number 1 is 17.0 MPG.

	Distance		Amount of Gasoline	
1)	826.7	miles	48.6	gallons
2)	463.8	miles	15.4	gallons
3)	406.1	miles	12.1	gallons
4)	170	kilometers	15.3	liters
5)	656.8	kilometers	61.9	liters
6)	474.1	miles	15.9	gallons
7)	1010.8	miles	53.4	gallons
8)	869.2	miles	27.3	gallons
9)	686.4	miles	17.6	gallons
10)	838.9	miles	39.5	gallons
11)	373.3	miles	24.8	gallons
12)	582.6	kilometers	71	liters
13)	901.3	miles	23.4	gallons
14)	777.4	miles	46.2	gallons
15)	602	kilometers	88.5	liters
16)	445.2	kilometers	35.9	liters
17)	133.7	miles	4.9	gallons
18)	204	miles	6.6	gallons
19)	1084.6	miles	78	gallons
20)	760.9	miles	29	gallons
21)	703.7	miles	21.4	gallons
22)	293.7	miles	11.1	gallons
23)	718.9	miles	17.6	gallons
24)	807.8	kilometers	164.8	liters
25)	859.4	miles	44.5	gallons

BASIC SKILL REVIEW

1) Norma's odometer read 4829.3 when she started her trip. It read 5127.1 when she finished her trip. How far did she travel?

2) Frank drove 400 miles per day for 35 days. How far did he drive?

3) Renee drove 432 miles in 8 hours. What was her average speed?

4) In 20 years, Eric drove 160,000 miles in his Volvo. He drove another 40,000 miles in his Buick. How far did Eric drive these two cars?

5) The air fare to Mexico is $486. Each child who flies with an adult pays only one-third of that. What would be the fare for one adult with two children?

6) Greg's bus traveled 150 miles in $3\frac{1}{3}$ hours. What was its average speed?

7) Marie drove for $3\frac{3}{4}$ hours. Then her husband drove for $2\frac{2}{5}$ hours. What was their combined driving time?

8) Mr. and Mrs. Katz shared driving for 6 hours. Mr. Katz drove for $3\frac{1}{3}$ hours. How long did Mrs. Katz drive?

9) The toll on a certain highway is $.12 per mile. Stephanie's toll was $3.24. How far did she travel on the highway?

10) The shipping charge to city A is $1.29 per pound. Find the shipping charge for 47 pounds.

11) The repair charge on Gabe's car was $628. The insurance company paid only $300.45. How much did Gabe pay himself?

Computer Program: COMPUTING MILEAGE

This program calculates the total mileage of several trips. Type it into a computer. Run it several times with different sets of data.

```
10   REM MILEAGE PROGRAM
15   REM TN = TRIP NUMBER
20   TN = 1
30   PRINT "TYPE IN THE ODOMETER READING AT THE":
     PRINT "BEGINNING OF TRIP NUMBER ";TN
40   PRINT "TYPE IN 0 (ZERO) TO SEE THE TOTAL MILE-
     AGE."
50   INPUT B
60   IF B = 0 THEN 130
70   PRINT "TYPE IN THE ODOMETER READING AT THE
     END OF TRIP NUMBER ";TN
80   INPUT E
90   REM TD = TOTAL DISTANCE OF ALL THE TRIPS
100  TD = TD + (E − B)
110  TN = TN + 1
120  GOTO 30
130  PRINT "AFTER ";TN − 1;" TRIPS YOU HAVE DRIVEN
     A TOTAL OF ";TD;" MILES."
140  END
```

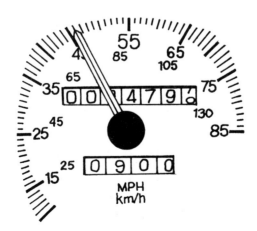

CHAPTER REVIEW

1) Dan will fly from New York to Atlanta first class. What is his air fare according to the chart on page 188?

2) What is the air fare for coach from Chicago to Phoenix to Los Angeles?

3) What is the air fare for two people flying coach from Houston to St. Louis to Washington, D.C.?

4) What is the cost per mile? Fred drove 22,000 last year. The insurance was $661. Maintenance, gas, and oil were $2,719. The loan interest was $330, and the depreciation was 15% of $9,000.

5) Edna drove 12,000 miles last year. Her insurance was $413. Maintenance, gas, and oil were $876. The loan interest was $507. The depreciation was 11% of $4,400. What was the cost per mile?

6) Don drove 9,000 last year. His insurance was $530. Maintenance, gas, and oil were $1,642. The loan interest was $280. The depreciation was 12% of $5,600. What was the cost per mile?

7) Tony rented a car for five days. The charges were $33 per day plus $.14 per mile. Tony drove 722 miles. What was the total charge?

8) Rose rented a car for three days. The charges were $18 per day plus $.15 per mile. She drove 258 miles. What was the total charge?

9) Helen rented a car for six days. The charges were $22 per day plus $.17 per mile. Her odometer reading was 17702.6 at the beginning, and 18429.2 at the end. What was the total charge?

10) Leroy drove a van 486 miles on 40 gallons of gas. Find the miles per gallon. Round to the nearest tenth.

Chapter **13**

Retail Sales

Much of the money spent in the United States is spent in retail stores. Most new businesses are started in the retail field. The earnings of retailers are unlimited. The more goods they sell, the more profit they earn.

In this chapter you will work with the mathematics of retailing.

UNIT PRICES AND COMPARISON SHOPPING

Business Vocabulary:

Comparison shopping — Shopping by comparing carefully the prices and quality of merchandise desired.

Unit price — The price per piece, per foot, per pound, and so forth.

People who do comparison shopping spend their money more wisely than people who buy on impulse. Comparison shoppers try to get the highest quality product at the lowest price. Different size packages of the same product may have different unit prices. You can find the best value by comparing unit prices.

Example: Wendy found computer diskettes selling 5 for $13.00, and 12 for $26.50. Which price was lower? Round to the next lower cent.

```
     $ 2.60  Per diskette          $ 2.208  ≈ $2.20
  5)$13.00                      12)$26.500      Per diskette
     10                            24
     30                            25
     30                            24
      0                            10
      0                             0
                                  100
                                   96
                                    4
```

Since $2.20 is less than $2.60, the lower price was $26.50 for 12.

▶ Find the unit prices of the two packages in each example. Tell which package has the lower price. Round to the next lower cent. The answer to Number 1 is Package 1, $.35; Package 2, $.25. Package 2 has the lower unit price.

	Package 1	Package 2
1)	$2.50 for 7 oz.	$2.75 for 11 oz.
2)	$8.82 for 9 sq. ft.	$10.07 for 9 sq. ft.
3)	$6.68 for 20 gal.	$6.30 for 10 gal.
4)	$4.02 for 5 gal.	$4.14 for 3 gal.
5)	$1.72 for 5 m	$.92 for 5 m
6)	$9.87 for 10 m	$11.07 for 8 m
7)	$7.83 for 8 yd.	$11.32 for 4 yd.
8)	$4.43 for 10 sq. ft.	$5.86 for 10 sq. ft.
9)	$3.99 for 7 m	$4.91 for 8 m
10)	$2.75 for 8 kg	$1.50 for 10 kg
11)	$8.46 for 13 gal.	$5.42 for 11 gal.
12)	$17.82 for 21 oz.	$8.73 for 18 oz.
13)	$10.62 for 16 ft.	$6.11 for 23 ft.
14)	$.10 for 4 m	$.05 for 2 m
15)	$.15 for 5 oz.	$.07 for 4 oz.
16)	$2.96 for 9 m	$3.62 for 13 m
17)	$.21 for 13 yd.	$.29 for 10 yd.
18)	$10.76 for 20 m	$8.73 for 15 m
19)	$11.67 for 14 gal.	$8.10 for 20 gal.
20)	$20.42 for 21 gal.	$30.21 for 28 gal.
21)	$11.48 for 16 m	$11.07 for 12 m
22)	$1.62 for 22 kg	$1.95 for 16 kg
23)	$2.69 for 4 m	$2.70 for 4 m
24)	$1.47 for 7 lb.	$1.39 for 9 lb.
25)	$12.62 for 20 ft.	$15.17 for 10 ft.

COMPUTING UNIT PRICES
With a Calculator

You can find a unit price by dividing the total price by the number of units included in the price. When the prices are high and the number of units is large, it is helpful to use a calculator.

Example A: Jim can spend $1,116.44 for 175 grams of a certain spice, or he can spend $1,488.21 for 190 grams of the same spice. Compute the unit prices and choose the better buy. Round answers down to the next lower cent.

Unit price = Total price ÷ Number of units

Offer 1: $1,116.44 ÷ 175 = $6.3796571
$6.37 (Rounded)

Offer 2: $1,488.21 ÷ 190 = $7.8326842
$7.83 (Rounded)

The unit price of Offer 1 is lower. Offer 1 is the better buy.

Example B: Nancy can spend $382.48 for 154 tiles, or she can spend $348.10 for 124 of the same tiles. Compute the unit prices and choose the better buy.

Offer 1: $382.48 ÷ 154 = $2.4836363
$2.48 (Rounded)

Offer 2: $348.10 ÷ 124 = $2.8072580
$2.80 (Rounded)

The unit price of Offer 1 is lower. Offer 1 is the better buy.

▶ Compute the unit prices and choose the better buy for each example below. Round answers down to the next lower cent. The answers to Number 1 are: Offer 1: $1.39; Offer 2: $2.22; Offer 1 is the better buy.

Offer 1	**Offer 2**
1) $232.98 for 167 lb.	$260.40 for 117 lb.
2) $688.16 for 177 m	$639.29 for 146 m
3) $607.13 for 165 oz.	$531.25 for 148 oz.
4) $203.68 for 32 gal.	$203.12 for 46 gal.
5) $1,113.92 for 165 in.	$1,429.03 for 112 in.
6) $536.16 for 143 oz.	$316.73 for 187 oz.
7) $826.91 for 176 in.	$983.20 for 245 in.
8) $1,308.82 for 146 sq. ft.	$1,374.42 for 119 sq. ft.
9) $419.37 for 53 sq. ft.	$391.53 for 37 sq. ft.
10) $836.19 for 85 gal.	$831.69 for 95 gal.
11) $1,714.44 for 211 gal.	$2,044.23 for 157 gal.
12) $319.96 for 47 in.	$286.59 for 60 in.
13) $173.35 for 190 gal.	$125.03 for 264 gal.
14) $750.70 for 118 sq. ft.	$385.41 for 108 sq. ft.
15) $28.17 for 77 in.	$20.72 for 85 in.
16) $217.57 for 47 yd.	$261.17 for 33 yd.
17) $130.81 for 15 oz.	$117.65 for 17 oz.
18) $1,129.25 for 149 sq. ft.	$1,466.34 for 208 sq. ft.
19) $206.87 for 84 ft.	$200.85 for 55 ft.
20) $1,724.94 for 180 yd.	$1,816.55 for 194 yd.
21) $100.44 for 137 gal.	$123.41 for 122 gal.
22) $1,161.11 for 135 in.	$1,515.59 for 115 in.
23) $46.98 for 20 ft.	$46.57 for 19 ft.
24) $1,628.82 for 211 oz.	$1,470.92 for 302 oz.
25) $1,574.19 for 187 gal.	$2,205.22 for 119 gal.

EXTENDING INVOICE PRICES

Business Vocabulary:

Invoice — A bill listing the products purchased and their prices.

Extended price — The amount obtained by multiplying the quantity sold by the unit price.

Retail — A business that sells directly to consumers, and sometimes to other businesses.

Wholesale — A business that sells only to retail businesses.

@ — Symbol for *at*. Often written before a unit price.

Retail businesses buy most of their goods from wholesalers. A wholesaler's bill includes the quantity, description, unit price, and extended price for each item ordered.

Example: Jacqueline ordered three types of wigs for her wig store: 4 @ $9.50; 12 @ $19.80; and 8 @ $25.15. Find the extended prices and the total bill.

Quantity		Unit Price		Extended Price
4	×	$ 9.50	=	$ 38.00
12	×	$19.80	=	237.60
8	×	$25.15	=	+201.20
				$476.80 Total

Jacqueline's total bill was $476.80.

▶ Find the total price for each set of items below. The answer to Number 1 is $164.34.

Merchandise Listed on Invoice

1) 4 @ $1.59, 6 @ $9.95, 11 @ $4.52, 8 @ $6.07
2) 6 @ $21.65, 3 @ $12.67, 1 @ $13.69, 3 @ $18.58
3) 11 @ $17.25, 9 @ $24.87, 5 @ $10.44, 12 @ $26.59
4) 2 @ $23.93, 7 @ $14.67, 7 @ $8.63, 10 @ $11.34,
   2 @ $30.36
5) 8 @ $24.23, 4 @ $15.58, 1 @ $14.95, 2 @ $19.31,
   10 @ $28.03, 2 @ $5.17
6) 2 @ $5.89, 10 @ $20.46, 3 @ $18.79, 11 @ $4.48,
   8 @ $21.44, 2 @ $29.75
7) 11 @ $28.58, 6 @ $20.16, 4 @ $30.27, 6 @ $8.89,
   11 @ $5.48
8) 12 @ $23.08, 12 @ $20.57, 4 @ $10.07, 10 @ $24.51
9) 12 @ $13.42, 9 @ $21.71
10) 12 @ $26.18, 9 @ $16.68, 9 @ $23.44, 8 @ $13.46,
    7 @ $22.96
11) 2 @ $24.31, 10 @ $25.27, 11 @ $5.95, 8 @ $24.69,
    4 @ $4.42, 4 @ $20.50
12) 7 @ $28.18, 8 @ $22.98, 4 @ $7.33, 6 @ $9.35,
    8 @ $7.41
13) 9 @ $13.74, 7 @ $23.72, 2 @ $12.89, 5 @ $27.72
14) 3 @ $17.42, 7 @ $24.12, 7 @ $15.91, 10 @ $15.44,
    3 @ $23.75
15) 4 @ $11.04, 6 @ $29.34, 4 @ $24.17, 3 @ $7.63,
    12 @ $30.34, 9 @ $22.09
16) 6 @ $7.51, 2 @ $24.22, 8 @ $13.67, 4 @ $17.87,
    5 @ $3.64
17) 2 @ $23.03, 4 @ $2.55, 8 @ $24.63, 2 @ $16.67
18) 5 @ $23.69, 9 @ $16.89, 3 @ $6.68
19) 8 @ $22.73, 4 @ $11.15
20) 2 @ $27.90, 12 @ $16.96, 2 @ $17.73, 4 @ $17.35,
    8 @ $29.14, 10 @ $24.82

MAKING CHANGE

When customers pay for their purchases at a cash register, the register may compute the amount of change automatically. However, there are many cashiers who have to calculate the change due. They begin with the purchase price and add coins and bills until they arrive at the amount given by the customer.

Example A: Rachel paid for purchases of $3.26 with $4.00. Compute her change.

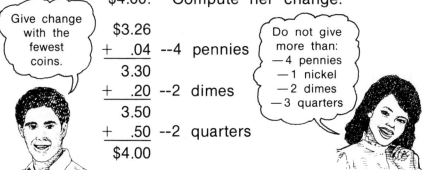

```
     $3.26
  +    .04  --4  pennies
     3.30
  +    .20  --2  dimes
     3.50
  +    .50  --2  quarters
     $4.00
```

Give change with the fewest coins.

Do not give more than:
— 4 pennies
— 1 nickel
— 2 dimes
— 3 quarters

Rachel's change was 4 pennies, 2 dimes, and 2 quarters.

Example B: Ward paid for a $2.67 purchase with $3.00. Compute his change.

```
     $2.67
  +    .03  -- 3 pennies
     $2.70
  +    .05  -- 1 nickel
     $2.75
  +    .25  -- 1 quarter
     $3.00
```

Ward's change was 3 pennies, 1 nickel, and 1 quarter.

▶ Compute the change for each of these purchases. The answer for Number 1 is 3 pennies, 1 nickel, 1 dime, and 2 quarters.

	Purchase Price	Cash		Purchase Price	Cash
1)	$2.32	$3	26)	$1.75	$2
2)	$3.72	$4	27)	$3.67	$4
3)	$ .16	$1	28)	$2.18	$3
4)	$3.44	$4	29)	$1.30	$2
5)	$ .60	$1	30)	$2.64	$3
6)	$2.80	$3	31)	$4.53	$5
7)	$3.75	$4	32)	$3.34	$4
8)	$1.70	$2	33)	$ .08	$1
9)	$1.95	$2	34)	$1.78	$2
10)	$4.50	$5	35)	$2.75	$3
11)	$ .11	$1	36)	$ .67	$1
12)	$4.74	$5	37)	$1.66	$2
13)	$3.78	$4	38)	$2.96	$3
14)	$4.80	$5	39)	$4.55	$5
15)	$4.76	$5	40)	$4.05	$5
16)	$1.40	$2	41)	$3.79	$4
17)	$3.41	$4	42)	$1.37	$2
18)	$2.99	$3	43)	$4.48	$5
19)	$1.91	$2	44)	$ .72	$1
20)	$1.59	$2	45)	$1.42	$2
21)	$3.67	$4	46)	$4.52	$5
22)	$4.74	$5	47)	$1.54	$2
23)	$3.13	$4	48)	$4.05	$5
24)	$4.85	$5	49)	$2.09	$3
25)	$2.81	$3	50)	$ .54	$1

CHECKING OUT A REGISTER

Business Vocabulary:

Starting cash — The amount of money in the register when the cashier starts working.

Final cash — The amount of money in the register when the cashier stops working.

The amount in a register should always equal the starting cash plus the total sales. Store managers check out each register to make sure that the cashiers are doing a careful job, and that the register contains the correct amount of money.

Example A: Mary's starting cash was $35. Her total sales were $227.22. Her register contains 27 pennies, 22 nickels, 41 dimes, 63 quarters, 10 half-dollars, 76 1-dollar bills, and 32 5-dollar bills. Does her register check out?

Step 1: Compute the final cash.

$$
\begin{aligned}
27 \times \$\ .01 &= \$\quad .27 \\
22 \times \$\ .05 &= \quad 1.10 \\
41 \times \$\ .10 &= \quad 4.10 \\
63 \times \$\ .25 &= \quad 15.75 \\
10 \times \$\ .50 &= \quad 5.00 \\
76 \times \$1.00 &= \quad 76.00 \\
32 \times \$5.00 &= +\,160.00 \\
\hline
&\quad \$262.22 \quad \text{Final cash}
\end{aligned}
$$

Step 2: Add the starting cash and the total sales.

$$
\begin{aligned}
\$\ 35.00 &\quad \text{Starting cash} \\
+\ 227.22 &\quad \text{Total sales} \\
\hline
\$262.22 &\quad \text{Amount that should be in the register}
\end{aligned}
$$

Mary's register checks out because the final cash equals the starting cash plus total sales.

Example B: Casey's starting cash was $25. His total sales were $186.62. His register contains 47 pennies, 23 nickels, 60 dimes, 32 quarters, 14 half-dollars, 39 1-dollar bills, and 28 5-dollar bills. Does his register check out?

Step 1: Compute the final cash.

$$
\begin{array}{rcl}
47 \times \$\,.01 &=& \$\quad\ .47 \\
23 \times \$\,.05 &=& 1.15 \\
60 \times \$\,.10 &=& 6.00 \\
32 \times \$\,.25 &=& 8.00 \\
14 \times \$\,.50 &=& 7.00 \\
39 \times \$1.00 &=& 39.00 \\
28 \times \$5.00 &=& +140.00 \\
\end{array}
$$

$201.62 Final cash

Step 2: Add the starting cash and the total sales.

$ 25.00 Starting cash
+186.62 Total sales
$211.62 Amount that should be in the register

Casey's register does not check out because the final cash ($201.62) does not equal the starting cash plus the total sales.

Since the register is missing $10, it is said to be "$10 under." If Casey's register had contained $10 too much, it would have been called "$10 over."

Some stores deduct missing funds from a cashier's paycheck.

▶ Check out these registers. Compute the final cash
and the sum of the starting cash and the total sales.
The answer to Number 1 is: The register checks out.
The final cash is $205.05.

	Pennies	Nickels	Dimes	Quarters	Halves	$1.00	$5.00	$10.00	$20.00	Starting Cash	Total Sales
1)	15	12	8	28	27	18	1	10	3	$40	$165.05
2)	41	4	0	33	23	26	41	23	34	$45	$1,106.36
3)	36	25	11	18	37	15	5	12	35	$25	$860.71
4)	24	38	18	0	5	42	5	42	30	$50	$1,043.44
5)	12	30	32	3	36	32	2	10	35	$50	$815.57
6)	11	21	18	7	5	1	25	32	26	$40	$935.34
7)	29	22	25	32	18	8	31	15	17	$35	$638.89
8)	5	27	41	21	20	31	29	7	33	$30	$896.75
9)	16	34	3	21	33	20	38	29	38	$40	$1,243.91
10)	13	23	38	9	34	9	18	12	15	$50	$493.33
11)	21	10	40	34	10	29	22	8	29	$45	$772.21
12)	11	36	3	38	9	38	22	27	18	$25	$769.21
13)	14	1	26	10	23	8	19	9	30	$25	$778.78
14)	41	28	32	38	34	18	15	10	6	$35	$309.51
15)	34	41	24	23	13	26	3	16	31	$40	$798.04
16)	36	15	34	14	3	10	20	21	9	$50	$459.51
17)	5	38	4	40	33	40	17	24	10	$35	$568.85
18)	20	11	38	7	21	19	15	30	13	$30	$640.80
19)	31	3	8	9	23	7	1	16	29	$35	$732.01
20)	17	27	33	32	24	25	40	8	31	$35	$914.82

BASIC SKILL REVIEW

1) David, the florist, sold $89,490 worth of flowers last year. He sold $120,699 the year before, and $182,997 the year before that. Find his total sales for these three years.

2) The XYZ Restaurant buys $125 worth of flowers per week. How much do they spend on flowers in 52 weeks?

3) Last month, Reuben sold $617,243 worth of building materials. Of that, $39,487 was returned. How much was *not returned*?

4) Marlene's laundry company had sales of $480,732 last year. What were the average sales per month?

5) Three-eighths of October's sales were charge sales. If the total sales were $74,000, what was the total of the charge sales?

6) Every sales trip in Greta's company lasts $3\frac{1}{2}$ weeks. How many sales trips can be scheduled in 49 weeks for one salesperson?

7) Robert's store sold $127,814 worth of goods. The total expenses were $200,125. Compute Robert's loss.

8) Tracy has received orders for 307 dolls. She will sell the dolls for $8.95 each. Compute Tracy's total sales for the 307 dolls.

9) Desiree's overhead costs were $629.14, $4,564, $75.47, and $1,463.33. Find Desiree's total overhead.

10) Crystal's invoice came to $1,008. If she pays the bill within 10 days, she can take a 2% discount. Find the discount. With the discount, how much will Crystal pay?

Computer Program: CAFETERIA COSTS

This program can compute the total cost of a meal in a school cafeteria. This type of program is called a spread sheet program because it takes a variety of numbers and prints out a chart. Spread sheet programs can quickly print out a new chart after a person has changed just one of the numbers.

Part of a sample run is shown on the next page.

```
10   REM SPREAD SHEET PROGRAM
20   PRINT "TYPE IN THE NUMBER OF STUDENTS."
30   INPUT NS
40   PRINT "TYPE IN THE NUMBER OF TEACHERS."
50   INPUT NT
60   PRINT "TYPE IN THE NO. OF OTHER STAFF MEMBERS."
70   INPUT NO
80   PRINT "TYPE IN THE PRICE OF A SERVING OF SOUP."
90   INPUT PS
100  PRINT "TYPE IN THE PRICE OF A HAMBURGER + ROLL."
110  INPUT PH
120  PRINT "TYPE IN PRICE OF SERVING OF FRENCH FRIES."
130  INPUT PF
140  PRINT "TYPE IN THE PRICE OF A SERVING OF CAKE."
150  INPUT PC
170  PRINT "△△△△△COST-STUDENTS-TEACHERS-OTHER
        STAFF."
180  PRINT "NUMBER------->" ;NS;"△△△△△△" ;NT;
        "△△△△△△△";NO
190  PRINT "SOUP△@$";PS;"△△$;NS * PS;"△△$";NT * PS;
        "△△△△$";NO * PS
200  PRINT "HAMB△@$";PH;"△$";NS * PH;"△△$";NT * PH;
        "△△△△$";NO * PH
210  PRINT "F.FR △@$";PF;"△△$";NS * PF;"△△$";NT * PF;
        "△△△△$";NO * PF
220  PRINT "CAKE△@$";PC;"△△$";NS * PC;"△△$";NT * PC;
        "△△△△$";NO * PC
230  PRINT "TOTALS△△△△△$";NS * (PS + PH + PF + PC):" $";
        NT * (PS + PH + PF + PC);"△△△$";NO * (PS +
        PH + PF + PC)
240  PRINT "△△△ GRAND TOTAL = $";NS * (PS + PH + PF +
        PC) + NT * (PS + PH + PF + PC) + NO * (PS +
        PH + PF + PC)
```

```
245   PRINT
250   PRINT "TYPE IN VARIABLE TO CHANGE."
260   PRINT "TYPE IN Q IF YOU WISH TO QUIT."
270   PRINT
280   PRINT "NS=NO. OF STUDENTS, NT=NO. OF TEACHERS"
290   PRINT "NO=NO.OF OTHER STAFF, PS=PRICE OF SOUP"
300   PRINT "PH=PRICE OF HAMBURGER, PF =PRICE OF FRIES"
310   PRINT "PC=PRICE OF CAKE"
320   INPUT A$
330   IF A$="Q" THEN 440
340   PRINT "TYPE IN THE NEW VALUE OF THE VARIABLE."
350   INPUT NV
360   IF A$="NS" THEN LET NS =NV
370   IF A$="NT" THEN LET NT=NV
380   IF A$="NO" THEN LET NO =NV
390   IF A$="PS" THEN LET PS =NV
400   IF A$="PH" THEN LET PH=NV
410   IF A$="PF" THEN LET PF=NV
420   IF A$="PC" THEN LET PC=NV
430   GOTO 170
440   END
```

```
]RUN
TYPE IN THE NUMBER OF STUDENTS.
?731
TYPE IN THE NUMBER OF TEACHERS.
?59
TYPE IN THE NO. OF OTHER STAFF MEMBERS.
?13
TYPE IN THE PRICE OF A SERVING OF SOUP.
?.83
TYPE IN THE PRICE OF A HAMBURGER + ROLL.
?1.03
TYPE IN  PRICE OF SERVING OF FRENCH FRIES.
?.71
TYPE IN THE PRICE OF A SERVING OF CAKE.
?.47
```

	COST—STUDENTS	—TEACHERS	—OTHER STAFF
Number------->	731	59	13
SOUP @$.83	$606.73	$48.97	$10.79
HAMB @$1.03	$752.93	$60.77	$13.39
F.FR @$.71	$519.01	$41.89	$9.23
CAKE @$.47	$343.57	$27.73	$6.11
TOTALS	$2222.24	$179.36	$39.52

GRAND TOTAL = $2441.12

CHAPTER REVIEW

1) Royal candy is $1.30 for 4 oz. Ben's candy is $2.30 for 9 oz. What are the unit prices? Round to the nearer cent.

2) Carlos can buy either 5 kg of fertilizer for $12, or 8 kg of fertilizer for $19.20. What are the unit prices?

3) An invoice lists 4 items at $1.59 each. What is the extended price?

4) An invoice lists 6 items at $4.56 each. What is the extended price?

5) Find the total bill: 3 @ $9.08, 5 @ $6.25, 7 @ $4.50, and 2 @ $6.00.

6) Find the total bill: 5 @ $8.75, 3 @ $5.98, 6 @ $8.32, and 12 @ $9.86.

▶ What is the change due? List the coins and bills.

7) The purchase price was $9.24. $10 was given.

8) The purchase price was $.63. $1.00 was given.

9) The purchase price was $1.48. $5.00 was given.

10) The purchase price was $10.33. $20 was given.

▶ Compute the final cash. Does the register check out?

11) Brian's starting cash was $25. The total cash sales were $244.81. His register had 26 5-dollar bills, 74 1-dollar bills, 5 halves, 26 quarters, 58 dimes, 15 nickels, and 26 pennies.

12) Vicki's starting cash was $70. Total sales were $308.05. Her register had 9 5-dollar bills, 155 1-dollar bills, 2 halves, 37 quarters, 23 dimes, 29 nickels, and 35 pennies.

Chapter 14

Mathematics Of Management

Successful business people need many skills and a great deal of knowledge. They must know what prices to charge. They must understand the tax laws. They must learn to recognize both the profitable and unprofitable parts of their business.

In this chapter you will work with the mathematics needed for business management.

Our sales are up, and our inventory is at an acceptable level.

COST OF PRODUCTION

Business Vocabulary:

Cost of production — The average cost for producing one unit.

Manufacturers use the cost of production as a guide in setting prices. The cost of production is the total of the labor cost, material cost, and the overhead cost, divided by the number of units produced.

Example: Maxine's company produced 2,800 brushes with costs of $5,342 for labor, $979 for materials, and $2,583 for overhead. Find the cost of production.

Step 1: Add the costs.
$$
\begin{array}{rl}
\$5,342 & \text{Labor} \\
979 & \text{Materials} \\
+2,583 & \text{Overhead} \\
\hline
\$8,904 & \text{Total cost}
\end{array}
$$

Step 2: Divide the total cost by the units produced.

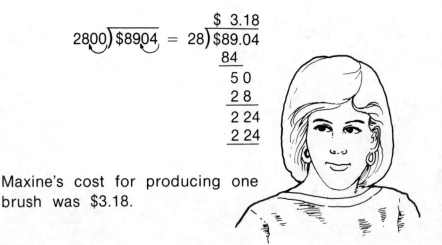

$$
2800\overline{)\$8904} = 28\overline{)\begin{array}{l}\;\;\;\$\ 3.18 \\ \$89.04 \\ \underline{84} \\ \;\;5\,0 \\ \;\;\underline{2\,8} \\ \;\;\;2\,24 \\ \;\;\;\underline{2\,24}\end{array}}
$$

Maxine's cost for producing one brush was $3.18.

▶ Compute the cost of production. The answer to Number 1 is $3.52.

Number of Units	Labor Cost	Materials Cost	Overhead Cost
1) 5,000	$9,500	$4,400	$3,700
2) 8,200	$37,018	$6,170	$12,900
3) 5,500	$17,787	$2,668	$9,190
4) 7,300	$36,135	$6,504	$29,631
5) 1,000	$6,188	$819	$2,093
6) 4,600	$23,621	$4,724	$7,995
7) 6,400	$14,336	$2,515	$8,301
8) 8,200	$43,079	$7,180	$15,013
9) 1,000	$5,630	$1,490	$1,160
10* 11,000	$640,024	$205,722	$297,154
11) 8,200	$17,513	$3,562	$8,609
12) 7,300	$24,179	$6,342	$9,118
13) 1,900	$2,432	$763	$1,574
14) 4,600	$13,823	$3,318	$10,505
15) 7,300	$20,465	$2,924	$9,096
16) 5,500	$21,375	$5,726	$11,069
17) 1,000	$1,423	$307	$460
18) 7,300	$35,483	$9,157	$12,592
19) 1,900	$969	$190	$741
20* 1,100	$57,890	$10,793	$29,437
21) 100	$164	$32	$92
22) 7,300	$40,604	$8,401	$21,002
23) 6,400	$38,568	$9,953	$13,687
24) 7,300	$19,898	$4,824	$5,427
25) 4,600	$5,046	$1,619	$2,857

COST OF GOODS SOLD

Business Vocabulary:

Inventory — A firm's stock of products to be sold, or the value of those products.

Cost of goods sold — The total cost of goods purchased for resale and then sold.

Businesses must make a profit to survive. Business owners can compute the total profit of a business from the markup percentage and the cost of goods sold. The cost of goods sold equals the beginning inventory plus purchases minus the ending inventory.

Example: Esther's Sweater Shop had a beginning inventory of $53,716. It made purchases of $145,033. Its ending inventory was $42,608. Find the cost of goods sold.

Step 1: Add.

$ 53,716 Beginning inventory
145,033 Purchases
――――――
$198,749

Step 2: Subtract.

$198,749
− 42,608 Ending inventory
――――――
$156,141 Cost of goods sold

The cost of goods sold was $156,141.

▶ Compute the cost of goods sold. The answer to Number 1 is $338,210.

	Beginning Inventory	Purchases	Ending Inventory
1)	$87,990	$324,060	$73,840
2)	$82,850	$248,550	$34,607
3)	$67,346	$505,095	$68,518
4)	$81,822	$605,482	$98,365
5)	$70,128	$231,422	$84,801
6)	$72,714	$756,225	$72,129
7)	$26,440	$161,284	$33,812
8)	$34,468	$110,297	$23,441
9)	$71,906	$222,908	$87,373
10*	$483,170	$5,218,236	$399,591
11)	$6,814	$21,804	$9,411
12)	$15,276	$180,256	$16,906
13)	$83,784	$829,461	$57,765
14)	$62,150	$590,425	$30,516
15)	$73,432	$697,604	$34,365
16)	$24,758	$252,531	$31,969
17)	$65,800	$296,100	$59,544
18)	$39,704	$142,934	$21,018
19)	$8,012	$63,294	$9,244
20*	$521,493	$3,702,600	$260,555
21)	$22,024	$79,286	$13,283
22)	$59,162	$420,050	$58,461
23)	$65,384	$405,380	$39,058
24)	$63,784	$357,190	$51,026
25)	$35,002	$157,509	$18,512

TURNOVER RATIO

The turnover ratio measures how the inventory compares with the total sales. The higher the ratio, the higher the profit.

$$\text{Turnover ratio} = \frac{\text{Cost of goods sold}}{\text{Average inventory}}$$

Example: Jerome's Auto Parts had a beginning inventory of $24,606. It made purchases of $246,788. Its ending inventory was $49,394. Compute Jerome's turnover ratio.

Step 1: Calculate the cost of goods sold.

Add: $ 24,606 Beginning inventory
+246,788 Purchases
$271,394

Subtract: $271,394
− 49,394 Ending inventory
$222,000 Cost of goods sold

Step 2: Calculate the average inventory.

Add: $24,606 Beginning inventory
+49,394 Ending inventory
$74,000

Divide: $37,000 Average inventory
2)$74,000

Step 3: Divide the cost of goods sold by the average inventory.

Divide: 6. Turnover ratio
$37,000.)$222,000.

Jerome's turnover ratio was 6.

▶ Compute the turnover ratio for each example. The answer to Number 1 is 4.7.

	Beginning Inventory	Purchases	Ending Inventory
1)	$87,286	$435,128	$94,714
2)	$21,540	$748,620	$152,460
3)	$4,492	$219,016	$75,508
4)	$29,488	$232,224	$74,512
5)	$50,508	$332,484	$119,492
6)	$6,866	$887,168	$175,134
7)	$55,998	$417,304	$102,002
8)	$14,222	$373,556	$105,778
9)	$7,274	$261,352	$54,726
10*	$148,941	$4,535,718	$858,059
11)	$29,412	$123,176	$22,588
12)	$41,926	$176,548	$42,074
13)	$47,572	$223,056	$26,428
14)	$11,256	$67,088	$20,744
15)	$10,520	$248,960	$109,480
16)	$41,636	$209,128	$44,364
17)	$23,932	$698,336	$158,068
18)	$44,870	$518,560	$113,130
19)	$56,392	$228,216	$67,608
20*	$262,599	$4,167,802	$1,181,401
21)	$17,628	$260,544	$50,372
22)	$6,556	$283,688	$99,444
23)	$55,608	$380,784	$108,392
24)	$20,530	$294,940	$119,470
25)	$4,220	$277,560	$105,780

RECOVERING AN INVESTMENT

To recover an investment means to accumulate enough net profit to pay off the initial expense completely. Many investments in equipment and facilities are judged worthwhile if they produce enough net profit to cover the original investment in a reasonable time.

For example, it is not wise to buy a $100,000 parking lot that has just one parking customer a month. However, the same parking lot is a great investment if it earns $40,000 net profit per year.

Example A: Manuel wants to buy a $2,550 coin-operated photocopy machine for his store. His gross profit will be $17 per week. His ongoing expenses will be $25 per week. How many weeks will Manuel need to recover his investment?

Manuel's expenses will exceed his net profit. Therefore, he will not recover his investment.

Example B: Antonia will save $75 per month in energy costs if she adds $2,000 of insulation to her attic. How many months will Antonia need to recover her investment? Her ongoing expenses will be $0.

Step 1: Subtract expenses from savings.

$$\begin{array}{r} \$75 \text{ Savings per month} \\ -\ 0 \text{ Expenses} \\ \hline \$75 \end{array}$$

Step 2: Divide the investment by the savings per time period.

$$\begin{array}{r} 26.6 \quad \text{Round up to 27} \\ \$75\overline{)\$2,000.0} \\ \underline{150} \\ 500 \\ \underline{450} \\ 500 \end{array}$$

Antonia will recover her investment in 27 months.

▶ Compute the number of time periods needed to recover each of these investments. Round up to the next whole time period. The answer to Number 1 is 104 months (or 8 years, 8 months).

	Investment	Gross Profit	Expenses
1)	$3,000	$46 per month	$17 per month
2)	$1,465	$52 per week	$56 per week
3)	$829	$52 per week	$48 per week
4)	$5,396	$91 per week	$63 per week
5)	$5,595	$34 per week	$27 per week
6)	$11,552	$390 per month	$113 per month
7)	$8,065	$13 per day	$13 per day
8)	$10,095	$52 per day	$43 per day
9)	$7,185	$11 per day	$7 per day
10)	$1,845	$78 per month	$48 per month
11)	$11,658	$73 per month	$21 per month
12)	$10,520	$76 per month	$74 per month
13)	$9,594	$30 per month	$15 per month
14)	$10,870	$54 per month	$33 per month
15)	$1,016	$42 per month	$43 per month
16)	$6,215	$52 per week	$21 per week
17)	$4,899	$13 per week	$9 per week
18)	$971	$88 per week	$95 per week

DEPRECIATION

Business Vocabulary:

Depreciation — The value lost by an object as it is used.

Recovery period — The number of years equipment is expected to last.

Businesses are allowed to deduct depreciation expenses when they calculate their taxes. This is called depreciating equipment. A recent tax law divided all equipment and buildings into three main classes, depending on their recovery period. Three-year property is that class of equipment and machinery that is expected to last about three years. The other two classes are five-year property and ten-year property.

Accelerated Cost Recovery System
Percentage Table

3-year property
1st year 25%
2nd year 38%
3rd year 37%

5-year property
1st year 15%
2nd year 22%
3rd through 5th year 21%

10-year property
1st year 8%
2nd year 14%
3rd year 12%
4th through 6th year 10%
7th through 10th year 9%

Example: Find the deduction for a $400, 3-year property in the second year.

The table shows that the second year of a 3-year property has a percentage of 38%.

Multiply the purchase price by 38%.
(38% = .38)

$400 Purchase price
×.38
3200
1200
$152.00 Deduction

The deduction is $152.00.

▶ Find the deduction for depreciation in each example
below. The answer for Number 1 is $2,465.55.

Purchase Price	Recovery Period	Year
1) $27,395	10 years	7
2) $16,659	3 years	3
3) $2,790	3 years	2
4) $19,841	10 years	3
5) $6,178	5 years	4
6) $12,868	3 years	2
7) $2,633	10 years	4
8) $15,617	10 years	6
9) $19,307	10 years	9
10* $186,967	10 years	4
11) $18,776	5 years	5
12) $5,585	10 years	5
13) $12,468	3 years	2
14) $18,709	10 years	1
15) $4	10 years	2
16) $1,690	10 years	8
17) $10,495	5 years	4
18) $6,763	10 years	2
19) $7,273	10 years	10
20* $45,034	10 years	8

THE SUM-OF-THE-YEARS'-DIGITS METHOD

Business Vocabulary:

Useful life — The amount of time that a piece of equipment should last.

Some pieces of older equipment must be depreciated with the sum-of-the-years'-digits method. This method allows for the greater part of the depreciation to be deducted early in the life of the item.

Example: Missy bought an $840 photocopy machine with a useful life of 6 years. Find the sum-of-the-years'-digits depreciation at the end of year 5.

Step 1: Add the digits of the years of useful life.

$$6 + 5 + 4 + 3 + 2 + 1 = 21$$

Step 2: Set up this fraction:

$$\frac{\text{Useful life} + 1 - \text{Year}}{\text{Sum of digits}}$$

$$\frac{6 + 1 - 5}{21} = \frac{2}{21} \quad \boxed{\text{End of year 5.}}$$

Step 3: Multiply the purchase price by the fraction.

$$\frac{\$840}{1} \times \frac{2}{21} = \frac{\$1680}{21} = \$80$$

Missy's deduction for depreciation at the end of year 5 was $80.

▶ Compute the sum-of-the-years'-digits depreciation for each example below. The answer to Number 1 is $2,700.

	Purchase Price	End of Year	Useful Life In Years
1)	$9,450	1	6
2)	$660	2	11
3)	$27,450	5	9
4)	$52,140	7	11
5)	$44,000	2	10
6)	$31,900	9	10
7)	$8,700	2	4
8)	$4,050	1	5
9)	$44,000	2	4
10*	$129,360	7	7
11)	$2,910	1	2
12)	$4,140	3	3
13)	$18,480	9	11
14)	$4,050	7	9
15)	$3,300	8	10
16)	$8,800	4	4
17)	$22,050	3	9
18)	$2,520	2	6
19)	$2,220	2	2
20*	$35,640	5	8
21)	$2,000	1	4
22)	$20,880	5	8
23)	$8,550	4	9
24)	$17,550	4	9
25)	$1,800	2	5

OVERHEAD PER DEPARTMENT

Business owners know that their departments have different amounts of overhead. Some owners divide up their total overhead expense according to floor area. Departments that occupy more space are responsible for more overhead. Owners study these area-by-area overhead figures when they need to change or eliminate departments.

Example: Roy's store has four departments and a total overhead of $10,920. Compute the overhead by department. The sizes of the four areas in square feet are 320, 324, 333, and 423.

Step 1: Calculate total square feet. Add.

320 + 324 + 333 + 423 = 1,400 square feet

Step 2: Find the overhead per square foot.
Divide the total overhead by total square feet.

$$1400 \overline{)\$10,920} \quad = \quad \begin{array}{r} \$\ \ 7.80 \text{ Overhead per sq. ft.} \\ 14\overline{)\$109.20} \\ \underline{98} \\ 11\ 2 \\ \underline{11\ 2} \\ 00 \end{array}$$

Step 3: Find the overhead for each department. Multiply the overhead per square foot by the area of each department. Round to the nearest dollar.

$7.80 × 320 = $2496 $7.80 × 333 = $2597.40
$7.80 × 324 = $2527.20 $7.80 × 423 = $3299.40

The four departments have overheads of $2,496, $2,527, $2,597, and $3,299.

► Compute the overhead for each department. Round to the nearest dollar. The answers for Number 1 are: $5,855, $6,225, and $14,920.

	Total Overhead	Area in Square Feet for Separate Departments
1)	$27,000	1,171, 1,245, 2,984
2)	$30,000	977, 888, 2,135
3)	$90,250	1,846, 1,940, 2,207, 3,507
4)	$15,250	1,056, 1,097, 740, 820, 2,387
5)	$4,200	645, 567, 492, 1,296
6)	$69,620	1,261, 1,553, 1,740, 3,846
7)	$15,680	160, 164, 162, 160, 954
8)	$1,920	189, 259, 209, 543
9)	$71,250	1,061, 763, 956, 1,375, 3,345
10)	$44,660	1,050, 1,017, 1,137, 2,596
11)	$26,190	619, 667, 638, 776
12)	$48,980	796, 908, 1,115, 1,132, 2,249
13)	$24,820	753, 1,221, 1,246, 1,098, 2,982
14)	$29,760	2,225, 1,935, 1,909, 3,231
15)	$17,280	500, 427, 443, 1,030
16)	$24,440	730, 1,010, 734, 2,226
17)	$47,520	1,811, 2,056, 3,333
18)	$7,920	998, 863, 1,739
19)	$11,130	1,343, 1,217, 2,740
20)	$29,120	598, 1,028, 794, 1,028, 1,752
21)	$1,920	189, 259, 209, 543
22)	$17,480	837, 898, 775, 2,090
23)	$30,450	2,484, 2,253, 3,963
24)	$30,940	772, 671, 636, 1,321
25)	$12,540	774, 883, 647, 1,496

COMPUTING PROFIT SHARES
IN A PARTNERSHIP
With a Calculator

Business Vocabulary:

Partnership — A business that is owned by at least two people.

Some people form partnerships because they do not have enough money by themselves to start a business. Other people form partnerships to share the work or to share the risk. In many partnerships, the partners share the profits (or the losses) based on the original amounts they invested.

Example: Partners A, B, C, and D divided a net profit of $7,800. Partner A had invested $75,292; Partner B had invested $9,201; Partner C had invested $85,641; and Partner D had invested $75,904. Find the profit share of each partner. Round shares to the next lower dollar.

Step 1: Add the investments.

$75,292	A
9,201	B
85,641	C
+ 75,904	D
$246,038	Total

Step 2: Find the investment share of each partner. Divide each investment by the total investment.

A: $75,292 ÷ 246,038 = .306017
B: $ 9,201 ÷ 246,038 = .037396
C: $85,641 ÷ 246,038 = .348080
D: $75,904 ÷ 246,038 = .308505

Step 3: Find the profit share of each partner. Multiply the net profit by each investment share.

A: $7,800 × .306017 = $2,386.93, or $2,386
B: $7,800 × .037396 = $291.68, or $291
C: $7,800 × .348080 = $2,715.02, or $2,715
D: $7,800 × .308505 = $2,406.33, or $2,406

The four shares were $2,386, $291, $2,715, and $2,406.

▶ Compute the profit shares in each example. Round to the next lower dollar. The answers to Number 1 are: $18,307, $12,098, and $34,931.

	Net Profit	Investments of Partners			
1)	$65,336	$24,729,	$16,342,	$47,185	
2)	$97,029	$10,411,	$1,871,	$78,034,	$55,283,
		$61,841			
3)	$85,644	$80,319,	$81,510,	$13,213,	$81,024
4)	$13,323	$59,296,	$26,900,	$42,021,	$87,983
		$36,937			
5)	$58,325	$83,732,	$11,662,	$81,611	
6)	$99,156	$89,093,	$42,802,	$2,369,	$12,459,
		$98,234,	$12,945		
7)	$29,946	$70,774,	$98,580,	$79,597	
8)	$7,800	$75,292,	$9,201,	$85,641,	$75,904
9)	$77,000	$82,943,	$89,228		
10)	$60,583	$25,789,	$50,593,	$43,481,	$17,003,
		$13,039,	$3,867		
11)	$10,963	$75,494,	$62,469,	$52,096	
12)	$76,482	$21,382,	$16,237,	$20,418,	$67,804,
		$51,839,	$58,917		
13)	$37,795	$43,000,	$19,837,	$73,581	
14)	$64,651	$37,604,	$25,477,	$12,991	
15)	$79,288	$95,708,	$49,829,	$48,258,	$73,378,
		$67,611,	$18,362		

Computer Program:
PROFITABILITY OF DEPARTMENTS

The goal of business owners is to maximize their profit. One way to do this is to expand those departments that are very profitable. Another way is either to decrease or eliminate those departments that are not as profitable. This program identifies each department as being either more profitable or less profitable. A more profitable department is one whose percent of net profit is at least equal to its percent of area.

Type this program into a computer. Run it several times with different sets of data.

```
10   REM THIS PROGRAM DETERMINES THE RELATIVE
     PROFITABILITY OF STORE DEPARTMENTS
20   REM LINES 40 AND 50 SET A MAXIMUM OF 35 DEPART-
     MENTS
30   REM AR(DE) = AREA OF DEPARTMENT NUMBER DE,
     NP(DE) = NET PROFIT OF DEPARTMENT NUMBER
     (DE)
40   DIM AR(35)
50   DIM NP(35)
60   REM TA = TOTAL AREA, TN = TOTAL NET PROFIT
70   PRINT "TYPE IN THE NUMBER OF DEPARTMENTS."
80   REM N = NUMBER OF DEPARTMENTS
90   INPUT N
100  REM DE = DEPARTMENT NUMBER
110  FOR DE = 1 TO N
120  PRINT "TYPE IN THE AREA OF DEPARTMENT ";DE
130  INPUT AR(DE)
140  LET TA = TA + AR(DE)
150  PRINT "TYPE IN THE NET PROFIT OF DEPART-
     MENT ";DE
160  INPUT NP(DE)
170  LET TN = TN + NP(DE)
180  NEXT DE
```

```
190  REM A DEPARTMENT IS LP (LESS PROFITABLE) IF
     ITS PERCENTAGE OF PROFIT < ITS PERCENTAGE
     OF AREA.
200  REM A DEPARTMENT IS MP (MORE PROFITABLE) IF
     ITS PERCENTAGE OF PROFIT >= ITS PERCENTAGE
     OF AREA.
210  PRINT
220  PRINT   "DEPT. △△%AREA△△%PROFIT△△PROFIT-
     ABILITY"
230  FOR DE = 1 TO N
240  REM LINES 250 AND 260 CHANGE THE AREA AND
     NET PROFIT FIGURES TO PERCENTS.
250  LET AR(DE) = INT (100 * AR(DE)/TA + .5)
260  LET NP(DE) = INT (100 * NP(DE)/TN + .5)
270  IF AR(DE) > NP(DE) THEN A$ = "LP"
280  IF AR(DE) <= NP(DE) THEN A$ = "MP"
290  PRINT   "△△";DE;"△△△△△";AR(DE);"%△△△△△";
     NP(DE);"%△△△△△△△";A$
300  NEXT DE
310  END
```

234 — Problem Solving

BASIC SKILL REVIEW

1) Mary earned a salary of $36,250. She also had rental income of $5,360 and interest income of $569. What was her total income?

2) Herschel earned $800 a week for 50 weeks. What was his income?

3) Sharonda's gross pay was $319. Her employer withheld $98 in taxes. What was her net pay?

4) Alicia paid $416 in social security taxes last year. This was paid in 52 equal deductions. How much was the deduction?

5) Gary's paycheck deductions totaled $198. Five-sixths of this amount was for federal tax. How much was deducted for federal tax?

6) Tom worked as a bus driver for $10\frac{1}{4}$ years. He drove new busses for $5\frac{3}{4}$ years. For how many years did he drive older busses?

7) Barbara's training period lasted 28 weeks. She spent 3 and one-half weeks in each store department. In how many departments did Barbara work?

8) Shira paid $\frac{1}{14}$ of her salary to social security. She paid $\frac{2}{7}$ of her salary in federal tax. Her other deductions totaled $\frac{1}{10}$ of her salary. What fraction of her gross pay went for deductions?

9) Steve had $2.67 deducted every week for state tax. In 37 weeks, what was Steve's total withholding for state tax?

10) The five deductions from Sandra's paycheck were $42.69, $6.74, $10.36, $2, and $.79. What was the total of the deductions?

11) Van's gross pay was $400. His deductions totaled $126.53. Find Van's net pay.

CHAPTER REVIEW

1) Find the cost of production when 1,900 units were produced with costs of $3,811 for labor, $646 for materials, and $2,003 for overhead.

2) Find the cost of production when 4,600 units were produced with costs of $5,925 for labor, $1,144 for materials, and $3,327 for overhead.

3) Find the cost of goods sold. The beginning inventory was $65,780. Purchases were $184,184. The ending inventory was $48,948.

4) Find the cost of goods sold. The beginning inventory was $45,470. Purchases were $109,128. The ending inventory was $51,264.

5) Find the turnover ratio. The beginning inventory was $47,942. Purchases were $316,616. The ending inventory was $102,058.

6) Find the turnover ratio. The beginning inventory was $51,366. Purchases were $81,768. The ending inventory was $30,634.

7) How many months are needed to recover an investment of $927? The profit per month is $59. The expenses per month are $42. Round to the next higher month.

8) How many weeks are needed to recover an investment of $2,317? The profit per week is $134. The expenses per week are $73. Round to the next higher week.

9) The purchase price of a piece of equipment was $8,743. The recovery period is 5 years. What is the depreciation for the fourth year? Refer to the chart on page 224.

CHAPTER REVIEW, Continued

10) The purchase price of a machine was $12,965. The recovery period is 10 years. What is the depreciation for the seventh year? Refer to the chart on page 224.

11) The purchase price of a piece of equipment was $4,200. The useful life was 5 years. Find the depreciation at the end of the third year. Use the sum-of-the-years'-digits method.

12) A machine with a useful life of 3 years was purchased for $6,000. Find the depreciation at the end of year 1. Use the sum-of-the-years'-digits method.

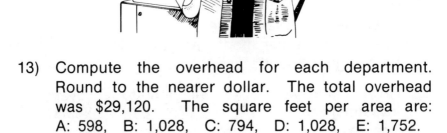

13) Compute the overhead for each department. Round to the nearer dollar. The total overhead was $29,120. The square feet per area are: A: 598, B: 1,028, C: 794, D: 1,028, E: 1,752.

14) Compute the overhead for each department. Round to the nearer dollar. The total overhead was $15,680. The square feet per area are: F: 160, G: 164, H: 162, I: 160, J: 954.

Chapter 15

Inflation

Economics is the study of business activity. It analyzes trends in manufacturing, commerce, taxation, unemployment, and foreign trade. Every facet of economics is affected by inflation.

In this chapter you will work with the concept of inflation and find out how inflation is measured.

INFLATION

Inflation increases prices. Inflation occurs when too many people want to buy a product, and when the prices of raw materials like copper and oil rise. As the cost of living increases, workers ask for higher wages. Firms increase their prices even more to pay the higher wage.

Example A: Suppose a package of pens costs $3.20. Then the price increases 15%. Find the new price.

15% = .15 $3.20 Old price $3.20 Old price
             ×   .15 Rate of increase   + .48 Increase
             1600 $3.68 New price
             320
             $.4800 Increase

    The new price is $3.68.

Example B: Suppose a one-minute radio advertisement costs $127. Then the price increases 9%. Find the new price.

9% = .09 $127 Old price $127.00 Old price
            ×   .09 Rate of increase   + 11.43 Increase
            $11.43 Increase $138.43 New price

    The new price is $138.43.

▶ Compute the new prices for these goods. If necessary, round up to the next cent. The answer to Number 1 is $15.65.

	Old Price	Rate of Increase		Old Price	Rate of Increase
1)	$14.35	9%	26)	$70.52	14%
2)	$9.07	7%	27)	$96.53	16%
3)	$68.78	11%	28)	$87.47	18%
4)	$4.76	16%	29)	$72.67	10%
5)	$65.83	18%	30*	$93.88	15.9%
6)	$73.99	17%	31)	$27.92	18%
7)	$80.68	14%	32)	$48.43	14%
8)	$44.24	7%	33)	$7.03	13%
9)	$68.33	6%	34)	$93.54	18%
10*	$80.54	10.3%	35)	$6.79	5%
11)	$16.64	20%	36)	$85.54	6%
12)	$34.06	10%	37)	$8.45	19%
13)	$1.06	19%	38)	$73.56	13%
14)	$82.29	12%	39)	$42.28	17%
15)	$14.59	17%	40*	$33.81	16.2%
16)	$63.79	14%	41)	$36.36	16%
17)	$83.29	6%	42)	$92.35	8%
18)	$74.31	7%	43)	$83.37	17%
19)	$20.43	14%	44)	$19.25	19%
20*	$99.20	15.3%	45)	$92.67	20%
21)	$30.89	11%	46)	$13.83	20%
22)	$61.98	15%	47)	$33.73	9%
23)	$7.13	12%	48)	$92.83	10%
24)	$13.16	20%	49)	$79.06	14%
25)	$33.77	17%	50*	$48.84	12.8%

THE CONSUMER PRICE INDEX

Business Vocabulary:
Base year — The year chosen for comparison purposes.

The federal government measures inflation with the Consumer Price Index (CPI). Recently, the CPI was 178.4. This meant that $10.00 worth of goods purchased in the base year would have cost $17.84. The CPI is affected by price changes in food, clothing, housing, health care, utilities, and so on. The CPI is computed from the prices of hundreds of things we regularly buy.

Pretend for a moment that we could spend money on only nine things. The CPI would then be computed like this:

	Base Year	This Year	Next Year (Predicted)
1 lb. chicken	$ .63	$ .89	$ .98
1 lb. carrots	.38	.45	.45
1 lb. bread	.39	.99	1.07
1 qt. milk	.42	.63	.65
1 bus fare	.25	.75	.80
1 day's housing	3.28	6.12	6.25
1 day's insurance	1.58	1.79	1.80
1 day's utilities	1.14	2.06	2.38
Doctor's visit (per minute)	+ 1.93	+ 2.44	+ 2.57
	$10.00	$16.12	$16.95

Example A: The cost to buy the nine items this year is $16.12. Therefore, the CPI is 16.12 × 10, or 161.2 this year.

Example B: The predicted cost of the nine items next year is $16.95. Therefore, the CPI is predicted to be 16.95 × 10, or 169.5 next year.

▶ Practice doing the same kind of computing as is done with the CPI. Find the cost of each set of nine items. Then multiply by 10. The answer to Number 1 is 156.6 (not $156.60).

1) $2.36, $1.86, $2.22, $1.03, $1.52, $2.44, $2.52, $ .45, $1.26

2) $2.95, $ .97, $2.78, $2.06, $1.88, $1.13, $1.91, $2.37, $1.44

3) $ .78, $1.89, $1.92, $1.95, $2.97, $2.90, $2.19, $ .30, $1.39

4) $2.33, $1.37, $ .93, $1.18, $ .97, $ .82, $2.46, $1.12, $1.73

5) $1.03, $2.64, $1.11, $1.07, $2.36, $ .33, $1.94, $1.18, $1.49

6) $2.22, $2.86, $1.91, $2.04, $ .49, $ .73, $2.14, $1.38, $1.04

7) $2.16, $2.06, $2.57, $2.28, $2.44, $2.46, $1.79, $1.46, $1.14

8) $2.12, $ .51, $2.46, $1.10, $1.02, $ .70, $2.90, $1.18, $1.33

9) $ .27, $2.79, $2.51, $1.51, $ .65, $2.39, $2.00, $1.87, $1.83

10) $ .49, $2.29, $ .63, $ .81, $1.94, $2.97, $2.12, $ .93, $1.30

11) $1.37, $1.95, $2.01, $ .44, $1.56, $ .61, $2.88, $1.17, $1.78

12) $2.18, $1.83, $2.90, $2.31, $2.65, $2.58, $2.24, $1.20, $1.93

13) $1.98, $2.92, $1.01, $2.58, $1.58, $1.96, $ .44, $1.75, $1.93

14) $2.50, $ .43, $ .25, $2.60, $ .52, $ .48, $2.81, $2.27, $1.52

15) $2.54, $2.37, $ .77, $2.80, $2.79, $2.95, $ .63, $2.91, $1.33

CONSUMER PRICE INDEX: PERCENT OF INCREASE

Percent of increase (or decrease) is a very important business concept. It is a measure of change. Labor unions use the percent of increase of the CPI to decide what size wage raise to request.

The formula for percent of increase (or decrease) is:

$$\frac{\text{Amount of change}}{\text{Original amount}}$$

Example: During the life of a labor contract, the CPI rose from 180 to 193.1. Find the percent of increase.

Step 1: Find the amount of change. Subtract.

$$\begin{array}{r} 193.1 \\ -180 \\ \hline 13.1 \end{array}$$

Step 2: Divide the amount of change by the original amount.

$$180\overline{)13.1} \qquad \text{Simplify to:} \qquad 18\overline{)\begin{array}{l}.0727 \\ 1.3100 \\ \underline{1\ 26} \\ 50 \\ \underline{36} \\ 140 \\ \underline{126} \\ 14 \end{array}}$$

.0727 is rounded to .073

.073 = 7.3%

The CPI rose 7.3%.

▶ Compute the percent of increase in the CPI. Round to the nearer tenth of a percent. The answer to Number 1 is 6.5%.

	CPI Jan. 1	CPI Dec. 31		CPI Jan. 1	CPI Dec. 31
1)	150	159.7	26)	120	138
2)	180	194.3	27)	120	128
3)	130	136.5	28)	150	165
4)	110	125.4	29)	190	203.3
5)	180	189	30)	147	161.7
6)	140	159.5	31)	130	136.5
7)	120	132	32)	120	128.3
8)	110	115.5	33)	120	133.1
9)	130	150.7	34)	180	190.7
10)	127	144.7	35)	150	175.5
11)	140	148.3	36)	110	126.5
12)	150	174	37)	140	145.5
13)	150	159	38)	170	197.2
14)	100	105	39)	190	197.5
15)	180	189	40)	144	151.1
16)	140	154	41)	110	117.7
17)	140	145.5	42)	170	181.9
18)	170	188.7	43)	100	110
19)	120	129.6	44)	180	198
20)	104	108.1	45)	110	115.5
21)	180	187.1	46)	160	185.6
22)	130	139	47)	170	185.6
23)	140	152.5	48)	140	162.3
24)	130	141.6	49)	130	149.5
25)	110	113.3	50)	125	137.5

READING A BAR GRAPH

Many business reports make use of graphs. Often, the best way to show information is with a graph. Quantities in a graph may be shown with bars, lines, or pictures. Look at the bar graph below.

Example:

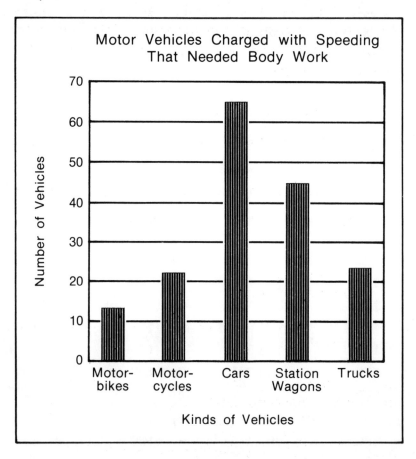

1) About how many of the motorcycles needed body work?

2) Which type of vehicle had the greatest number needing body work?

Solutions:

1) Find the bar that represents the number of motor-cycles. Notice that the bar extends to just above the level of the 20 at the left. This means that there were about 22 or 23 motorcycles that needed body work.

2) Look at all the bars. Find the bar that is the longest. The bar for cars is the longest. This means that more cars needed body work than did any other kind of vehicle.

▶ Answer these questions.

1) About how many station wagons needed body work?

2) About how many trucks needed body work?

3) Which type of vehicle had the fewest number need-ing body work?

4) About how many more trucks than motorcycles needed body work?

5) About how many more cars than motorbikes needed body work?

▶ List the kinds of vehicles in order from most to least in number needing body work.

READING A LINE GRAPH

Look at this example of a line graph.

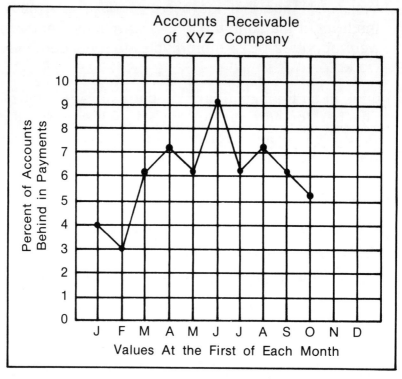

Accounts Receivable
of XYZ Company

1) About what percent of the accounts were behind in September?

2) During which month was the rise in accounts behind the greatest?

Solutions:

1) Find the abbreviation for September along the bottom of the graph. Trace the line upwards until you meet the dot. Then look at the scale at the left to find what percent is at that level. The dot for September is just above the line for 6%. This means that a little more than 6% of the accounts were behind in September.

2) To find the month with the greatest rise, look for the steepest part of the graph that is rising. That steepest part lies between February and March. Therefore, the month with the greatest rise was February. Note that the graph is also very steep between June and July. However, between June and July the graph is falling, not rising.

▶ Answer these questions.

1) About what percent of the accounts were behind in February?

2) About what percent were behind in October?

3) What month had the highest percent of accounts behind?

4) What month had the second lowest percent of accounts behind?

5) What month had the steepest fall?

6) During what months did the percent fall?

7) Was there any month when the percent seemed to remain the same as the month before?

8) What two months seem to have the same percent of accounts behind?

9) What four months seem to have the same percent behind?

10) During what two months was there a steady decline?

11) During what two months did the percent continue to rise?

12) What is a possible reason for the percent behind to rise steeply in June?

13) What percent do you suppose will be behind in November? Make a reasonable prediction.

DRAWING GRAPHS

Before you draw a graph, examine the data. There are usually several possible ways to show the information. Decide what variable you will use on the vertical scale, and what variable on the horizontal scale. Decide what size units to mark off on each scale.

Example: The sales force of XYZ Co. consisted of 18 people in 1983, 26 in 1984, 27 in 1985, 30 in 1986, 31 in 1987, and 32 in 1988. Show this on a graph.

One solution, using a bar graph:

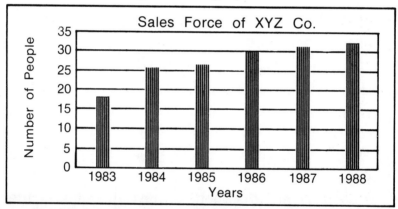

One solution, using a line graph:

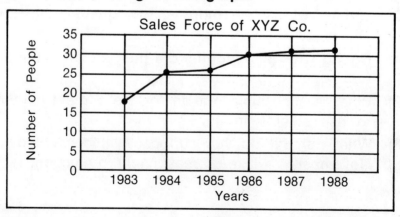

▶ Draw a bar graph for each set of data. Add your own descriptions.

1) 1984 - 4, 1985 - 9, 1986 - 2, 1987 - 10, 1988 - 6

2) 1 - 523, 2 - 833, 3 - 142, 4 - 789, 5 - 994

3) 1985 - 11, 1986 - 3, 1987 - 5, 1988 - 6

4) 1 - 50, 2 - 63, 3 - 70, 4 - 48, 5 - 68

5) June - 24, July - 39, Aug. - 45, Sept. - 36

6) Mon. - 987, Tues. - 649, Wed. - 550, Thur. - 718

7) Men - 75, Women - 80, Children - 45

8) Red - 4, Blue - 8, Green - 12, Orange - 15

9) 1 - 22, 2 - 11, 3 - 15, 4 - 36, 5 - 53

10) Spring - 200, Summer - 650, Fall - 530, Winter - 390

▶ Draw a line graph for each set of data. Add your own descriptions.

11) 1960 - 40, 1970 - 80, 1980 - 60, 1990 - 85

12) A - 125, B - 325, C - 250, D - 475, E - 350

13) 1 - 43, 2 - 9, 3 - 13, 4 - 38, 5 - 25

14) W - 475, X - 300, Y - 650, Z - 550

15) Jan. - 5, Feb. - 17, Mar. - 10, Apr. - 13, May - 7

16) Sun. - 940, Mon. - 875, Tues. - 658, Wed. - 790

17) 1 - 50%, 2 - 30%, 3 - 85%, 4 - 65%, 5 - 95%

18) Winter - 23, Spring - 54, Summer - 84, Fall - 46

19) Red - 163, Blue - 140, Green - 178, Yellow - 135

20) 6 - 15, 7 - 30, 8 - 45, 9 - 25, 10 - 35

COMPUTING REAL DOLLARS
With a Calculator

Inflation decreases the value of money. As prices rise, a dollar buys less and less. Suppose Anita was hired at $8,000 per year. Over the next 11 years, prices as measured by the CPI doubled. Anita's salary also doubled, to $16,000. In real or constant dollars, though, her salary remained the same. Her salary would buy just the same amount of goods and services as before. A calculation in real dollars allows us to compare the buying power of an amount of money in different years.

Example A: Ray earns $343 per week. The CPI is 253. Compute his salary in real dollars compared to when the CPI was 173.1. Round to the nearer dollar.

$$\text{Real dollars} = \frac{\text{Current earnings} \times \text{CPI Then}}{\text{CPI Now}}$$

$343 × 173.1 ÷ 253 = $234.67
$235   (Rounded)

In real dollars, Ray's salary is $235.

Example B: Bobby earns $67,798 per year, and the CPI is 185.3. Compute his salary in real dollars compared to when the CPI was 168.4. Round to the nearer dollar.

$67,798 × 168.4 ÷ 185.3 = $61,614.58
$61,615   (Rounded)

In real dollars, Bobby's salary is $61,615 per year.

▶ Compute each of these salaries in real dollars. Round to the nearer dollar. The answer for Number 1 is $14,125.

	Current Earnings	CPI Then	CPI Now
1)	$16,300	127.3	146.9
2)	$14,031	136.1	145
3)	$88,822	112.9	166.4
4)	$357	182.7	272.1
5)	$85,666	114.5	126.4
6)	$21,518	119.2	164.5
7)	$372	147.7	165.2
8)	$75,497	190.8	218.3
9)	$87,052	142.8	163.9
10)	$197	156.9	179.6
11)	$474	181.9	197.3
12)	$59,811	140.9	153.9
13)	$432	125.4	163.8
14)	$362	111.5	199.1
15)	$318	131.9	172.1
16)	$282	145.3	163.7
17)	$59,238	185.8	210.6
18)	$407	150	240.3
19)	$156	177.1	224.6
20)	$82,490	126.3	158
21)	$18,155	120.4	172.4
22)	$91,717	186.5	228.2
23)	$495	191.8	202.9
24)	$28,556	115.3	132.1
25)	$51,655	102.1	152.9

Computer Program:
SALARY SCALE RAISES

Large firms commonly have a salary scale for each set of employees. There are four different salary scales for clerks at the General Rotors Corporation. Clerks rise one step on their scale for each year with the company. The management has offered to raise each of these four salary scales 5%. Use a calculator to find the increase for each step and the total increase a worker will get as he moves from one step to the next.

Example: Level 1, Step 1 is now $10,558.
Level 1, Step 2 is now $11,041.
What is the proposed amount for Step 2?

First: Find the proposed amount by multiplying $11,041 × 105%.

$11,041 × 1.05 = $11,593.05
$11,593   Rounded

Next: Find the step increase by subtracting.

$11,593 − $11,041 = $552

Then: Find the total increase by subtracting the old amount on Step 1 from the new amount on Step 2.

$11,593 − $10,558 = $1,035

▶ Use your calculator to compute the missing amounts in the table on page 253. Round to the nearer dollar. The answers for Step 4 are: Proposed, $12,607. Step increase, $600. Total increase, $1,083.

LEVEL 1				
	Salary		**Increase**	
Step	**Present**	**Proposed**	**Step**	**Total**
1	$10,558	$11,086		
2	$11,041	$11,593	$552	$1,035
3	$11,524	$12,100	$576	$1,059
4	$12,007			
5	$12,490			
6	$12,973			

This program can compute the increase for each step after Step 1. Type it into a computer and run it several times. Is it easier to use a calculator or a computer to find the missing amounts?

```
10   REM PROGRAM FOR PROPOSED SALARY SCALE
20   REM SS = SALARY STEP
30   PRINT "TYPE IN THE NUMBER OF THE FIRST":PRINT "SALARY
         STEP THAT YOU WANT TO COMPUTE."
40   INPUT SS
50   REM P = PERCENT INCREASE FOR THE SALARY SCALE
60   PRINT "TYPE IN THE PERCENT INCREASE FOR THE":PRINT
         "WHOLE SALARY SCALE."
70   INPUT P
80   REM SP = SALARY FOR PREVIOUS STEP
90   PRINT "TYPE IN THE PRESENT SALARY FOR THE":PRINT "PREVI-
         OUS STEP: NUMBER ";SS − 1
100  INPUT SP
110  REM PS = PRESENT SALARY
120  PRINT "TYPE IN THE PRESENT SALARY FOR":PRINT "STEP:
         NUMBER ";SS
130  INPUT PS
140  PRINT
150  PRINT "PRESENT = $";PS
160  PRINT "PROPOSED SALARY = $"; INT ((1 + P / 100) * PS + .5)
170  PRINT "STEP INCREASE = $"; INT (PS * P / 100 + .5)
180  PRINT "TOTAL INCREASE = $"; INT ((1 + P / 100) * PS + .5) − SP
190  PRINT
200  PRINT "DO YOU WISH TO SEE THE FIGURES FOR THE":PRINT
         "NEXT SALARY STEP (NUMBER ";SS + 1;")?  (Y/N)"
210  INPUT A$
220  IF A$ = "N" THEN 260
230  LET SS = SS + 1
240  LET SP = PS
250  GOTO 120
260  END
```

BASIC SKILL REVIEW

1) In March there were 9.1 million people unemployed. In April there were 7.9 million people unemployed. What was the difference in the figures for March and April?

2) Inflation rose 9.6% last year. Ths figure was three times the rise for the year before that. What was the rate of inflation before it was 9.6%?

3) The Consumer Price Index (CPI) rose 1% in April, .7% in May, 1.2% in June, .9% in July, and .5% in August. Find the overall rise in the CPI.

4) In 1920 there were .76 million people unemployed. There were 5.4 times as many people unemployed in 1931. How many people were unemployed in 1931?

5) The increases in the number of employed people in a certain state were 92,435 in May; 109,765 in June; 116,799 in July; and 87,600 in August. Find the total increase in employment.

6) Ghosttown had to lay off 2317 municipal workers to meet its budget. Before the layoff, there were 10,000 municipal workers. How many are there now?

7) Sun Motor Company employs 60,000 people in 25 assembly plants. Each plant has an equal number of employees. How many employees are there at a Sun plant?

8) The net profit for a company was twice as big this year as last year. Their net profit last year was $375,849. Find their net profit this year.

9) Thirteen-twentieths of 1500 workers received pay raises this year. How many received pay raises?

10) The CPI for the base year (last year) was 100. The CPI rose 10.1% this year. What is the CPI now?

CHAPTER REVIEW

1) The price of a wrench was $4.15. Then the price increased 6%. What was the new price? Round up to the next higher cent.

2) A box of tiles cost $61.45. The price increased 27%. What was the new price? Round up to the next higher cent.

3) Calculate a consumer price index from these nine items: $1.12, $2.02, $1.17, $1.23, $1.98, $.56, $1.89, $1.57, $.98.

4) Calculate a consumer price index from these nine items: $1.16, $2.09, $1.17, $1.24, $2.34, $.79, $1.98, $1.44, $1.02.

5) The CPI on January 1 was 150. On December 31, it was 160. What was the percent of increase?

6) The CPI was 110 on January 1. On December 31, it was 119. What was the percent of increase?

7) Read Graph A. Find the inflation rate for 1983.

8) Read Graph A. Find the inflation rate for 1985.

Graph A: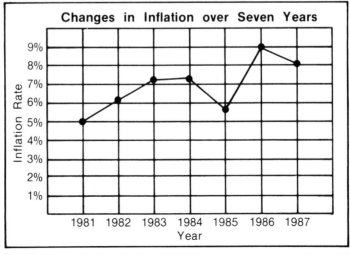

9) Tom earns $21,000 per year. The CPI is 140. Compute his salary in real dollars compared to when the CPI was 120.

10) Elaine earns $30,000 per year. The CPI is 150. Compute her salary in real dollars compared to when the CPI was 100.

11) Read Graph B. How many vehicles carried two passengers?

12) Read Graph B. How many vehicles carried six passengers?

Graph B:

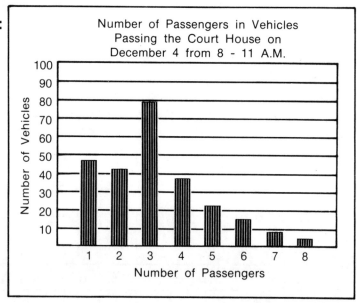

Number of Passengers in Vehicles Passing the Court House on December 4 from 8 - 11 A.M.

13) Draw a bar graph to show this information. Make up your own descriptions.

1981 - 3,   1982 - 0,   1983 - 5,   1984 - 5

1985 - 4,   1986 - 2

14) Draw a line graph to show this information. Make up your own descriptions.

1 - 6,   2 - 5,   3 - 4,   4 - 8,   5 - 3,   6 - 7

Chapter **16**

Personal Applications of Business Math

The mathematics used in business can affect our personal lives to a great degree. A good understanding of business mathematics helps us to be wise and informed workers, spenders, savers, and investors.

In this chapter you will work with several topics that influence your personal life as well as your business life.

Should I pay cash for the TV or....

Should I charge it on my credit card and pay finance charges?

CREDIT CARD FINANCE CHARGES

Business Vocabulary:

Finance charge — A penalty in the form of interest that is added to an unpaid bill.

Most credit card companies will not add a finance charge to a bill if you pay it in two or three weeks. However, many credit cards add a 1-and-one-half percent finance charge to overdue bills less than $500. They add a 1% finance charge to that part of the overdue bill over $500.

Example A: Joe's $372 credit card bill is overdue. Find the $1\frac{1}{2}$ % finance charge.

$1\frac{1}{2}$ % = 1.5% = .015

$$
\begin{array}{r}
\$372 \text{ Bill} \\
\times\ .015 \text{ Finance charge rate} \\
\hline
1860 \\
372 \\
\hline
\$5.58\cancel{0} \text{ Finance charge}
\end{array}
$$

Joe's finance charge was $5.58.

Example B: Miguel's $1,372 credit card bill is overdue. Find the total finance charge. He owes more than $500, so there are four steps.

Step 1: Find the excess over $500. Subtract.

$$\$1,372 - \$500 = \$872$$

Step 2: Find the finance charge for first $500.

$$
\begin{array}{r}
\$500 \\
\times\ .015 \\
\hline
2500 \\
500 \\
\hline
\$7.50\cancel{0} \text{ Finance charge}
\end{array}
$$

Step 3: Find the finance charge for amount over $500.

$872 × .01 = $8.72

Step 4: Add the two finance charges.

$ 8.72
+ 7.50
$16.22 Total finance charge

Miguel's finance charge was $16.22.

▶ Compute the total finance charge on each of these overdue bills. Round fractions of a cent up. The answer to Number 1 is $2.54.

Amount Due	Finance Charge
1) $127	2% up to $500, 1% over $500
2) $848	1% up to $500, 1/2% over $500
3) $949	1% up to $500, 1/2% over $500
4) $1,832	1% up to $500, 1/2% over $500
5) $807	1% up to $500, 1/2% over $500
6) $884	1 1/2% up to $750, 1% over $750
7) $720	1 1/2% up to $750, 1% over $750
8) $449	1% up to $500, 1/2% over $500
9) $647	2% up to $600, 1 1/2% over $600
10) $611	1 1/2% up to $750, 1% over $750
11) $1,080	2% up to $600, 1 1/2% over $600
12) $617	1 1/2% up to $750, 1% over $750
13) $1,622	1 1/2% up to $750, 1% over $750
14) $825	1% up to $500, 1/2% over $500
15) $607	1% up to $500, 1/2% over $500

REPOSSESSION REFUNDS

Under the installment plan, a customer makes a down payment to the merchant and takes the merchandise home. The customer agrees to make regular payments, including interest, to the merchant. The customer also agrees that if he or she stops making payments before the item is paid off, the merchant may repossess (take back) the item.

Some states require stores to make a partial refund when they repossess goods. The refund equals:

(Total payment + Resale price)　minus
　　　A　　　　　　　　**B**

(Original price + Repossession and Resale costs)
　　　C　　　└───── **D** ─────┘

Refund = (A + B) − (C + D)

Example: Jay made total payments of $350 on a TV before it was repossessed. The resale price was $200. The original price was $500. The repossession and resale costs were $15 and $5. Find Jay's refund.

Step 1: Add A + B.

$350 Total payment
+200 Resale price
$550

Step 2: Add C + D.

$500 Original price
　15 Repossession cost
+　5 Resale cost
$520

Step 3: Subtract.

$550
−520
$ 30 Refund

Jay's refund after paying $350 was only $30!

▶ Compute the refund after each of these reposses-
sions. If there is no refund, write "None." The
answer to Number 1 is $207.

	Total Payment A	Resale Price B	Original Price C	Costs of Repossession and Resale D
1)	$410	$337	$ 500	$25, $15
2)	$1,226	$551	$1,877	$15, $7
3)	$1,253	$428	$1,884	$14, $13
4)	$1,264	$832	$2,253	$16, $5
5)	$615	$674	$1,404	$16, $7
6)	$406	$686	$ 972	$10, $6
7)	$1,492	$819	$1,836	$15, $14
8)	$1,252	$482	$1,721	$22, $12
9)	$653	$451	$1,291	$22, $11
10)	$2,216	$896	$2,379	$10, $8
11)	$1,198	$503	$1,918	$16, $7
12)	$687	$228	$ 816	$24, $7
13)	$1,225	$588	$2,138	$25, $5
14)	$959	$526	$1,632	$24, $14
15)	$1,222	$358	$1,612	$13, $11
16)	$521	$915	$1,223	$23, $13
17)	$1,575	$754	$1,879	$21, $9
18)	$536	$155	$ 692	$26, $8
19)	$475	$854	$ 967	$16, $8
20)	$382	$170	$ 421	$19, $6
21)	$1,470	$681	$1,959	$26, $5
22)	$899	$947	$1,886	$22, $14

Computer Program:
AVERAGE DAILY BALANCE

The average daily balance of a charge account is the average amount a person owes during a month. The average daily balance depends upon the total amount of a person's charge purchases and when those purchases were made.

This program computes the average daily balance. Type it into a computer. Run it several times with different data. A sample run is shown on page 263.

```
10   REM AVERAGE DAILY BALANCE PROGRAM
20   REM WP=WEIGHTED PURCHASE TOTAL: TP=TOTAL PUR-
     CHASE
30   LET WP = 0
40   LET TP = 0
50   REM ND=NUMBER OF DAYS IN THIS MONTH
60   PRINT "TYPE IN THE NUMBER OF DAYS IN THIS MONTH."
70   INPUT ND
80   REM PN=PURCHASE NUMBER
90   LET PN = 1
100  PRINT "TYPE IN THE DATE OF PURCHASE NUMBER ";PN
110  REM DA=DATE OF PURCHASE
120  INPUT DA
130  REM AM=AMOUNT OF PURCHASE
140  PRINT "TYPE IN THE AMOUNT OF PURCHASE NUMBER ";
     PN
150  INPUT AM
160  LET WP = WP + (ND + 1 - DA) * AM
170  LET TP = TP + AM
180  PRINT "TYPE IN 0 (ZERO) IF THERE WERE NO":PRINT
            FURTHER PURCHASES.":PRINT
190  PRINT "IF THERE WAS ANOTHER PURCHASE,":PRINT
            "TYPE IN THE DATE OF THAT PURCHASE."
200  INPUT DA
210  IF DA = 0 THEN 240
220  LET PN = PN + 1
230  GOTO 140
```

```
240  LET AV = INT (100 * WP/ND + .999)/100
250  PRINT "THE AVERAGE DAILY BALANCE FOR THE ";PN;
     " PURCHASES TOTALING $";TP;" WAS $";AV
260  END
```

```
RUN
TYPE IN THE NUMBER OF DAYS IN THIS MONTH.
?31
TYPE IN THE DATE OF PURCHASE NUMBER 1
?4
TYPE IN THE AMOUNT OF PURCHASE NUMBER 1
?67.08
TYPE IN 0 (ZERO) IF THERE WERE NO FURTHER PURCHASES.
IF THERE WAS ANOTHER PURCHASE, TYPE IN THE DATE OF
THAT PURCHASE.
?21
TYPE IN THE AMOUNT OF PURCHASE NUMBER 2
?764.99
TYPE IN 0 (ZERO) IF THERE WERE NO FURTHER PURCHASES.
IF THERE WAS ANOTHER PURCHASE, TYPE IN THE DATE OF
THAT PURCHASE.
?0
THE AVERAGE DAILY BALANCE FOR THE 2 PURCHASES
TOTALING $832.07 WAS $332.04.
```

UNIT CONVERSIONS WITHIN THE CUSTOMARY SYSTEM

The system of measure that we use in the United States is called the Customary System, or the English System. Measuring and converting from one unit to another is an important skill because we use it so often. Study this list of important conversions:

1 foot = 12 inches
1 yard = 3 feet = 36 inches
1 English ton = 2,000 pounds
1 pound = 16 ounces
1 dozen = 12 items
1 gross = 12 dozen = 144 items
1 gallon = 4 quarts
1 quart = 2 pints
1 square yard = 9 square feet
1 year = 12 months = 52 weeks

Converting between units of measure requires either multiplying or dividing.

When you convert from a larger unit to a smaller unit, you multiply.

When you convert from a smaller unit to a larger unit, you divide.

An easy way to remember this is SLD (Smaller-Larger: Divide), and LSM (Larger-Smaller: Multiply).

Example A: 46 inches = ___feet, ___inches
This is an SLD example.   Divide.

$$\begin{array}{r} 3 \\ 12\overline{)46} \\ \underline{36} \\ 10 \end{array}$$

The answer is 3 feet and 10 inches.

Example B: 5 gross = ___dozen

This is an LSM example. Multiply.

12 × 5 = 60

The answer is 60 dozen.

▶ Convert each measurement to the specified unit. The answer to Number 1 is 108 months.

1) 9 years = ___ months
2) 3 feet = ___ inches
3) 237 yards = ___ feet
4) 19 yards = ___ inches
5) 22 English tons = ___ pounds
6) 504 ounces = ___ pounds ___ ounces
7) 247 quarts = ___ gallons ___ quarts
8) 554 pints = ___ quarts
9) 50 square yards = ___ square feet
10) 27 years = ___ months
11) 2 years = ___ weeks
12) 387 items = ___ dozen ___ items
13) 1322 items = ___ gross ___ items
14) 52 yards 1 foot = ___ feet
15) 22 feet 11 inches = ___ inches
16) 295 inches = ___ feet ___ inches
17) 296 feet = ___ yards ___ feet
18) 9 yards = ___ inches
19) 31 English tons = ___ pounds
20) 39 pounds = ___ ounces
21) 25 gailons = ___ quarts
22) 288 quarts = ___ pints
23) 124 square yards = ___ square feet
24) 16 years = ___ months

UNIT CONVERSIONS
WITHIN THE METRIC SYSTEM

Many products sold in the United States are measured with metric units. The most important metric units in everyday life are those listed below.

Study the chart. The SLD and LSM methods work for these metric conversions, too.

1 centimeter (cm) = 10 millimeters (mm)
1 meter (m) = 100 centimeters = 1,000 millimeters
1 kilometer (km) = 1,000 meters
1 kilogram (kg) = 1,000 grams (g)
1 gram = 1,000 milligrams (mg)
1 liter (L) = 1,000 milliliters (mL)
1 kiloliter (kL) = 1,000 liters
1 metric ton (t) = 1,000 kilograms

Example A: 46 mm = ___cm

This is an SLD example. Divide.

$$
\begin{array}{r}
4.6 \\
10\overline{)46.0} \\
\underline{40} \\
6\,0 \\
\underline{6\,0}
\end{array}
$$

46 millimeters = 4.6 centimeters.

Example B: 18 t = ___kg

This is an LSM example. Multiply.

18 × 1,000 = 18,000

18 metric tons = 18,000 kilograms

▶ Convert each measurement to the specified unit. The answer to Number 1 is 10,000 millimeters.

1) 10 m = ___mm

2) 9 m = ___mm

3) 2,155 mm = ___cm

4) 18,488 m = ___km

5) 24,635 cm = ___m

6) 5,716 mL = ___L

7) 200 kL = ___L

8) 5,380 g = ___kg

9) 113 t = ___kg

10) 2 g = ___mg

11) 19 m = ___mm

12) 222 cm = ___mm

13) 25 km = ___m

14) 18 m = ___cm

15) 32 L = ___mL

16) 24,169 L = ___kL

17) 8,547 g = ___kg

18) 34 t = ___kg

19) 12,264 mg = ___g

20) 15 mm = ___m

21) 247 cm = ___mm

22) 4,377 m = ___km

23) 26 m = ___cm

24) 5,013 mL = ___L

25) 22,300 L = ___kL

26) 6169 g = ___kg

27) 102 t = ___kg

28) 24,586 mg = ___g

29) 101 mm = ___m

30) 1,740 mm = ___cm

31) 3 km = ___m

32) 6,684 cm = ___m

33) 2,042 mL = ___L

34) 216 kL = ___L

35) 629 kg = ___g

36) 122 t = ___kg

37) 30,596 mg = ___g

38) 438 mL = ___L

39) 285 kL = ___L

40) 90 kg = ___g

41) 10 t = ___kg

42) 3,666 mg = ___g

43) 281 mm = ___m

44) 158 cm = ___mm

45) 22,769 m = ___km

46) 36,665 cm = ___m

47) 19 L = ___mL

48) 282 kL = ___L

49) 25,051 g = ___kg

50) 126 t = ___kg

METRIC EQUIVALENTS

Occasionally, business people need to be able to convert from one system of measure to the other. The table below lists some of the more important equivalents between the Customary and Metric Systems.

1 inch	2.54 centimeters
1 centimeter	0.393 inch
1 inch	25.4 millimeters
1 millimeter	0.039 inch
1 foot	0.305 meter
1 meter	3.28 feet
1 yard	0.914 meter
1 meter	1.09 yards
1 mile	1.61 kilometers
1 kilometer	0.621 mile
1 ounce	28.4 grams
1 gram	0.035 ounce
1 pound	0.454 kilogram
1 kilogram	2.2 pounds
1 English ton	0.909 metric ton
1 metric ton	1.1 English tons
1 ounce	30 milliliters
1 milliliter	0.033 ounce
1 quart	0.946 liter
1 liter	1.06 quarts
1 gallon	3.79 liters
1 liter	0.264 gallon

Conversions from one system to the other can be done with multiplication, as long as you consult the table first. That is why the numbers in the table are called multipliers.

Example A: Jon has 900 meters of wire in stock. He just received an order for 930 yards of the wire. Is there enough wire in stock to fill the order?

Since 1 meter = 1.09 yards, multiply the number of meters by 1.09.

$$
\begin{array}{rl}
900 & \text{Meters} \\
\times\ 1.09 & \text{Multiplier} \\
\hline
8100 & \\
9000\ \ \ & \\
\hline
981.00 & \text{Yards}
\end{array}
$$

900 meters equal 981 yards. Jon has enough wire in stock.

Example B: Fran needs 4,000 pounds of concrete for her patio. Are her seventeen 100-kilogram bags enough?

One kilogram = 2.2 pounds.

17 100-kilogram bags hold 1700 kilograms.

Multiply 1700 by 2.2.

$$
\begin{array}{rl}
1700 & \text{Kilograms} \\
\times\ \ \ 2.2 & \text{Multiplier} \\
\hline
3400 & \\
3400\ \ \ & \\
\hline
3740.0 & \text{Pounds}
\end{array}
$$

1700 kilograms equal 3,740 pounds. Fran needs more concrete.

▶ Convert each measurement to the specified unit. Multiply in each problem. The answer to Number 1 is 304.8 centimeters.

1) 120 inches = ___centimeters

2) 309 millimeters = ___inches

3) 237 inches = ___centimeters

4) 19 feet = ___meters

5) 22 yards = ___meters

6) 504 kilometers = ___miles

7) 247 quarts = ___liters

8) 554 gallons = ___liters

9) 50 milliliters = ___ounces

10) 27 pounds = ___kilograms

11) 13 ounces = ___grams

12) 387 English tons = ___metric tons

13) 247 inches = ___millimeters

14) 267 centimeters = ___inches

15) 68 meters = ___feet

16) 500 meters = ___yards

17) 44 miles = ___kilometers

18) 300 liters = ___quarts

19) 223 gallons = ___liters

20) 122 milliliters = ___ounces

21) 26 pounds = ___kilograms

22) 140 grams = ___ounces

23) 384 English tons = ___metric tons

24) 2280 millimeters = ___inches

25) 157 inches = ___centimeters

26) 507 meters = ___feet

27) 28 meters = ___yards

28) 468 kilometers = ___miles

29) 160 liters = ___quarts

30) 103 liters = ___gallons

31) 159 ounces = ___milliliters

32) 187 kilograms = ___pounds

33) 552 grams = ___ounces

34) 106 English tons = ___metric tons

35) 39 yards = ___meters

36) 24 miles = ___kilometers

37) 207 liters = ___quarts

38) 274 liters = ___gallons

39) 487 ounces = ___milliliters

40) 25 pounds = ___kilograms

41) 52 ounces = ___grams

42) 25 metric tons = ___English tons

43) 2067 millimeters = ___inches

44) 195 centimeters = ___inches

45) 10 feet = ___meters

46) 36 yards = ___meters

47) 36 miles = ___kilometers

48) 135 quarts = ___liters

49) 150 liters = ___gallons

50) 103 milliliters = ___ounces

THE 24-HOUR CLOCK

Some businesses use a 24-hour clock instead of a 12-hour clock. With the 24-hour clock, each hour's number is used only once during the day. This avoids some of the confusion caused by the 12-hour clock. You may need to use a 24-hour clock for parking lot tickets or for some airline schedules.

The chart below shows how the 12-hour clock compares to the 24-hour clock.

12-Hour Clock	24-Hour Clock
12:01 A.M.	0001 hours
1:00 A.M.	0100 hours
2:00 A.M.	0200 hours
3:00 A.M.	0300 hours
4:00 A.M.	0400 hours
5:00 A.M.	0500 hours
6:00 A.M.	0600 hours
7:00 A.M.	0700 hours
8:00 A.M.	0800 hours
9:00 A.M.	0900 hours
10:00 A.M.	1000 hours
11:00 A.M.	1100 hours
12:00 noon	1200 hours
1:00 P.M.	1300 hours
2:00 P.M.	1400 hours
3:00 P.M.	1500 hours
4:00 P.M.	1600 hours
5:00 P.M.	1700 hours
6:00 P.M.	1800 hours
7:00 P.M.	1900 hours
8:00 P.M.	2000 hours
9:00 P.M.	2100 hours
10:00 P.M.	2200 hours
11:00 P.M.	2300 hours
12:00 midnight	2400 hours

The time up to 10 A.M. uses a 0 before the number.

9:30 A.M. ──────────→ 0930 hours

At 10 A.M. there is no 0 before the numbers.

10:01 A.M. ──────────→ 1001 hours
11:45 A.M. ──────────→ 1145 hours

After 12:59 P.M. add 12 to the numbers.

1:30 P.M. ──────────→ 1330 hours
9:15 P.M. ──────────→ 2115 hours
11:25 P.M. ──────────→ 2325 hours

Example A: What is 7:45 A.M. on a 24-hour clock?

0745 hours

Example B: What is 7:45 P.M. on a 24-hour clock?

1945 hours

▶ Change each of these 12-hour times to its 24-hour time. Be sure to write the word "hours." The answer to Number 1 is 0400 hours.

1) 4:00 A.M.	16) 7:36 A.M.	31) 12:30 P.M.
2) 4:00 P.M.	17) 9:44 P.M.	32) 12:30 A.M.
3) 6:30 A.M.	18) 8:31 P.M.	33) 1:08 A.M.
4) 7:10 A.M.	19) 6:54 P.M.	34) 1:07 P.M.
5) 11:25 A.M.	20) 10:42 A.M.	35) 7:24 P.M.
6) 9:15 P.M.	21) 8:32 P.M.	36) 6:08 A.M.
7) 6:20 P.M.	22) 3:29 A.M.	37) 2:04 P.M.
8) 4:12 P.M.	23) 11:47 A.M.	38) 1:08 P.M.
9) 12:04 P.M.	24) 12:35 A.M.	39) 5:54 P.M.
10) 3:18 A.M.	25) 7:06 P.M.	40) 2:27 A.M.
11) 8:10 A.M.	26) 10:21 P.M.	41) 3:22 A.M.
12) 5:05 P.M.	27) 12:27 P.M.	42) 12:57 A.M.
13) 4:52 A.M.	28) 5:54 A.M.	43) 12:15 P.M.
14) 11:42 A.M.	29) 3:45 P.M.	44) 1:45 P.M.
15) 1:15 P.M.	30) 4:01 P.M.	45) 11:10 P.M.

TIME ZONES

Since the sun cannot shine on the entire earth at once, there are 24 time zones around the world. The map below shows four of the zones as they cover the United States. There is a one-hour difference as you move from one zone to the next.

When it is 1200 hours in Atlanta, it is 0900 in Los Angeles. When it is 1300 hours in Dallas, it is 1100 hours in San Diego. When it is 1200 hours in Denver, it is 1400 in Pittsburgh.

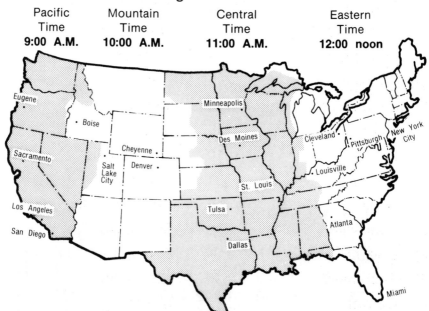

Pacific Time	Mountain Time	Central Time	Eastern Time
9:00 A.M.	10:00 A.M.	11:00 A.M.	12:00 noon

Example A: When it is 0037 hours in Eugene, what time is it in Miami?

Miami is 3 time zones to the east of Eugene. Therefore, the time in Miami is 3 hours later: 0337 hours.

Example B: When it is 1451 hours in New York, what time is it in Salt Lake City?

Salt Lake City is 2 time zones to the west of New York. Therefore, the time in Salt Lake City is 2 hours earlier: 1251 hours.

▶ Find the missing times. Write your answers in 24-hour time. The answer to Number 1 is 2146 hours.

If the time in...	Is:	The time in...	Is?
1) Pittsburgh	0046	San Diego	
2) Cleveland	2048	St. Louis	
3) Los Angeles	2150	Atlanta	
4) Des Moines	1052	Cheyenne	
5) Boise	0750	Sacramento	
6) Eugene	1453	New York City	
7) Salt Lake City	0358	Los Angeles	
8) San Diego	1759	Pittsburgh	
9) Cleveland	1745	Cheyenne	
10) Sacramento	1804	Miami	
11) Los Angeles	2245	Atlanta	
12) Denver	1010	Minneapolis	
13) St. Louis	1531	Pittsburgh	
14) Boise	1011	New York City	
15) Louisville	0922	Salt Lake City	
16) Cheyenne	1557	Eugene	
17) Sacramento	0438	Cleveland	
18) Denver	0230	Miami	
19) Pittsburgh	2241	Boise	
20) Atlanta	2219	Minneapolis	
21) Louisville	0547	Atlanta	
22) Los Angeles	0722	Denver	
23) New York City	1214	Des Moines	
24) Miami	0641	Cleveland	
25) Dallas	1747	San Diego	

BALANCING A CHECKING ACCOUNT
With a Calculator

Business Vocabulary:

Deposit — Money you add to your checking account.

Bank statement — A list of your checks and deposits that the bank handled during a month.

Bank balance — The last amount on the bank statement; the amount of money in your account when the statement was printed.

Checkbook balance — Your current balance according to your own records.

Many people and businesses balance their checking accounts every month. This process takes three steps. It reveals any errors in the account. You need your monthly bank statement before you begin. The bank statement is usually three or four days old when you receive it.

Example A: Checkbook balance = $1,017

Step 1: Add the bank balance to all recent deposits that do not appear on your statement. These are called outstanding deposits.

$ 826 Bank balance
286 Outstanding deposit
+ 397 Outstanding deposit
$1,509 Amount A

Step 2: Add any recent checks that do not appear on your statement. These are outstanding checks.

$172 Outstanding check
46 Outstanding check
+274 Outstanding check
$492 Amount B

Step 3: Subtract B from A.

$$\begin{array}{r} \$1,509 \text{ Amount A} \\ -\underline{492} \text{ Amount B} \\ \$1,017 \end{array}$$

This answer, $1,017, equals the $1,017 balance in your checkbook. Therefore, the account balances.

Example B: Checkbook balance = $900

Step 1: Add the bank balance to all recent deposits that do not appear on your statement.

$$\begin{array}{r} \$1,046.19 \text{ Bank balance} \\ 45.00 \text{ Outstanding deposit} \\ 951.07 \text{ Outstanding deposit} \\ +\underline{983.30} \text{ Outstanding deposit} \\ \$3,025.56 \text{ Amount A} \end{array}$$

Step 2: Add any recent checks that do not appear on your statement.

$$\begin{array}{r} \$947.15 \text{ Outstanding check} \\ +\underline{841.11} \text{ Outstanding check} \\ \$1,788.26 \text{ Amount B} \end{array}$$

Step 3: Subtract B from A.

$$\begin{array}{r} \$3,025.56 \text{ Amount A} \\ -\underline{1,788.26} \text{ Amount B} \\ \$1,237.30 \end{array}$$

This answer does not equal your $900 balance. Your account does not balance. This means that either you made an error, or the bank made an error.

▶ Use the three-step method to find if these accounts balance. If the account does balance, write "Balances." If the account does not balance, write the answer to step 3. The answer to Number 1 is: Step 3, $727.

	Checkbook Balance	Bank Balance	Outstanding Deposits	Outstanding Checks	
1)	$427.00	$ 846.00	$100.00 259.00 54.00	$206.00	$326.00
2)	906.44	5,348.35	814.24	22.71 556.83 965.29 807.19 136.13	784.34 622.41 552.15 819.10
3)	73.59	1,965.96	894.93 432.02 27.69	373.37 285.11 120.62 578.25	128.23 841.32 820.11
4)	219.03	3,547.55	261.89 509.93 438.81	96.01 763.04 251.98 896.28	860.41 73.00 833.43 765.00
5)	237.37	1,515.46	593.17 759.82 434.00	628.69 104.63 166.37 682.04	524.96 217.82 208.18 522.39
6)	832.88	4,788.52	187.62	133.91 961.08 486.58 680.11	641.51 502.29 737.78

	Checkbook Balance	Bank Balance	Outstanding Deposits	Outstanding Checks	
7)	$503.38	$3,085.96	$654.57	$ 95.74	$515.12
			901.46	789.91	474.83
			323.35	900.83	694.00
				894.79	
8)	743.36	4,994.43	252.21	374.18	988.75
				627.35	499.63
				248.44	948.40
				817.53	
9)	382.89	4,736.69	18.41	280.26	851.02
			460.73	96.23	896.83
				226.32	889.68
				525.95	641.18
				425.47	
10)	620.46	712.06	877.07	202.93	467.94
			673.27	219.19	705.42
				160.96	56.46
11)	23.32	4,012.10	323.44	369.24	251.29
			613.96	167.42	475.85
				648.36	806.72
				963.30	585.89
				558.11	
12)	831.96	4,017.35	119.44	79.86	239.91
			946.27	478.95	496.49
				228.38	840.80
				846.81	144.03
				905.87	

BASIC SKILL REVIEW

1) Last week Carey received contracts from 54, 106, 97, 120, and 186 customers. How many contracts did he receive?

2) Sherri's property was 4,000 square feet before she sold a 926-square foot piece. How much property did she have left?

3) With every 28 payroll deductions of $3.00, Gail buys one share of company stock. What is Gail's price per share?

4) How many $75 tents can be purchased with $3,000?

5) The weights for 5 shipments were 14 kg, 98.14 kg, 13.6 kg, 2.071 kg, and 39.66 kg. Find the total weight.

6) Each group dental policy costs $201.17. Find the cost for 80 policies.

7) How many tools weighing .15 kg each can be packed into a box that will hold only 36 kg?

8) A non-stop trip takes 4 hours. If you have been traveling for $1\frac{1}{4}$ hours, how much longer must you travel?

9) How many $2\frac{3}{4}$″ books can be placed on a 77″ shelf?

10) Of 2,000 employees, 16.7% need safety glasses. How many need safety glasses?

11) Andrew paid 5% of his $210.20 salary to state tax. How much state tax did he pay?

CHAPTER REVIEW

1) Larry's $842 credit card bill is overdue. The finance charge rate is 2% of the first $500 and 1% of the amount over $500. What is Larry's finance charge?

2) Sue's $1,697 credit card bill is overdue. The finance charge rate is $1\frac{1}{2}$ % of the first $500 and 2% of the amount over $500. What is Sue's finance charge?

3) Janie made total payments of $684 on an electric range before it was repossessed. The resale price was $215. The original price was $750. The repossession cost was $10. The resale cost was $10. What was Janie's refund?

4) Tony made total payments of $920 on a computer before it was repossessed. The resale price was $400. The original price was $950. The reposession cost was $5, and the resale cost was $25. What was Tony's refund?

5) How many quarts equal 8 gallons, 1 quart?

6) How many feet and inches equal 82 inches?

7) How many centimeters equal 63 meters?

8) How many kilograms equal 6700 grams?

9) How many miles equal 82 kilometers?

10) How many liters equal 500 gallons?

11) What is 0621 hours on a 12-hour clock?

12) What is 1400 hours on a 12-hour clock?

13) What is 7:30 A.M. on a 24-hour clock?

14) What is 1:40 P.M. on a 24-hour clock?

15) If it is 1341 hours in Atlanta, what time is it in San Diego?

16) If it is 2130 hours in Denver, what time is it in St. Louis?

17) Does Mike's checking account balance? His checkbook balance is $513.77. The bank balance is $2,637.58. Outstanding deposits are $190.49 and $495.23. Outstanding checks are: $249.17, $781.73, $266.32, $126.25, $484.67, and $901.39.

18) Does Karen's checking account balance? Her checkbook balance is $1,172.45. The bank balance is $3,156.78. An outstanding deposit is $41.16. Her outstanding checks are: $797.86, $738.28, $75.00, $192.62, $227.81, $561.87, and $180.33.

Chapter 17

Basic Skill
Practice

Decimal Drill A

1) Add: 7.11 + .185 + 28 + .3 + .8654 + .95

2) Subtract: 17.1 − 4.6

3) Multiply: 5.61 × 1.47

4) Divide: 15.7 ÷ 5

5) Divide: 1672.8 ÷ 2.4

6) Divide: 4.1705 ÷ .095

Decimal Drill B

1) Add: 5.78 + .437 + 90 + .3 + .8581 + .29

2) Subtract: 11.8 − 8.7

3) Multiply: .09 × 8.27

4) Divide: 7.1 ÷ 5

5) Divide: 1269.6 ÷ 2.3

6) Divide: .4296 ÷ .024

Decimal Drill C

1) Add: 4.79 + .504 + 91 + .5 + .7354 + .46
2) Subtract: 13.1 − 8.6
3) Multiply: 5.81 × 6.01
4) Divide: 22.8 ÷ 5
5) Divide: 724.8 ÷ 1.2
6) Divide: 2.2814 ÷ .061

Decimal Drill D

1) Add: 2.38 + .363 + 35 + .4 + .9645 + .74
2) Subtract: 16 − 3.2
3) Multiply: 4.2 × .63
4) Divide: 66.71 ÷ 7
5) Divide: 1662.5 ÷ 3.5
6) Divide: 1.0261 ÷ .031

Decimal Drill E

1) Add: 9.79 + .657 + 84 + .7 + .5926 + .82
2) Subtract: 17.3 − 5.4
3) Multiply: 1.9 × 6.81
4) Divide: 10.89 ÷ 3
5) Divide: 258.3 ÷ 2.1
6) Divide: 1.7446 ÷ .061

Decimal Drill F

1) Add: 6.84 + .12 + 52 + .5 + .7221 + .43
2) Subtract: 13.5 − 4.1
3) Multiply: .83 × 7.16
4) Divide: 5.8 ÷ 5
5) Divide: 1711.2 ÷ 3.1
6) Divide: 1.9282 ÷ .062

Decimal Drill G

1) Add: .47 + .983 + 29 + .5 + .3419 + .61
2) Subtract: 10.1 − 6.7
3) Multiply: 7.85 × .44
4) Divide: 10.83 ÷ 3
5) Divide: 919.2 ÷ 2.4
6) Divide: 1.525 ÷ .05

Decimal Drill H

1) Add: 8.41 + .881 + 40 + .2 + .3071 + .83
2) Subtract: 17.9 − 3.7
3) Multiply: 5.99 × 9.43
4) Divide: 19.65 ÷ 5
5) Divide: 1670.4 ÷ 3.2
6) Divide: .3538 ÷ .029

Decimal Drill I

1) Add: .53 + .459 + 34 + .7 + .7704 + .23
2) Subtract: 15.4 − 3.2
3) Multiply: 2.46 × 4.71
4) Divide: 54.27 ÷ 9
5) Divide: 1544.4 ÷ 3.3
6) Divide: 2.2411 ÷ .073

Decimal Drill J

1) Add: 1.37 + .731 + 94 + .1 + .6326 + .26
2) Subtract: 14.9 − .4
3) Multiply: 6.8 × 6.24
4) Divide: 26.64 ÷ 3
5) Divide: 1795.5 ÷ 3.5
6) Divide: 1.926 ÷ .06

▶ Rename these decimals as percents.

1)	2.4	13)	0.07	25)	0.0036
2)	8.9	14)	0.09	26)	84
3)	4.2	15)	7.01	27)	4.1
4)	0.4	16)	31.8	28)	1.12
5)	3.0	17)	69	29)	8.9
6)	4.8	18)	5.7	30)	14.5
7)	5	19)	0.222	31)	84.9
8)	1.30	20)	0.0009	32)	0.0211
9)	8	21)	4.221	33)	57
10)	21.6	22)	3.011	34)	2.9
11)	91	23)	26	35)	7.0
12)	43	24)	5.02	36)	0.32

▶ Rename these percents as decimals.

1)	300%	13)	29%	25)	400%
2)	2%	14)	22.9%	26)	77%
3)	10%	15)	69%	27)	7.002%
4)	45%	16)	0.45%	28)	3000%
5)	6%	17)	8.12%	29)	5.10%
6)	8.2%	18)	30%	30)	58%
7)	34.4%	19)	13%	31)	9.2%
8)	35%	20)	1.9%	32)	7.4%
9)	12%	21)	94%	33)	5.14%
10)	5.2%	22)	0.005%	34)	87%
11)	25%	23)	8%	35)	15%
12)	0.4%	24)	3%	36)	75%

▶ Find the missing percentages. Round to the nearest hundredth.

1) 8% of 74 is ___   26) 0.38% of 74 is ___

2) 4% of 25 is ___   27) 18% of 200 is ___

3) 2% of 10 is ___   28) 7.2% of 44 is ___

4) 10% of 270 is ___   29) 55% of 609 is ___

5) 8% of 37 is ___   30) 90% of 2,000 is ___

6) 40% of 1,000 is ___   31) 8% of 16 is ___

7) 50% of 2,000 is ___   32) 6.3% of 7.02 is ___

8) 7% of 67 is ___   33) 7% of 70 is ___

9) 5% of 56 is ___   34) 10% of 400 is ___

10) 0.9% of 7 is ___   35) 2% of 4.8 is ___

11) 8% of 24 is ___   36) 23% of 45 is ___

12) 90% of 304 is ___   37) 5% of 60 is ___

13) 85% of 4,000 is ___   38) 3% of 80 is ___

14) 38% of 4.7 is ___   39) 90% of 245 is ___

15) 70% of 384 is ___   40) 30% of 9 is ___

16) 4.2% of 44 is ___   41) 42.5% of 70.5 is ___

17) 55% of 100 is ___   42) 6.01% of 9.01 is ___

18) 25% of 0.57 is ___   43) 32% of 1,000 is ___

19) 6.01% of 0.01 is ___   44) 23% of 57 is ___

20) 5% of 69 is ___   45) 2.7% of 3,000 is ___

21) 60% of 9 is ___   46) 9% of 95 is ___

22) 4% of 37 is ___   47) 4% of 20 is ___

23) 75% of 450 is ___   48) 6% of 12 is ___

24) 39% of 300 is ___   49) 7% of 30 is ___

25) 8% of 49 is ___   50) 24% of 54 is ___

Powers of Ten Drill A

Multiply: *Divide:*

1) .4 × 10   4) 6.18 ÷ .01
2) 879.5 × .001   5) 767.1 ÷ 1,000
3) 2.59 × .01   6) 31.5 ÷ .01

Powers of Ten Drill B

Multiply: *Divide:*

1) 8.7 × 10   4) 5.5 ÷ .1
2) .43 × 10   5) 72.54 ÷ .001
3) 12.84 × .001   6) .85 ÷ 100

Powers of Ten Drill C

Multiply: *Divide:*

1) 1.2 × 10   4) 2.5 ÷ .1
2) 8.95 × 100   5) .44 ÷ .1
3) 7.14 × .01   6) 73.35 ÷ 1,000

Powers of Ten Drill D

Multiply: *Divide:*

1) 4.7 × 100   4) 417.6 ÷ .001
2) 1.02 × 100   5) 257.3 ÷ .001
3) 5.26 × 100   6) 51.45 ÷ 1,000

Powers of Ten Drill E

Multiply: *Divide:*

1) 214.3 × .001   4) 8.5 ÷ .01
2) 42.15 × 1,000   5) 801.7 ÷ 1,000
3) 21.4 × .01   6) 1.6 ÷ 10

Powers of Ten Drill F

Multiply:

1) 44.97 × .001

2) 4.1 × 10

3) 4 × .1

Divide:

4) 36.9 ÷ .001

5) .54 ÷ 10

6) .18 ÷ .01

Powers of Ten Drill G

Multiply:

1) 2.07 × 100

2) 8.6 × .1

3) 378 × 100

Divide:

4) .37 ÷ 10

5) 52 ÷ 100

6) 67.08 ÷ 1,000

Powers of Ten Drill H

Multiply:

1) 4.93 × 100

2) 2.6 × 100

3) 5.1 × .1

Divide:

4) 42.3 ÷ 100

5) 32.3 ÷ 100

6) 4.11 ÷ .01

Powers of Ten Drill I

Multiply:

1) .15 × 10

2) 88.3 × 100

3) 5.1 × .1

Divide:

4) .04 ÷ 10

5) 3.4 ÷ .1

6) 7.56 ÷ .01

Powers of Ten Drill J

Multiply:

1) 207.1 × .001

2) 539.9 × 1,000

3) 422.1 × .001

Divide:

4) 5 ÷ .01

5) 6.1 ÷ .1

6) 29.18 ÷ .001

Powers of Ten Drill K

Multiply:

1) .5 × .1

2) 6.34 × 100

3) 8.41 × .01

Divide:

4) 4.4 ÷ 10

5) .16 ÷ 10

6) 89.49 ÷ .001

Powers of Ten Drill L

Multiply:

1) 62.2 × 100

2) 1.69 × 100

3) 85.2 × 100

Divide:

4) 16.3 ÷ .01

5) 1.3 ÷ 100

6) 507.3 ÷ 1,000

Powers of Ten Drill M

Multiply:

1) 8.33 × .01

2) 848.5 × .001

3) 3.9 × .1

Divide:

4) 74.24 ÷ .001

5) 8.4 ÷ .1

6) .29 ÷ .1

Powers of Ten Drill N

Multiply:

1) 40 × 100

2) 3.1 × 10

3) 21.51 × .001

Divide:

4) .66 ÷ .1

5) 4.9 ÷ 10

6) 7.17 ÷ .01

Powers of Ten Drill O

Multiply:

1) .12 × .1

2) 5.68 × .1

3) 84.8 × .01

Divide:

4) 758.4 ÷ .001

5) 7 ÷ .1

6) 86.1 ÷ .01

INDEX